Learning to Glow

Gift of the Knapp Foundation
2002-2003

Learning to Glow

(A NUCLEAR READER)

Edited by

John Bradley

The University of Arizona Press   Tucson

First printing
The University of Arizona Press
⊛ This book is printed on acid-free, archival-quality paper.
Manufactured in the United States of America
05 04 03 02 01 00   6 5 4 3 2 1

Library of Congress Cataloging-in-Publication Data
Learning to glow : a nuclear reader / edited by John Bradley.
    p. cm.
Includes bibliographical references and index.
ISBN 0-8165-1955-2 (cloth : acid-free paper)
ISBN 0-8165-1956-0 (paper : acid-free paper)
    1. Nuclear energy—United States—Public opinion. 2. Nuclear energy—
Political aspects—United States. 3. Nuclear energy—Social aspects—
United States. 4. Nuclear energy—Environmental aspects—United States.
I. Bradley, John, 1950–
TK9155.L425 2000
333.792'4—dc21   99-006961

British Library Cataloging-in-Publication Data
A catalog record for this book is available from the British Library.

Publication of this book is made possible in part by the proceeds
of a permanent endowment created with the assistance of a
Challenge Grant from the National Endowment for the Humanities,
a federal agency.

For

**Mordechai Vanunu and Aleksandr Nikitin
nuclear prisoners of conscience**

Contents

Foreword

THE PRACTICE OF HUMANITY

The difficulty of living in the Nuclear Age is that so many aspects of it are unthinkable: the technology penetrates to a reality so minute as to be unimaginable, yet the weapons resulting are gargantuan in their destructive power; the poisons are invisible, yet speckle everyone's bones and air; the responsibility for the invention, deployment, and continued "improvement" of nuclear weapons is something we own and invest in as taxpaying Americans; corporate and government officials have used the authority of science to quell public debate about nuclear risks; and our individual fears are so profound that the most successful coping mechanisms for the past fifty-plus years have been psychic numbing and denial. Yet for all of us who find the powers and dangers of nuclear technology unthinkable, there are countless others for whom thinking about these matters is a daily responsibility. They work in power plants, waste disposal sites, submarines, military bases, offices, and laboratories devoted to advancing the technology of war, factories making and unmaking weapons of mass destruction. This anthology compels its readers to think about the unthinkable, to ask questions born of "our special responsibility," in John Bradley's apt phrase, as Americans, people of the first nation to test nuclear weapons and the only nation to inflict their powers on another's citizens.

The images and language of nuclear America tend in the public eye to be arrested in the 1950s, when this technology first became a part of our public and private lives. It is easy to conjure up the black-and-white renditions of the mushroom cloud, the wind- and firestorms after the blast, the irradiated silhouettes of vaporized bodies in Hiroshima, safely humming nuclear power plants, and cafes along Route 66 sporting catchy names that transform terror into a chuckle served with burger and fries. These images were fixed in the minds of those of us growing up in the "duck and cover" era. I saw civil defense films in elementary and junior high school aimed at educating me about the threat of nuclear war while calming my fears by showing me "fail-safe" devices, bomb shelters, Geiger counters, and images of families reemerging into post-Holocaust bliss. I now try, and fail, to conjure up the scriptwriting and editorial meetings at which educated civic leaders believed these films could do anything but make us feel like sitting ducks. It is hard, however, to contemplate that the names of those still dying due to the explosion of "Little Boy," name after name after name, are written annually into sacred volume after volume after volume of the lost, kept in the Cenotaph at Hiroshima. It is hard to contemplate that the U.S. government considers parts of the American West to be "National Sacrifice Zones," the land and its citizens disposable in the interest of poisons that are not. It is hard to contemplate that bullets used in the Gulf War were made from "depleted uranium" posing significant danger to soldiers who were never told the nature of the materials they handled.

This anthology offers a wealth of anecdotal evidence to update the bank of images and language with which we attempt to understand and protect ourselves from such dangers and cruelties. It employs the methods of the discipline we call "the humanities": story, myth, philosophy, and the humanizing sciences of psychology and sociology. Anecdotal evidence is considered in the sciences to be irrelevant—merely a story, one person's view. But that is exactly the view that is needed to counteract the militaristic thinking that denies the dignity of individual life. The wisdom of the anthology, while no easy reading, is profound in its encouragement regarding the human capacity for transformation. Hearing each other's stories helps us, as Ed Dougherty writes, "to recognize our common humanity." And through such recognition comes the hope of "Hiroshima having more meaning for the future than the past," as we learn to transform its legacy into more prudent and just means to solve our disagreements. Awareness motivates activism, and despair, as Randy Morris writes, "awakens and liberates the moral imagination." This anthology drinks deeply at the well of our history, a history saturated with grief and despair. But the end result is one of affirmation. What we can imagine signals what we can become, and this work invites us to face the darkest lessons in our history and transcend them, through the practice of humanity, into faith in the possibility of human goodness.

Alison Hawthorne Deming

Introduction

INVISIBILITY

*W*hen you hear the phrase "the Nuclear Age," what comes to mind? Robert Oppenheimer at Trinity, making his famous statement "I am become Death"? A watch, found in the ashes of Hiroshima, frozen at 8:15? Mushroom clouds rising over Bikini or Nevada? The "doomsday clock" of the *Bulletin of the Atomic Scientists* ticking toward a midnight we hope will never arrive? Bert the Turtle urging us to "duck and cover"? Gigantic mutant ants in the film *Them!*? Slim Pickins in *Dr. Strangelove* a-whoopin' and a-hollerin' like some demented cowboy as he rides his nuclear bomb down upon the Russians? Haunting images all, but more and more I think about the everyday people, ordinary working folks who placed their trust in the words of government officials and who had that trust betrayed. People like the young women in a factory in Ottawa, Illinois.

In the summer of 1995, I did something I had wanted to do for some time—I visited Ottawa, Illinois, a town of 17,400, located about eighty miles southwest of Chicago. I wanted to see a friend, Dan Ursini, who grew up in this town, but there was another reason lurking in the back of my mind. For years Dan had been telling me about a little-known (even to those who live in Illinois) event in our nation's nuclear history—the town's radium dial plants. I wanted to see the site of the original plant and try to learn more about this mysterious story.

What I heard from Dan is confirmed by Catherine Quigg in her essay "The Society of the Living Dead," in this anthology. Young women, enticed by relatively high wages for a small midwestern town, worked at the Radium Dial Company's factory in Ottawa. The workers, allegedly encouraged by management, licked their brushes, and hence the radium, to make a fine tip for applying the substance that made the numerals on watches and instruments glow. This wasn't all that glowed. In playful moments, the young women painted mustaches on their faces, or painted their teeth so they would glow in the dark. Despite illnesses and even occasional deaths of some of the workers, these women were repeatedly reassured by the factory owner and management that radium was perfectly safe. A lawsuit brought by one of the workers eventually led to the Ottawa factory's closing in 1936, though a new factory soon opened a few blocks away. That original factory has long been demolished and largely forgotten, another missing chapter in our nation's nuclear history.

I stood there in Ottawa in disbelief, asking Dan if this really could have been the site of a radium factory. If it wasn't for the knowledge of this native Ottowan, I would never have known that anything extraordinary happened here. What could be seen looked like a picture in any small town—a concrete lot adjacent to a tiny white bungalow, the kind that might be used for the selling of Christmas trees or for children's conversations with Santa. A few cars and pickup trucks and a jeep with a rusty plow testified to the current use of the site—a used car lot. "Hot" sales? Later, when I watched Carol Langer's documentary *Radium City,* on the radium dial painters in Ottawa, I learned that the site I stood on was indeed, as I suspected at the time, still hot. Despite this rather unsurprising fact, the lot had been used at one time for a farmers market. The people of Ottawa were radiating their tomatoes, corn, and other fresh farm produce, the food they would feed their own children.

Wanting to preserve a visual record of the site, I tried to take a photograph of the lot that day, but where, I wondered, should I point the camera? At the concrete lot? The little white bungalow? Some used cars and trucks? How do you communicate the history of this place, the invisible danger? I took the picture, knowing, as the camera clicked, that I had failed. All I was able to do was show the innocuousness of a radioactive site.

No wonder it's so difficult for us to comprehend the dangers of radioactivity. Radioactivity is something so abstract, so imperceptible to our senses, that it seems to exist only in our imaginations. And that instinctual response has received lots of official encouragement. During the era of atomic bombs going off above ground at the Nevada Test Site, from 1951 to 1963, our Atomic Energy Commission assured us that "There is virtually no danger from radioactive fallout."[1] In fact, they encouraged watching the bomb tests as "entertaining and educational."[2] Those who questioned the safety of such practices were called "charlatans" and "terror-mongers."[3] When Americans, particularly women, in Utah, living downwind of the Nevada Test Site, went to hospitals for burned skin and loss of hair due to fallout, they were diagnosed as "neurotic."[4] As late as 1984, the U.S. Department of Energy went so far as to award an $85,000 contract to a Phobia Society to find ways to overcome the public's "nuclear phobia."[5] In the former Soviet Union, citizens sick with radioactivity from Chernobyl were said by government officials to be suffering from "radiophobia," as poet Lyubov Sirota, who was exposed to Chernobyl's radiation, writes in her poem "Radiophobia."[6] Fear of radiation, scientific "experts" continually suggest, is completely unfounded. Tell that to the women who worked at the Radium Dial plants, who, if they survived the initial exposure, lived lives of disfigurement and pain. Tell that to Terry Tempest Williams, who watched her mother die of cancer due to fallout from the Nevada nuclear bomb tests. Tell that to Bill Witherup, who watched his father die of cancer from working at the Hanford nuclear reservation in Washington state. Stories such as these are dismissed by many as merely "anecdotal," as Valerie Kuletz notes in her essay "Tragedy at the Center of the Universe." Thus are ordinary citizens, especially those who have firsthand knowledge of the dangers of radioactivity, stripped of all credibility.

Compound physical invisibility, then, of both radioactivity and its victims with the willful ignoring and hiding of this century's nuclear history, and you have a truly frightening situation, ripe for accidents and deliberate misuse. In an incident eerily reminiscent of the radium dial workers, we learn through Bill Mesler's essay, "The Pentagon's Radioactive Bullet," of how our Gulf War soldiers were never informed that they were dealing with uranium-coated ammunition. Whether it was through "friendly fire" (U.S. shells mistakenly fired by U.S. soldiers at other U.S. soldiers), or from cleanup of exposed tanks, or from bringing home a radioactive war souvenir, many of our Persian Gulf soldiers were radiated. Not to mention the Iraqis who were left to deal with irradiated tanks and shells. The U.S. government has yet to officially acknowledge or take responsibility for this situation. In a more recent example of invisibility, an Associated Press news release (in one of those articles the size of a postage stamp) states that "in Gore, Oklahoma, a uranium-processing plant gets rid of low-level radioactive waste by licensing it as a liquid fertilizer and spraying it over 9,000 acres of grazing land."[7] "What we don't know can't harm us" seems to be an operating belief. A variation of the axiom is that we know it all and that we are in complete control. Words that seem made for an epitaph.

The dangers of radioactivity can be seen around the world. While it was my intention to present an anthology of essays that would address this international scope, several factors intervened to limit the focus to the United States. Limitation of the size of the anthology was one factor, as was the availability of essays by Americans. The more I considered narrowing the focus to America, the more appropriate it seemed. Given the testing of the first atomic bomb in the New Mexican desert on July 16, 1945, and the first use of atomic bombs by the United States on the Japanese cities of Hiroshima and Nagasaki, and the emergence of the United States as the only superpower following the collapse of the Soviet Union, it would seem that Americans have a special responsibility in nuclear matters. Yet Americans seem to think that with the destruction of the Berlin Wall and the end of the Cold War, the Nuclear Age is somehow over. Even as the United States continues research on and development of nuclear weapons, there's little to no public discussion of whether such research should go on, whether plutonium should be floating overhead in our space shuttles, whether domestic reactors should burn weapons-grade plutonium, whether Nevada's Yucca Mountain is the proper place to dump our nuclear waste, whether nuclear waste should be transported past our homes on highways and rails, to name but a few neglected issues. Upon reflection, I came to the conclusion that American voices desperately need to be heard in this anthology.

This collection of essays, I hope, will make radiation a little less abstract and invisible. They will demonstrate the folly and consequences of secrecy, of disinterest, of assuming someone else will take care of our nuclear problems for us. I also hope the essays will encourage Americans to start asking more questions. Most important, I hope these stories show a glaring need for change in the way we live—that humans are not *apart* from the landscape, but *a part* of it. As Linda Hogan has noted,

"We have forgotten that this land and every life-form is a piece of god, a divine community, with the same forces of creation in plants as in people."[8] How will the Earth, how will any of us, survive without such a stance?

While all of the essays in some manner raise this question, they are organized into three sections. In the opening section, "In the Belly of the Beast," we hear personal testimonies on what it was like to come of age during the Cold War. The writers vividly portray growing up in a climate of suspicion and fear. In "A Roller-Coaster Ride through the Nuclear Age," David Seaborg calls a telephone operator to find out if San Francisco has been hit by a nuclear bomb. This striking incident illustrates the very real psychological effects of nuclear fear, of living with the fact that the world we know could be obliterated at any moment, an abstract idea at best in histories of the Cold War era. It is easy to see how politicians and military officials would justify the development of bigger bombs as a way to placate such fears. And bigger bombs, of course, generate even more fear. In the next section, "Coyote Learns to Glow," we learn of health and environmental costs of our nuclear policies and practices. Americans have paid a terrible price—often with their very lives—for supposedly "winning" the Cold War, as we see in these essays. But despite politicians telling us that the "nuclear nightmare is over," nuclear threats have not ended. As Karl Grossman shows in "Brighter than the Brightest Star," we live with the very real possibility of plutonium from an errant missile launch coming back to haunt us, to cite but one ongoing concern. The last group of essays, "Beyond Despair," offers some responses to the Nuclear Age other than fear and paralysis, understandable reactions yet ultimately ineffectual. Many of the writers in this section suggest that we revisit Hiroshima—physically, spiritually, emotionally—as a means of honestly facing our past. It will better enable us, these writers seem to imply, to face future nuclear decisions. I find these personal interactions with Hiroshima to be inspiring. How can we not be moved, like Kenneth Robbins in "The Cenotaph," at the sight of book after book of the names of those who have died from what happened at 8:15 A.M. on August 6, 1945, in Hiroshima? The emotional courage shown by Kenneth Robbins and the other writers who revisit Hiroshima is surely needed now. How else can we offer moral or ethical guidance to nations such as India and Pakistan, now embracing nuclear weapons? For if we ignore and deny Hiroshima, ignore and deny what happened at ground level after the *Enola Gay* dropped its cargo, ignore and deny the testimony of our own nuclear witnesses, how can we expect citizens of other nations, eager to possess the power and prestige of the Bomb, not to proceed as if blindfolded? Facing the past is surely part of the process of breaking the spell of fear, apathy, and invisibility.

Like those women in Ottawa whose lives were forever changed by contact with radium, we also interact daily—simply by drawing breath, by drinking a glass of water—with deadly substances, substances of our own creation, substances we do not fully understand. This, too, is part of the legacy of the Nuclear Age. May we have the humility and courage to admit our ignorance and to act accordingly.

I wish to thank all those who contributed, directly or indirectly, to the creation of this anthology. Bill Witherup served as catalyst as well as contributing editor, and thus deserves recognition as prime mover. Beth Bentley, Edward Dougherty, Patricia Brodsky, and Todd Davis provided forums for presenting these issues to those who are the most affected by them—the public. Alison Deming, Ray Gonzalez, Craig McGrath, Richard Minear, and Scott Slovic suggested authors, provided manuscripts, and offered encouragement. Craig also deserves thanks for reading the manuscript, offering comments, and locating a contributor. Finally, I wish to thank my wife, Jana, for her loving support; without her help I could not have edited this manuscript.

The essays you are about to read offer an alternative to the official version of nuclear history told to us by our school textbooks, scientists, military authorities, government agencies, and nuclear industry officials. These are stories told by individuals—or by writers who have listened carefully to individuals—who suffered the consequences of the decisions made by those in power. These are stories by people no different from yourself. These are stories that have been largely ignored, dismissed, or suppressed, a part of the people's history of the atom. We need to hear many more such testimonies in the coming years in order to find our way. For as poet Muriel Rukeyser wrote: "The universe is made of stories,/not of atoms."[9]

John Bradley

NOTES

1. Catherine Caufield, *Multiple Exposures: Chronicles of the Radiation Age* (Chicago: University of Chicago Press, 1989), 106.

2. Ibid.

3. Ibid., 171.

4. Carole Gallagher, *American Ground Zero: The Secret Nuclear War* (Cambridge, MA: MIT Press, 1993), xxx.

5. Caufield, 177.

6. John Bradley, ed., *Atomic Ghost: Poets Respond to the Nuclear Age* (Minneapolis: Coffee House Press, 1995), 106.

7. "Toxins Reused as Fertilizers, Paper Reports," *Chicago Tribune*, 7 July 1997.

8. Linda Hogan, "Creations," in Linda Hogan, ed., *Dwellings: A Spiritual History of the Living World* (New York: Norton, 1995), 96.

9. Muriel Rukeyser, "The Speed of Darkness," in *Out of Silence: Selected Poems* (Oak Park, Ill.: TriQuarterly Books, 1992), 135.

PART I

In the Belly of the Beast

At Play in the Paradise of Bombs

SCOTT RUSSELL SANDERS

Twice a man's height and topped by strands of barbed wire, a chain-link fence stretched for miles along the highway leading up to the main gate of the Arsenal. Beside the gate were tanks, hulking dinosaurs of steel, one on each side, their long muzzles slanting down to catch trespassers in a cross fire. A soldier emerged from the gatehouse, gun on hip, silvered sunglasses blanking his eyes.

My father stopped our car. He leaned out the window and handed the guard some papers that my mother had been clutching nervously.

"With that license plate, I had you pegged for visitors," said the guard. "But I see you've come to stay."

His flat voice ricocheted against the rolled-up windows of the back-seat where I huddled beside my sister. I hid my face in the upholstery, to erase the barbed wire and tanks and mirror-eyed soldier, and tried to wind myself into a ball as tight as the fist of fear in my stomach. By and by, our car eased forward into the Arsenal, the paradise of bombs.

This was in April of 1951, in Ohio. We had driven north from Tennessee, where spring had already burst the buds of trees and cracked the flowers open. Up here on the hem of Lake Erie the earth was bleak with snow. I had been told about northern winters, but in the red clay country south of Memphis I had seen only occasional flurries, harmless as confetti, never this smothering quilt of white. My mother had been crying since Kentucky. Sight of the Arsenal's fences and guard shacks looming out of the snow brought her misery to the boil. "It's like a concentration camp," she whispered to my father. I had no idea what she meant. I was not quite six, born two months after the gutting of Hiroshima and Nagasaki. My birth sign was the mushroom cloud. "It looks exactly like those pictures of the German camps," she lamented. Back in Tennessee, the strangers who had bought our farm were clipping bouquets from our garden. Those strangers had inherited everything—the barn and jittery cow, the billy goat fond of corn silks, the crops of beans and potatoes already planted, the creek bottom cleared of locust trees, the drawling voices of neighbors, the smell of cotton dust.

My father had worked through the Second World War at a munitions plant near his hometown in Mississippi. Now his company, hired by the Pentagon to run this Ohio Arsenal, was moving him north to supervise the production lines where artillery shells and land mines and bombs were loaded with explosives. Later I would hear stories about those loadlines. The concrete floors were so saturated with TNT that any chance spark would set off a quake. The workers used tools of brass to guard against sparks, but every now and again a careless chump would drop a pocketknife or shell casing, and lose a leg. Once a forklift dumped a pallet of barrels and blew out an entire factory wall, along with three munitions lockers.

In 1951 I was too young to realize that what had brought on all this bustle in our lives was the war in Korea; too green to notice which way the political winds were blowing. Asia was absorbing bullets and bombs as quickly as the Arsenal could ship them. At successive news conferences, President Truman meditated aloud on whether or not to spill *the* Bomb—the sip of planetary hemlock—over China. Senator Joseph McCarthy was denouncing Reds from every available podium, pinning a single handy label on all the bugbears of the nation. Congress had recently passed bills designed to hamstring unions and slam the doors of America in the faces of immigrants. The Soviet Union had detonated its own atomic weapons, and the search was on for the culprits who had sold our secret. How else but through treachery could such a benighted nation ever have built such a clever bomb? In the very month of our move to the Arsenal, Julius and Ethel Rosenberg were sentenced to death. Too late, J. Robert Oppenheimer was voicing second thoughts about the weapon he had helped build. In an effort to preserve our lead in the race toward oblivion, our scientists were perfecting the hydrogen bomb.

We rolled to our new home in the Arsenal over the impossible snow, between parking lots filled with armored troop carriers, jeeps, strafing helicopters, wheeled howitzers, bulldozers, Sherman tanks, all the brawny machines of war. On the front porch of our Memphis home I had read GI Joe comic books, and so I knew the names and shapes of these death-dealing engines. In the gaudy cartoons the soldiers had seemed like two-legged chunks of pure glory, muttering speeches between bursts of their machine guns, clenching the pins of grenades between their dazzling teeth. Their weapons had seemed like tackle worthy of gods. But as we drove between those parking lots crowded with real tanks, past guardhouses manned by actual soldiers, a needle of dread pierced my brain.

Thirty years later the needle is still there, and is festering. I realize now that in moving from a scrape-dirt farm in Tennessee to a munitions factory in Ohio, I had leaped overnight from the nineteenth century into the heart of the twentieth. I had landed in a place that concentrates the truth about our condition more potently than any metropolis or suburb. If, one hundred years from now, there are still human beings capable of thinking about the past, and if they turn their sights on our time, what they will see in the crosshairs of memory will be a place very like the Arsenal, a fenced wilderness devoted to building and harboring the instruments of death.

Our house was one of twenty white frame boxes arrayed in a circle about a swatch of lawn. Originally built for the high-ranking military brass, some of these governmental quarters now also held civilians—the doctors assigned to the base hospital, the engineers who carried slide rules dangling from their belts, the accountants and supervisors, the managerial honchos. To us children, this hoop of houses became the Circle, the beginning and ending point of all our journeys. Like campers drawn up around a fire, like wagons wound into a fearful ring, the houses faced inward on the Circle, as if to reassure the occupants, for immediately outside that tamed hoop the forest began, tangled, beast-haunted woods stretching for miles in every direction.

Through our front door I looked out on mowed grass, flower boxes, parked cars, the curve of concrete, the wink of windows. From the back door I saw only the trees, bare dark bones thrust up from the snow in that first April, snarled green shadows in all the following summers. Not many nights after we settled in, I glimpsed a white-tailed deer lurking along the edge of the woods, the first of thousands I would see over the years. The Arsenal was a sanctuary for deer, I soon learned, and also for beaver, fox, turkey, geese, every manner of beast smaller than wolves and bears. Protected by that chain-link fence, which kept out hunters and woodcutters as well as spies, the animals had multiplied to very nearly their ancient numbers, and the trees grew thick and old until they died with their roots on. So throughout my childhood I had a choice of where to play—inside the charmed Circle or outside in the wild thickets.

Viewed on a map against Ohio's bulldozed land, the Arsenal was only a tiny patch of green, about thirty square miles; some of it had been pasture as recently as ten years earlier, when the government bought the land. It was broken up by airstrips and bunkers and munitions depots; guards cruised the perimeter and bored through its heart twenty-four hours a day. But to my young eyes it seemed like an unbounded wilderness. The biggest parcel of land for the Arsenal had belonged to a U.S. senator who—in the selfless tradition of public servants—grew stinking rich from the sale. The rest was purchased from farmers, some of them descendants of the hardbitten New England folks who had settled that corner of Ohio, most of them reluctant to move. One of the old-timers refused to budge from his house until the wrecking crew arrived, and then he slung himself from a noose tied to a rafter in his barn. By the time I came along to investigate, all that remained of his place was the crumbling silo; but I found it easy to imagine him strung up there, roped to his roof beam, riding his ship as it went down. Every other year or so, the older children would string a scarecrow from a rafter in one of the few surviving barns, and then lead the younger children in for a grisly look. I fell for the trick only once, but the image of that dangling husk is burned into my mind.

Rambling through the Arsenal's twenty-one thousand acres, at first in the safe backseats of our parents' cars, then on bicycles over the gravel roads, and later on foot through the backcountry, we children searched out the ruins of those abandoned farms. Usually the buildings had been torn down and carted away, and all that remained were the cellar holes half-filled with rubble, the skewed limestone foundations, the stubborn flowers. What used to be lawns were grown up in sumac, maple, blackberry. The rare concrete walks and driveways were shattered, sown with ferns. Moss grew in the chiseled names of the dead on headstones in backyard cemeteries. We could spy a house site in the spring by the blaze of jonquils, the blue fountain of lilacs, the forsythia and starry columbine; in the summer, by roses; in the fall, by the glow of mums and zinnias. Asparagus and rhubarb kept pushing up in the meadows. The blasted orchards kept squeezing out plums and knotty apples and bee-thick pears. From the cellar holes wild grapevines twisted up to ensnarl the shade trees. In the ruins we discovered marbles, bottles, the bone handles of knives, the rusty heads of hammers, and the tips of plows. And we dug up keys by the fistful, keys of brass and black iron, skeleton keys to ghostly doors. We gathered the fruits of other people's planting, staggering home with armfuls of flowers, sprays of pussy willow and bittersweet, baskets of berries, our faces sticky with juice.

Even where the army's poisons had been dumped, nature did not give up. In a remote corner of the Arsenal, on land which had been used as a Boy Scout camp before the war, the ground was so filthy with the discarded makings of bombs that not even the guards would go there. But we children went, lured on by the scarlet warning signs. DANGER. RESTRCTED AREA. The skull-and-crossbones aroused in us dreams of pirates. We found the log huts overgrown with vines, the swimming lake a bog of algae and cattails, the stone walls scattered by the heave of frost. The only scrap of metal we discovered was a bell, its clapper rusted solid to the rim. In my bone marrow I carry traces of the poison from the graveyard of bombs, as we all carry a smidgen of radioactivity from every atomic blast. Perhaps at this very moment one of those alien molecules, like a grain of sand in an oyster, is irradiating some cell in my body, or in your body, to fashion a pearl of cancer.

Poking about in the ruins of camp and farm, I felt a wrestle of emotions, half sick with loss, half exultant over the return of forest. It was terrifying and at the same time comforting to see how quickly the green wave lapped over the human remains, scouring away the bold marks of occupation. The displaced farmers, gone only a decade, had left scarcely more trace than the ancient Indians who had heaped up burial mounds in this territory. We hunted for Indian treasure, too, digging in every suspicious hillock until our arms ached. We turned up shards of pottery, iridescent shells, fiery bits of flint; but never any bones. The best arrow points and ax heads we invariably discovered not by looking, but by chance, when jumping over a creek or scratching in the dirt with a bare incurious toe. This was my first lesson in the Zen of seeing, seeing by not-looking.

With or without looking, we constantly stumbled across the more common variety of mound in the Arsenal, the humpbacked bunkers where munitions were stored. Implausibly enough, they were called igloos. There were rows and rows of them, strung out along rail beds like lethal beads. Over the concrete vaults grass had been planted, so that from the air, glimpsed by enemy bombers, they would look like undulating hills. Sheep kept them mowed. The signs surrounding the igloos were larger and more strident than those warning us to keep away from the waste dumps. These we respected, for we feared that even a heavy footfall on the grassy roof of a bunker might set it off. Three or four had blown up over the years, from clumsy handling or the quirk of chemicals. Once a jet trainer crashed into a field of them and skidded far enough to trigger a pair. These numbers multiplied in our minds, until we imagined the igloos popping like corn. No, they were set far enough apart to avoid a chain reaction if one should explode, my father assured me. But in my reckoning the munitions bunkers were vaults of annihilation. I stubbornly believed that one day they all would blow, touched off by lightning, maybe, or by an enemy agent. Whenever I stole past those fields of bunkers or whenever they drifted like a flotilla of green humpbacked whales through my dreams, I imagined fire leaping from one to another, the spark flying outward to consume the whole creation. This poison I also carry in my bones, this conviction that we build our lives in minefields. Long before I learned what new sort of bombs had devoured Hiroshima and Nagasaki, I knew from creeping among those igloos full of old-fashioned explosives that, on any given day, someone else's reckless step might consume us all.

Of course we played constantly at war. How could we avoid it? At the five-and-dime we bought plastic soldiers, their fists molded permanently around machine guns and grenades, their faces frozen into expressions of bravery or blood lust. They were all men, except the weaponless nurse who stood with uplifted lantern to inspect the wounded; and those of us who toyed at this mayhem were all boys. In the unused garden plot behind the Circle, we excavated trenches and foxholes, embedded cannons inside rings of pebbles, heaped dirt into mounds to simulate ammo bunkers. Our miniature tanks left tread marks in the dust exactly like those cut into the blacktop roads by real tanks. Running miniature trucks, our throats caught the exact groan of the diesel convoys that hauled army reservists past our door every summer weekend. When we grew tired of our Lilliputian battles, we took up weapons in our own hands. Any stick would do for a gun, any rock for a bomb. At the drugstore we bought war comics, and on wet afternoons we studied war movies on television to instruct us in the plots for our games. No one ever chose to play the roles of Japs or Nazis or Commies, and so the hateful labels were hung on the smallest or shabbiest kids. For the better part of my first three years in the Arsenal I was a villain, consigned to the Yellow Peril or the Red Plague. Like many of the runts, even wearing the guise of a bad guy I refused to go down, protesting every lethal shot from the good guys. If all the kids eligible to serve as enemies quit the game, the Americans just blasted away at invisible foes, GIs against the universe.

Whenever we cared to, we could glance up from our play in the garden battlefield and see the dish of a radar antenna spinning silently beyond the next ridge. We knew it scoured the sky for enemy bombers and, later, missiles. The air was filled with electronic threats. Every mile or so along the roads there were spiky transmitters, like six-foot-tall models of the Empire State Building, to magnify and boom along radio messages between security headquarters and the cruising guards. Imagining dire secrets whispered in code, I keened my ears to catch these broadcasts, as if by one particular resonance of brain cells I might snare the voices inside my skull. What I eventually heard, over a shortwave radio owned by one of the older boys, were guards jawing about lunch, muttering about the weather, about wives or bills or bowling, swearing aimlessly, or counting deer.

Our favorite family outing on the long summer evenings, after supper, after the washing of the dishes, was to drive the gravel roads of the Arsenal and count deer. We would surprise them in clearings, a pair or a dozen, grass drooping from their narrow muzzles, jaws working.

They would lift their delicate heads and gaze at us with slick dark eyes, some of the bucks hefting intricate antlers, the fresh does thick-uddered, the fawns still dappled. If the herd was large enough to make counting tricky, my father would stop the car. And if we kept very still, the deer, after studying us a while, would go back to their grazing. But any slight twitch, a throat cleared or the squeak of a window crank, would startle them. First one white tail would jerk up, then another and another, the tawny bodies wheeling, legs flashing, and the deer would vanish like smoke. Some nights we counted over three hundred.

There were so many deer that in bad winters the managers of the Arsenal ordered the dumping of hay on the snow to keep the herds from starving. When my father had charge of this chore, I rode atop the truckload of bales, watching the tire slices trail away behind us in the frozen crust. Still the weak went hungry. Sledding, we would find their withered carcasses beside the gnawed stems of elderberry bushes. A few generations earlier, wolves and mountain lions would have helped out, culling the slow of foot. But since the only predators left were two-legged ones, men took on the task of thinning the herds, and naturally they culled out the strongest, the heavy-antlered bucks, the meaty does. Early each winter the game officials would guess how many deer ought to be killed, and would sell that many hunting tags. Most of the licenses went to men who worked on the Arsenal, the carpenters and munitions loaders and firemen. But a quantity were always reserved for visiting military brass.

They rolled into the Arsenal in chauffeured sedans or swooped down in star-spangled planes, these generals and colonels. Their hunting clothes smelled of mothballs. Their shotguns glistened with oil. Jeeps driven by orderlies delivered them to the brushwood blinds, where they slouched on canvas chairs and slugged whiskey to keep warm, waiting for the deer to run by. The deer always obligingly ran by, because men and boys hired from nearby towns had been out since dawn beating the bushes, scaring up a herd, and driving it down the ravine past the hidden generals, who pumped lead into the torrent of flesh.

Each deer season of my childhood I heard about this hunt. It swelled in my imagination to the scale of myth, outstripped in glory the remote battles of the last war, seemed more grand than even the bloody feuds between frontiersmen and Indians. I itched to go along, cradling my own shotgun, but my father said no, not until the winter after my thirteenth birthday. If I couldn't carry a gun, I begged, let me watch the hunt with empty hands. And so, the year I turned eleven, he let me join the beaters, who would be herding deer for a party of shooters from the Pentagon.

A freezing rain the night before had turned the world to glass. As we fanned out over the brittle snow, our bootsteps sounded like the shattering of windows. We soon found our deer, lurking where they had to be, in the frozen field where hay had been dumped. Casting about them our net of bodies, we left open only the path that led to the ravine where the officers waited. With a clap of hands, we set them scurrying, the white tails like an avalanche, black hoofs punching the snow, lank hams kicking skyward. Not long after, we heard the crackle of shotguns. When the shooting was safely over, I hurried up to inspect the kills. The deer lay with legs crumpled beneath their bellies or jutting stiffly out, heads askew, tongues dangling like handles of leather. The wounded ones had stumbled away, trailing behind them ropes of blood; my father and the other seasoned hunters had run after them to finish them off. The generals were tramping about in the red snow, noisily claiming their trophies, pinning tags on an ear of each downed beast. The local men gutted the deer. They heaped the steaming entrails on the snow and tied ropes through the tendons of each hind leg and dragged them to the waiting jeeps. I watched it all to the end that once; rubbed my face in it; and never again asked to work as a beater, or to watch the grown men shoot, or to hunt.

With the money I was paid for herding deer, I bought the fixings for rocket fuel. That was the next stage in our playing at war, the launching of miniature missiles. We started by wrapping tinfoil around the heads of kitchen matches, graduated to aluminum pipes crammed with gunpowder, and then to machined tubes that burned zinc or magnesium. On the walls of our bedrooms we tacked photos of real rockets, the V-2 and Viking; the homely Snark, Hound Dog, Bullpup, Honest John, Little John, Mighty Mouse, Davy Crockett; and the beauties with godly names—Atlas, Titan, Jupiter, Juno, Nike-Hercules—the pantheon of power. By then I knew what rode in the nose cones, I knew what sort of bombs had exploded in Japan two months before my birth, I even knew, from reading physics books, how we had snared those fierce bits of sun. But I grasped these awesome facts in the same numb way I grasped the definition of infinity. I carried the knowledge in me like an ungerminated seed.

There was a rumor among the children that atomic bombs were stored in the Arsenal. The adults denied it, as they denied our belief that ghosts of Indians haunted the burial mounds or that shades of strung-up farmers paced in the haylofts of barns, as they dismissed all our bogies. We went searching anyway. Wasting no time among the igloos, which were too obvious, too vulnerable, we searched instead in the boondocks for secret vaults that we felt certain would be surrounded by deadly electronics and would be perfect in their camouflage. Traipsing along railway spurs, following every set of wheel tracks, we eventually came to a fenced compound that satisfied all our suspicions. Through the gridwork of wire and above the earthen ramparts we could see the gray concrete skulls of bunkers. We felt certain that the eggs of annihilation had been laid in those vaults, but none of us dared climb the fence to investigate. It was as if, having sought out the lair of a god, we could not bring ourselves to approach the throne.

In our searches for the Bomb we happened across a good many other spots we were not supposed to see—dumps and man-made deserts, ponds once used for hatching fish and now smothered in oil, machine guns rusting in weeds, clicking signal boxes. But the most alluring discovery of all was the graveyard of bombers. This was a field crammed with the ratty hulks of World War II Flying Fortresses, their crumpled green skins painted with enigmatic numbers and symbols, their wings twisted, propellers shattered, cockpits open to the rain. In one of them we found a pair of mannequins rigged up in flight gear, complete with helmets, wires running from every joint in their artificial bodies. What tests they had been used for in these crashed planes we had no way of guessing; we borrowed their gear and propped them in back to serve as navigators and bombardiers. Most of the instruments had been salvaged, but enough remained for us to climb into the cockpits and fly imaginary bombing runs. Sitting where actual pilots had sat, clutching the butterfly wings of a steering wheel, gazing out through a cracked windshield, we rained fire and fury on the cities of the world. Not even the sight of the deer's guts steaming on the red snow had yet given me an inkling of how real streets would look beneath our storm of bombs. I was drunk on the fancied splendor of riding those metal leviathans, making them dance by a touch of my fingers. At the age when Samuel Clemens sat on the bank of the Mississippi River, smitten by the power of steamboats, I watched rockets sputter on their firing stand, I sat in the gutted cockpits of old bombers, hungry to pilot sky ships.

The sky over the Arsenal was sliced by plenty of routine ships: the screaming fighters, droning trainers, groaning transports, percussive helicopters; but what caught the attention of the children were the rare, rumored visitations of flying saucers. To judge by reports in the newspaper and on television, UFOs were sniffing about here and there all over the Earth. We studied the night sky hopefully, fearfully, but every promising light we spied turned into a commonplace aircraft. I was beginning to think the aliens had declared the Arsenal off-limits. But then a neighbor woman, who sometimes looked after my sister and me in the afternoons, told us she had ridden more than once in a flying saucer that used to come fetch her in the wee hours from the parking lot behind the Bachelor Officers' Quarters. Mrs. K. was about fifty when we knew her, a stunted woman who gave the impression of being too large for her body, as if at birth she had been wrapped in invisible cords that were beginning to give way; she had a pinched face and watery eyes, a mousy bookkeeper for a husband, and no children. She was fastidious about her house, where the oak floors gleamed with wax, bathrooms glittered like jeweled chambers, and fragile knickknacks balanced on shelves of glass. When my mother dropped us by her place for an afternoon's stay, we crept about in terror of sullying or breaking something. In all her house there was nothing for children to play with except, stashed in the bottom drawer of her desk, a dog-eared pack of cards, a pair of dice, and a miniature roulette wheel. Soon tiring of these toys, my sister and I sat on the waxed floor and wheedled Mrs. K. into talking. At first she maundered on about her life on military bases around the world, the bridge parties and sewing circles; but eventually her eyes began to water and her teeth to chatter, and she launched into the history of her abduction by the aliens.

"They're not at all like devils," she insisted, "but more like angels, with translucent skin that glows almost as if there were lights inside their bodies." And their ship bore no resemblance to a saucer, she claimed. It was more like a diamond as large as a house, all the colors of the rainbow streaming through the facets. The angelic creatures stopped her in the parking lot during one of her stargazing walks, spoke gentle English inside her head, took her on board their craft, and put her to sleep. When she awoke she was lying naked, surrounded by a ring of princely aliens, and the landscape visible through the diamond walls of the ship was the vague purple of wisteria blossoms. "They weren't the least bit crude or nasty," she said, the words coming so fast they were jamming together in her throat, "no, no, they examined me like the most polite of doctors, because all they wanted was to save us from destroying ourselves, you see, and in order to do that, first they had to understand our anatomy, and that's why they had chosen me, don't you see, they had singled me out to teach them about our species," she insisted, touching her throat, "and to give me the secret of our salvation—me, of all people, you see, *me!*"

My sister had the good sense to keep mum about our baby-sitter's stories, but I was so dazzled by hopes of meeting these aliens and learning their world-saving secrets that I blabbed about the possibility to my mother, who quickly wormed the entire chronicle from me. We never visited Mrs. K. again, but we often saw her vacuuming the lawn in front of her house. "Utterly crazy," my mother declared.

Mrs. K. was not alone in her lunacy. Every year or so one of the career soldiers, having stared too long into the muzzle of his own gun, went berserk or broke down weeping. A guard began shooting deer from his jeep, leaving the carcasses in heaps on the roads. A janitor poured muriatic acid into the swimming pool and then down his own throat. One Christmas, the lieutenant colonel who played Santa Claus started raving at the annual gift-giving and terrified the children out of their wits. It took five fathers to muscle him down and make him quit heaving presents from his bag of geegaws. To this day I cannot see Santa's white beard and red suit without flinching. Life on military reservations had also crazed many of the army wives, who turned to drink and drugs. Now and again an ambulance would purr into the Circle and cart one of them away for therapy. When at home, they usually kept hidden, stewing in bedrooms, their children grown and gone or at school or buried in toys. Outside, with faces cracked like the leather of old purses, loaded up with consoling chemicals, the crazed women teetered carefully down the sidewalk, as if on a tightrope over an abyss.

The Arsenal fed on war and the rumors of war. When the Pentagon's budget was fat, the Arsenal's economy prospered. We could tell how good or bad the times were by reading our fathers' faces, or by counting the pickup trucks in the parking lots. The folks who lived just outside the chain-link fence in trailers and tarpaper shacks did poorly in the slow spells, but did just fine whenever an outbreak of Red Scare swept through Congress. In the lulls between the wars, the men scanned the headlines, looking for omens of strife in the way farmers scanned the horizon for promises of rain.

In 1957, when the Arsenal was in the doldrums and parents were bickering across the dinner table, one October afternoon, between innings of a softball game, somebody read aloud the news about the launching of *Sputnik*. The mothers clucked their tongues and the fathers groaned; but soon the wise heads among them gloated, for they knew this Russian feat would set the headlines humming, and it did.

Our model rocketeering took on a new cast. It occurred to us that any launcher capable of parking a satellite in orbit could plant an H-bomb in the Circle. If one of those bitter pills ever landed, we realized from our reading, there would be no Circle, no dallying deer, no forests, no Arsenal. Suddenly there were explosives above our heads as well as beneath our feet. The cracks in the faces of the crazed ladies deepened. Guards no longer joked with us as we passed through the gates on our way to school. We children forgot how to sleep. For hours after darkness we squirmed on our beds, staring skyward. "Why don't you eat?" our mothers scolded. Aged thirteen or fourteen, I stood one day gripping the edge of the marble-topped table in our living room, staring through a glass bell at the spinning golden balls of an anniversary clock, and cried, "I don't ever want to be a soldier, not ever, ever!"

Each weekend in summer the soldiers still played war. They liked to scare up herds of deer with their tanks and pin them against a corner of the fence. Snooping along afterward, we discovered tufts of hair and clots of flesh caught in the barbed wire as the deer leaped over. Once, after a weekend soldier's cigarette had set off a brushfire, we found the charred bodies of a dozen deer jammed against a fence. We filled ourselves with that sight, and knew what it meant. There we lay, every child in the Arsenal, every adult, every soul within reach of the bombs—twisted black lumps trapped against a fence of steel. I have dreamed of those charred deer ever since. During the war in Vietnam, every time I read or heard about napalm, my head filled with visions of those blackened lumps.

To a child, it seemed the only salvation was in running away. Parents and the family roof were no protection from this terror. My notebooks filled with designs for orbiting worlds that we could build from scratch and for rocket ships that would carry us to fresh, unpoisoned planets. But I soon realized that no more than a handful of us could escape to the stars; and there was too much on Earth—the blue fountains of lilacs, the red streak of a fox across snow, the faces of friends—that I could never abandon. I took longer and longer walks through the backwoods of the Arsenal, soaking in the green juices; but as I grew older, the forest seemed to shrink, the fences drew in, the munitions bunkers and the desolate chemical dumps seemed to spread like a rash, until I could not walk far in any direction without stumbling into a reminder of our preparations for doom.

Because the foundations of old farms were vanishing beneath the tangle of barriers and saplings, for most of my childhood I had allowed myself to believe that nature would undo whatever mess we made. But the scars from these new chemicals resisted the return of life. The discolored dirt remained bare for years and years. Tank trucks spraying herbicides to save the cost of mowing stripped the roads and meadows of wildflowers. Fish floated belly-up in the scum of ponds. The shells of bird eggs, laced with molecules of our invention, were too flimsy to hold new chicks. The threads of the world were beginning to unravel.

In a single winter a hired trapper cleared out the beavers, which had been snarling the waterways, and the foxes, which had troubled the family dogs. Our own collie, brought as a puppy from Memphis, began to chase deer with a pack of dogs. At night he would slink home with bloody snout and the smell of venison on his laboring breath. The guards warned us to keep him in, but he broke every rope. Once I saw the pack of them, wolves again, running deer across a field. Our collie was in the lead, gaining on a doe, and as I watched, he bounded up and seized her by the ear and dragged her down, and the other dogs clamped on at the belly and throat. I preferred this wild killing to the shooting-gallery slaughter of the hunting season. If our own dogs could revert to wildness, perhaps there was still hope for the Earth. But one day the guards shot the whole wolfish pack. Nature, in the largest sense of natural laws, would outlast us; but no particular scrap of it, no dog or pond or two-legged beast, was guaranteed to survive.

There was comfort in the tales forever circulating among the children of marvelous deer glimpsed at dusk or dawn, bucks with white legs, a doe with pale fur in the shape of a saddle on her back, and, one year, a pair of ghostly albinos. Several of the children had seen the all-white deer. In 1962 I spent most of the summer sunsets looking for them, needing to find them, hungering for these tokens of nature's prodigal energies. By September I had still seen neither hide nor hair of them. That October was the showdown over the placement of Soviet missiles in Cuba; Kennedy and Khrushchev squared off at the opposite ends of a nuclear street, hands hovering near the butts of their guns. For two weeks, while these desperadoes brooded over whether to start the final shooting, I quit going to school and passed all the hours of daylight outdoors, looking for those albino deer. Once, at the edge of a thicket, on the edge of darkness, I thought I glimpsed them, milky spirits, wisps of fog. But I could not be sure. Eventually the leaders of the superpowers lifted their hands a few inches away from their guns; the missiles did not fly. I returned to my studies, but gazed stupidly at every page through a meshwork of fear. In December the existence of the albino deer was proved beyond a doubt, for one afternoon in hunting season an army doctor and his wife drove in the Circle with the pair of ghostly bodies tied to the hood of their car.

The following year—the year when John Kennedy was killed and I registered for the draft and the tide of U.S. soldiers begin to lap against the shores of Asia—my family moved from the Arsenal. "You'll sleep better now," my mother assured me. "You'll fatten up in no time." During the twelve years of our stay inside the chain-link fences, almost every night at suppertime outdated bombs were detonated at the ammo dump. The concussion rattled the milk glass and willowware in the corner cupboard, rattled the forks against our plates, the cups against our teeth. It was like the muttering of local gods, a reminder of who ruled our neighborhood. From the moment I understood what those explosions meant, what small sparks they were of the engulfing fire, I lost my appetite. But even outside the Arsenal, a mile or an ocean away, every night at suppertime my fork still stuttered against the plate, my teeth still chattered from the remembered explosions. They still do. Everywhere now there are bunkers beneath the humped green hills; electronic challenges and threats needle through the air we breathe; the last wild beasts fling themselves against our steel boundaries. The fences of the Arsenal have stretched outward until they circle the entire planet. I feel, now, I can never move outside.

White Sands

RAY GONZALEZ

*I*t was like playing on the moon as we rolled down the white sand dunes when we were kids. By the time we came to a stop at the bottom, we were covered in white dirt, looking like ghost children. The memory of family picnics at the White Sands National Monument near Alamogordo, New Mexico, in the 1950s is blurred now, but I still cling to a few vivid images of miles and miles of a white world where I had fun playing in the dunes, building white sand castles without knowing we were only a few miles from the government test site where Trinity, the first atomic bomb, was detonated on July 16, 1945.

Until I studied World War II in high school, I did not know the white desert playground of the park distracted visitors from the fact that they were near the historic site. After seeing what I was reading, my mother casually told me she and my father, along with thousands of El Pasoans, had seen a bright flash in the sky on July 16. My parents were high school students at El Paso Technical when the bomb went off one hundred miles to the north. No one knew what the flash was until years later, but she told me that day felt very unusual. The sudden light made many people nervous because the war was still on.

My parents had witnessed a turning point in history when they saw that bright light in the sky. As a child, I spent many weekends playing in the white sands of the future, just another kid amazed at the endless horizon of white hills and dunes, the light falling from the desert sun to wither everything in ninety-five-degree heat, making us play harder as the light intensified.

I can't forget the first day we walked through the park museum.

Besides the usual geological charts and relief maps, I saw displays of mounted white mice, white rabbits, a white coyote—even white tarantulas. These creatures had adjusted to this white world so that they could survive in the heat and desolation of the bleached landscape. Each species evolved to take advantage of constant camouflage. When I learned about Trinity, I wondered how many of the animals had been affected by the radiation of history. Had they truly changed color to blend into the white sand for protection and survival against predators, or were this ivory land, and its creatures, mutations from the first blast?

Nuclear fallout was not a hot topic for high school students in an isolated West Texas town during the 1960s. No one thought about it. It was not an issue. I knew nature had created the white sands thousands of years ago, and the evolution of white animals had nothing to do with the atomic bomb, but as I remembered that day in the museum, I sensed that the whiteness of every living thing around me was connected to the darkness of the brilliant flash of 1945.

I first read Leslie Groves's eyewitness account of the Alamogordo explosion when my American history class studied the development of the atomic bombs the United States dropped on Hiroshima and Nagasaki. As director of the Manhattan Project, a top-secret government program, Groves described what he saw across the white sands as an intense and blinding flash of light, a tremendous ball of fire that turned into the first mushroom cloud any of them had ever seen. He watched as the steel tower vaporized in the blast generated by the equivalent of fifteen to twenty thousand tons of explosives.

When I read this in high school and recognized the area as the place where we enjoyed family outings, I had not been to White Sands in years. Groves's account did not really strike me until a decade later. In high school, it was just another assigned chapter to read. For whatever reasons, my high school friends and I never went to White Sands, even though it was less than two hours from El Paso. I enjoyed the white fields only as a small boy.

I didn't make the connection between the bomb, my parents seeing the flash, and my innocent childhood in the sand until 1977, as I drove alone across southern New Mexico. I was on my way back to El Paso after living for two years in San Diego. I drove south past Albuquerque.

But instead of taking the straight, short route to El Paso, I headed east from Las Cruces over the Organ Mountains.

The high pass took me to the eastern side of the range, directly above the vast flatness of the desert floor and White Sands, forty miles away. I don't know why I chose to return to El Paso from that direction, but driving past White Sands brought it all back. Perhaps I thought of those days because friends of mine in San Diego had mentioned their participation in antinuclear groups protesting at the nuclear power plant near San Clemente. The last demonstration had taken place a few days before I said good-bye to them and headed home.

It was an early evening in April when I headed down the long stretch of highway bordering the eastern end of White Sands. The setting sun ignited the peaks of the Organ Mountains and washed the miles of white sand with a peach-colored hue. I drove past the fenced-off land whose barbed-wire barriers held small signs every few hundred feet: "Property of United States Government. No Trespassing."

A simple warning like that was enough to keep people away and draw them to the park instead. Thousands of visitors came each year to gawk at the white sand dunes, miles and miles of them. Roads had been cut to reach the interior dunes. After the shock of the white world had worn off, families could eat at the picnic tables scattered throughout the park.

I spotted the museum building about a mile down the road and began to relive our family picnics. It must have been 1958. As a six-year-old, I thrilled in climbing the steep dunes to pretend I was going to get lost out there and scare my parents into coming to look for me. When I stood at the top of the dunes, my father and mother looked tiny and faraway as they sat at the picnic table at the bottom.

I waved and yelled until I caught their attention. They waved back, but I couldn't hear what they were saying. I turned and started hiking across the deep sand. The white powder seeped into my sneakers and pant cuffs. I never hiked more than a hundred yards before I began to get scared at the realization that I was standing in an endless sea of whiteness. I would turn and retrace my deep footprints back to the family.

Now, as I drove past the museum, I had the urge to stop and find out if the display of white animals was still there. I slowed down and saw the "Closed" sign on the doors. Almost twenty years after my first visit to the museum, I couldn't go in to look at the white kangaroo rats, the snarling white coyote, or the huge albino rattlesnake that was the most vivid, shocking animal mounted in the museum.

I sped past the closed building and continued toward El Paso, remembering how the white rattlesnake had startled me as a boy. After peering into the glass-enclosed exhibits of rats and lizards, I came upon the coiled body of the rattlesnake. The sight of a white reptile, and the fact that it had come from the sands where I loved to play, increased my wonder. It was one of the first times I felt I belonged in the desert.

My nose barely cleared the bottom of the display, so I had to stand on tiptoe to get a good look. I stared at the huge snake. I couldn't believe its pale skin and transparent rattle. Its head was a dirty, milky white with tiny black eyes, the only dark spots on the body. I had seen rattlesnakes in El Paso, but I never guessed they could turn white to live in these sands.

The rest of that long-ago day is a blur. I think I ran out of the museum to find my parents and sister, who were walking back to the picnic area. I didn't say a word to them about the white rattlesnake. I sat at the table and kept looking up at the walls of white sand as we ate, wondering if I had rolled over any snakes in my adventures in the dunes. I can still see the brightness of the white sand, intensifying while we ate. It must have been noon on a hot day, because I see myself sitting at the table, sweating and biting into my sandwich as the blinding sunlight draws the white earth closer to me.

I drove toward El Paso, and the heat of the picnic faded. I couldn't recall the last time my family took me to White Sands. As I approached Alamogordo, the image of the white rattlesnake changed from a coiled shape to a mushroom cloud rising above the desert.

I have never been an antinuclear activist or protester and have never even read books about Hiroshima, but as I drove through the area where Trinity was detonated, I thought about those childhood picnics, the white animals in the museum, and the brilliance of the sands. I discovered a certain light, a clarity of understanding, a radiance burning through the dunes of family history.

Its energy came from many sources. The innocence of childhood produced the light on those white hills. Our family outings generated the heat because they were part of growing up with a sense that the concept of family could never be broken. Those picnics on the dunes represented the outlook of a small boy growing up in the late 1950s, a boy who thought the world was made up of nothing but good times.

The energy of the blinding desert also came from the fact that the U.S. government chose this area in which to conduct experiments that would change world history. If someone had interrupted my fun on the dunes to tell me that the Manhattan Project had reached its climax a few miles away, I couldn't have comprehended it. As a child, I would have thought the idea of a big bomb in the desert was kind of neat. Nothing could have destroyed my playground.

Twelve years after my solitary drive past the dunes toward home, the first test of a Star Wars laser weapon was successfully completed at White Sands. In 1989, the U.S. government finally shot down a missile with a laser. The flight and destruction of the missile took place over White Sands. Forty-four years after the first atomic flash startled the people of El Paso, there had been another turning point over the white dunes.

As before, the energy for the laser weapon came from the white desert, from energy spilling over from the atomic bomb. Yet it was power derived from the desert itself.

In *Masked Gods,* his classic book on Navajo history, Frank Waters writes about the kiva ceremonies of native people, and he reflects on the future of mankind and how studying native religions gives many clues to our turbulent century. He describes a visit to Los Alamos, the town near Santa Fe founded in 1945 to house scientists working on the Manhattan Project. The atomic reactor constructed there was named Clementine after the miner's daughter of the folk song. Waters states that the Clementines were an Egyptian religious sect in the first century A.D. who believed in the female spirit. He compares this female power to the force rising out of the kivas near Los Alamos. He points out that the Sun Temple at Mesa Verde is the most intense example of female power because elaborate ceremonies of light and fire were held there, ceremonies to end life cycles and begin new ones, the whole process forming out of the sheer power of Mother Earth and her underground forces.

Waters writes about the Sun Temple of Mesa Verde and its parallel to the atomic reactor. He feels it is not far-fetched to see the parallel in their meanings. He compares the physical energy locked inside the atom to the energy inside our psyches. Both involve the transformation of matter into creative energy. This creation arises from a dependence on what he calls "the reconciliation" of the primitive forces of life. This fusion results in a birth of new energy.

Tremendous conflict—from the smallest, most insignificant act of a small boy rolling down the white dunes, to Trinity detonating nearby—explodes past the spiritual kivas toward the end of the twentieth century and the Star Wars forming high above the desert. If Frank Waters is correct, and if the white rattlesnake is my most vivid memory of the White Sands museum, then the first atomic blast that startled my parents was destined to take place in the desert of New Mexico. It is a flow of light from the ancient people to the builders of the test tower melting at ground zero, to me rolling down the white dunes as rattlesnakes coiled undetected nearby—all the way to the final act of driving past the closed museum.

As I drove past Alamogordo and neared El Paso, the white sands were left behind. To my right, the Franklin Mountains rose in a purple haze. I was coming home to live again in El Paso.

I made my way through the northeast suburb of my hometown and tried to picture what it must have been like to see the flash on July 16, 1945. My mother said it lasted only an instant, and life went on. I stared at the mountains and noticed how new housing developments were creeping up the canyons. It meant cutting into the desert, disrupting the ancient landscape, uprooting cacti, and forcing wildlife to readjust. It also meant that many new home owners in the foothills of the Franklins would find rattlesnakes in their yards. I wondered how many they would kill, or if any of those people in the new suburbs would get bitten. It was a small ecological problem. The snakes would disappear.

I drove into El Paso knowing that none of these homeowners would ever be startled or frightened by a white rattlesnake. They would never learn that albino rattlesnakes lived one hundred miles to the north of their new homes. These new residents of El Paso had no reason to discover the secrets that lay hidden in their magnificent desert. It was too vast, too much land. They would have no urge to explore beyond the city limits of their dreams. Retirees from nearby military installations and new high-tech company employees weren't interested in local history. It's not part of the dream. After all, the stark, brown mountains a few miles from their backyards give off a beautiful light each evening, enough heat to satisfy them in their moment under the Southwestern sun.

Mother Witherup's Top-Secret Cherry Pie

BILL WITHERUP

I

I have come back to the A-type, government-built, double-decker du-
plex where I grew up in the Fifties, to visit my ailing father, seventy-
seven, who has terminal bone cancer. Merv, as his brothers and friends
call him, retired from N-Reactor in 1972, after thirty years at the Hanford Atomic Engineering Works.

Father and I disagree on nuclear matters and foreign policy. And on
the virtue of holding a steady job. But I pull my Oedipal punches, in
deference to his cancer. It is not for the Prodigal Son to pass judgment—
Dad's labors in the mills of the National Security State fed, clothed, and
housed a family of six.

Merv is frail now, down to 135 pounds. But his opinions have kept
their weight and vigor. He keeps trying to bait me into a nuclear discussion, much like the hired hand in the Robert Frost poem, who wants one
more chance to teach the college boy how to build a load of hay.

When one of the hospice's nurses stops in to take his blood pressure,
Pop gets in a dig.

"This is my oldest son, Bill. He grew up here, but he's been trying to
shut the place down ever since."

Rictus-like grin, on my part. In the past, when he was healthy, we
could never have it out anyway. Rose, my mother, would not allow
arguments or heated discussions in her territory. She would shut us off
with "It's time for dinner" or "How about some pie and ice cream?"

Behind every good man there stands a baker of pies, her rolling pin raised like a gavel to rap the house to order.

Here lies the crust of a tale.

II

It is an October afternoon, 1987. A high-pressure ridge vaults up along the West Coast, and it is unseasonably warm. Seattle, two hundred miles northwest, is talking water rationing. Due west, Mount St. Helens heats a fresh cauldron of Lava Soup. Some thirty miles northeast of Richland, N-Reactor is on hold and simmer—11,000 cooks, preps, and dishwashers sweat a layoff. The reactor has been temporarily closed by the Public Health Service: cockroaches were found swimming in the Uranium Soup; rats burrowing in the Plutonium Soufflé.

We have just finished an early dinner. Since Father's retirement the elders have supped at 4:30 P.M. so they can catch *People's Court* at 5:00 on the boob. Mother apologizes for serving leftovers, even though her leftovers would put the main course at a classy restaurant to shame.

Merv has gone back to the living room couch, where he holds court now, attired in black Playboy pajamas with red piping. Wasting and bird-boned, he reminds me of a red-winged blackbird perched on a cattail.

Here Mother says a variation of her standard line.

"I don't know why I bother cooking. Your father doesn't eat enough to keep a bird alive."

Papa Witherup grew up during the Great Depression, one of four children of a grocer in Kansas City, Missouri. After he married Mother, he first went to work in a paint store. Following Pearl Harbor, he was hired by Remington Arms, a DuPont subsidiary, in the Quality Control section to check the annealing on cartridges.

When the Manhattan Project kicked into gear, DuPont contracted to build the world's first plutonium reactor at Hanford, Washington. Dad was recruited to come west. His first job was, again, in Quality Control. He helped record each graphite block that made up the core of Ur-Reactor.

Mama Witherup, nee Nita Rosemond Allen, was the youngest of six children. Her father was a drummer who sold drugstore supplies across Missouri, Kansas, and Nebraska.

Rose is one hell of a cook. Her forte has always been dessert—especially pie. Her crusts are so light that the wedges levitate on their own and float into your mouth.

Dessert was always the bait and the reward for eating your veggies. Dinner opened with a Blessing and ended with a blessing—provided we four cubs could see our teeth in the cleaned plates.

III

Mother always eats her dessert, with a cup of decaf, directly after the main course, whereas Father's habit, after retirement, is to have his pie and ice cream later in the evening.

Though I'm bloated from overeating, I signal weakly that I will join mother over her dessert. My extended visit has given her the excuse to be liberal with the commissary. Food is Love. It is also part of my wages for helping to spit-shine and buff the decks of The Good Ship Witherup—a working-class frigate that has patrolled the Columbia River against the assaults of dirt and communism for almost half a century!

We have our pie at the dining room table while Father kibitzes from the sofa. With each visit home I've prodded the old folks to tell me about their childhood and about the parts of the Richland/Hanford Saga that I wasn't privy to as a youngster.

Neither of my parents is a great conversationalist—they are laconic, matter-of-fact, hardworking, Show-Me Missourians still. But as it is Saturday and there is no *People's Court,* mother allows herself a bit of free-associating. She tells me about the time, not too long after the move to Richland, when her cherry pie was classified TOP SECRET.

IV

Hanford was one of three highly secret death factories engineered by General Leslie Groves to produce atomic bombs. The other two plants were at Los Alamos, New Mexico (Brain Center), and Oak Ridge, Tennessee (Uranium Milling).

All the engineers and production workers on the assembly line were kept in the political and moral dark about the product of their labors. They knew only that they were performing essential war work.

The workers were not supposed to tell their wives what they were doing at Hanford, or if working women, to discuss it with their boyfriends or husbands. Children had even less of an idea. During my nine years of boyhood in Richland, I never knew what it was my father did, exactly, as he left each day or swing or grave shift on the gray bus called the *Grey Goose,* on the way to the satanic mills.

Hanford workers and their families, however, were checked and re-checked for political spots or moral stains. Every six months the plain-clothes guys from Military Intelligence would knock on the neighbors' doors and inquire about the Witherups; would rap on our door and discuss the neighbors.

Before the unions were voted in at Hanford, it was hard to make do for a family of six. My mother cooked up the idea to cater desserts for a little extra grocery money. Her masterwork, the Cadillac of pies, was her cherry pie, with freshly picked Yakima Valley cherries as the nuclear core. She decided to advertise her wares in the local paper, *The Villager.*

V

Shortly after the advertisement appeared, the man from Military Intelligence sniffed the wind and came knocking on our door. He had seen the advertisement, he said, and he had dropped by to sample the product. Rose invited him in—she had a pie cooling in the kitchen. She set out a piece with a cup of coffee; hoped perhaps he was a local businessman.

"My, my," he said. "This is some pie. Sakes alive!"

Then he flashed his Gumshoe Glow-in-the-Dark Badge.

"I'm sorry, Mrs. Witherup. We can't let you advertise your pies. It violates security precautions. But you keep on making these," he said generously, dabbing his mouth with a government issue hanky.

"You can sell these to friends, or by word of mouth, but any advertising by Hanford workers or their families is CLASSIFIED. Security, you know. We wouldn't want the Axis to find out what we are up to here, would we?"

VI

It is 4 A.M. I'm asleep in my old room upstairs. I always wake up about this time when I'm visiting, gasping for air like a carp out of water: my folks have converted the original government model to an airtight, filter-controlled residence (a Defense System to protect Mother's sinuses from dust and nefarious pollens).

This particular morning I bolt upright, awakened by a pulsing, steady siren.

"Christ!" I think, "N-Reactor has gone critical!"

I throw on a robe and hurry downstairs, open the front door as quietly as I can, and listen intently to the radioactive air. Relieved, I decide the siren is merely a car alarm that has triggered, only a few blocks away.

But as I stand there, I notice bulky shadows lurking about the remodeled A, B, C, D, E, and F houses—and I know it is the KGB snuffling window sills for the home-baked pies. For there, deep in the sweet juices and sexual hearts of cherry, peach, and apple pie, lie the state-of-the-art secrets of the U.S. nuclear weaponry!

A Roller-Coaster Ride through the Nuclear Age

DAVID SEABORG

I was born in 1949, four years after the two nuclear bombs were dropped on Japan, and World War II ended, and about the time the Nuclear Age, the Cold War, and the arms race began. The date of my birth was April 22, which later became Earth Day. I was born in Berkeley, in a house several blocks from the University of California campus that was the site of many major scientific discoveries that fueled the Nuclear Age, as well as a major site of protest against many of its manifestations. My mother, who had worked as the secretary of Ernest O. Lawrence, the inventor of the cyclotron (the atom smasher so crucial in the discovery by my father of radioactive elements heavier than uranium, such as plutonium), did not have time to leave for the hospital before my sudden birth on the front porch of my parents' house. I came out so rapidly that I would have hit the front porch had my father not stepped in and caught me! This man who both fathered and delivered me in this unusual birth is Glenn T. Seaborg, the scientist who discovered many of the heavy elements created by Lawrence's cyclotron. He is a Nobel Prize winner in chemistry and discoverer of plutonium, the element used in the atomic bomb and nuclear reactors. I was born at the right time and place, and had the right parents, for a firsthand roller-coaster ride through the Nuclear Age.

My father was very famous for as long as I can remember, having won the Nobel Prize when I was two years old. Hence, I have had the experience of having a famous father in the field of nuclear science for my entire life. I am often asked what it is like to be the son of a Nobel Prize–winning scientist. It had both extremely positive and extremely negative effects on me. It made for an interesting childhood, with many discussions about science and scientific issues with my dad, as well as the opportunity to meet eminent scientists, congressmen, and heads of state, and other prominent people, including athletes, because of my dad's interest in sports. Also, my dad took me to many interesting places, including two Nobel Prize ceremonies in Stockholm, the second one being the ninetieth anniversary of the Nobel Prize. Attending the latter one were many former Nobel Prize winners, with whom I had an opportunity to speak. My dad also took me on a behind-the-scenes tour of Oak Ridge National Laboratory, a major site of nuclear research in Tennessee, when I was on break from college. My family received special treatment at the Montreal World's Fair, where we did not have to wait in line like the rest of the people. These were some of the opportunities I experienced because of my parentage.

Both my parents encouraged my early interest in biology, tolerating my constantly collecting and keeping as pets various species of snakes, lizards, salamanders, and insects. I am forever grateful to them both, since this greatly influenced my choice to major in zoology in college and graduate school, and to pursue evolutionary biology as a career. It also was important in my development into a dedicated, active environmentalist.

One day my dad brought a small cube of uranium to my elementary school class and gave a talk on the radioactive elements. It was a nice experience for me at that age. The reflected glory and respect I received from my classmates that day were quite satisfying. I was the star of the class that week. The cube of uranium was heavy and fun to play with. (It was not dangerous.)

I did have some fun as a young child with my father's fame, at his expense. On one occasion, at the International House at the University of California at Berkeley, where I later lived as a graduate student, there was a gathering of the U.C. faithful before a Cal football game that my parents, my brother Steve, and I attended. I was ten years old and Steve was eight. After the MC of the event said some words honoring my father, he announced that my mother was present, and then said, "And

Dr. Seaborg's sons, Dave and Steve, are present today." They had us stand, and the audience applauded us. We put our hands together and held them over our heads, moving them up and down in a most immodest bow that embarrassed both our parents. This got a good laugh from the audience. I initiated the performance; Steve merely followed his older brother's lead. Our tolerant parents did not punish either of us for this act.

I took a phone call one day from a woman who asked for Dr. Seaborg. I told her to wait a minute, and went looking for my dad. I did not find him right away, and, being a child of about twelve with priorities suited to that age, forgot about the call and went to play baseball. About half an hour later, I saw my dad walking by. I said, "Oh, by the way, Dad, you have a phone call." My dad came back from the call a few minutes later, not pleased with me. "Dave," he said, "do you know who you just kept waiting for half an hour on the phone? The president of the United States!" It was President Kennedy. Once again, I did not get punished for my faux pas. Actually, my dad thought it was pretty funny.

Since my dad was appointed by Kennedy as chairman of the U.S. Atomic Energy Commission (AEC; it is now the Department of Energy), and hence the head governmental person on nuclear issues, we moved from California to Washington, D.C., when I was twelve years old. My father had a good relationship with Kennedy. He had scheduled to have my siblings and me meet Kennedy, a meeting that would have taken place just a few days after President Kennedy was shot. It has always been a disappointing memory for me that I just missed meeting this president, in addition to the loss of someone I admired so much. I remember sitting alone for a few minutes in my room on the top floor of our house in Washington, a few hours or perhaps a day or two after President Kennedy was shot. My stomach hurt, and I felt an awful, overwhelming fear, a terror, for both myself and the human race. It was very intuitive and emotional; exactly what I was afraid of was not very clear. I felt that a wise, compassionate leader who knew how to lead us was lost; that there were sinister forces operating that I could not comprehend; and, above all, over the years, if not very soon, the assassination and its related consequences could lead to a nuclear holocaust of unimaginable terror and destruction.

I believe that because I was raised by the man who discovered plutonium, the threat of a nuclear holocaust arose in my consciousness more than would be the case with most people. Of course, during the Cold War, we all faced the possibility of sudden extinction, so I cannot be sure that the average American did not worry just as much as I did. During my years in middle school and high school, in Washington, the government had a plan to save the chairman of the AEC and his family in the event of a nuclear war. The AEC's main office was in Washington, and this is where my father normally went to work. However, the government decentralized the AEC to make it less vulnerable to a nuclear attack. It therefore had another office in Germantown, Maryland, about an hour from Washington by car, where my dad sometimes worked. The plan was that as soon as we got word that the unthinkable had actually happened, our family—my parents, five siblings, and I—would load into the car and drive (or be driven by the chauffeur the government provided my dad) to a bomb shelter in Germantown, where we would be sequestered in safety. It was a joke. And I knew it. To get a family with six children to the car before a Soviet missile launched from a submarine just off the coast hit us would be a feat in itself. Reaching Germantown took almost an hour in good traffic conditions. The roads, of course, would be jammed with angry, terrified motorists having little regard for traffic laws or courtesy. Even if by some miracle we made it to our destination, the Soviets surely knew about Germantown, and would target it, so our bomb shelter was at ground zero. If Germantown went unscathed or our shelter withstood a direct hit, the radiation and other environmental disruptions, such as nuclear winter and increased ultraviolet radiation due to destruction of the ozone layer, would make survival for any length of time impossible. I could not have known, of course, about nuclear winter or the destruction of the ozone layer then; such knowledge would not have made my assessment of our chances of survival any more bleak.

Although most of the time my thoughts were occupied with my schoolwork and other activities, which kept my conscious mind mercifully off nuclear war, I periodically experienced episodes of absolute terror. Some were worse than others. The following were the two worst episodes. The first episode began at a rally to protest Nixon's blockade of North Vietnam during the Vietnam War, when I was an undergraduate student at the University of California at Davis. A student speaker announced that he had received word that the Soviets were going to run the blockade. I do not know in retrospect if the speaker was dishonestly trying to drum up support for further protest action or was simply misinformed, but I believed him at the time. I thought this would lead to World War III.

I left the rally and phoned my mother in Washington, imploring her to ask my father to speak to Nixon right away and ask him to remove the blockade. She did not want to do this. She told me that she did not know why I was so worried. She spoke to me about how much my dad had done for world peace. I guess she thought a talk with Nixon would be of no help and would not be well received. I went to the student travel office and asked the student working there when I could get a plane to Australia, because I felt nuclear war was impending. I remember his words, spoken almost thirty years ago, so well: "Buddy, it ain't going to make any difference where you are." I knew he was right. Feeling out of options, I stayed put and hoped the world would go on. I want you to imagine, to get a clear concept of the terror I felt, believing the entire world would end in such a hideous way because of human foolishness. And note that my reasoning was not based on entirely irrational thinking. In this case, it was based on misinformation, but there have been other times when the world has come dangerously close to destroying all higher forms of life on Earth in a few hours.

In my second episode, I was a graduate student at the University of California at Berkeley. I woke in the middle of the night. I heard sirens. Since I had just awakened and it was the middle of the night, I was in a strange psychological state, easily suggestible, full of anxiety. Perhaps I had had a dream. At any rate, I thought the sirens were the emergency alarm system warning that nuclear war had broken out. I think I perceived screaming or people driving off in their cars. I looked out a window of the house I was living in, at San Francisco and the bay. Part of San Francisco appeared to be missing. I did not realize that Angel Island was blocking out the lights of the city from my vantage point. I dialed the operator. I was too embarrassed to ask if a nuclear war had started, for I partly believed it hadn't. So I said to the operator, "Is everything all right?"

"Everything's just fine, sir," she said.

I figured there was no nuclear war going on, since I would not have received an answer if there were. I breathed a sigh of relief bigger than the Grand Canyon. We talked a bit more, until I was sure.

In these two incidents, my fears proved to be unfounded. However, they illustrate the constant fear I lived with. I think the fact that we lived with the threat that the human race could destroy itself totally, at any moment, without warning, had profound negative psychological effects on all of us who lived through the Cold War. These effects have not been adequately studied; they should be.

One night my father threw a party at our house in Washington for Andronik Petrosyants and his entourage. Petrosyants was my father's Russian counterpart, the chairman of the Soviet State Committee on Atomic Energy, their equivalent of the AEC. A number of Americans who worked with my father also attended. With great fanfare and, I must say, charm, Petrosyants gave my father a number of gifts. Everyone applauded after each gift was given. The most interesting present was a model of part of the moon, shaped like part of a globe. Attached to it by a plastic rod was a metal Soviet satellite. A button on the moon could be pushed to make the satellite beep. This was a source of amusement for me and my siblings. One day it broke; the satellite failed to beep at the push of the button. My eldest brother and his friend, both good at electronics, opened up the model of the moon to fix it. Inside, they found far more wiring than would be necessary to make a beep at the push of a button. My brother said the Soviets were either very poor electricians or very good ones! The theory that he and his friend had was that the extra wiring was a bug capable of transmitting my father's conversations back to the Soviet embassy, about two miles from our house. Perhaps they hoped he would keep it in his downtown office, where they could hear some really interesting conversations. When my brother told my father of his discovery, my father said he would have the appropriate people examine it. The next night at the dinner table, we all waited anxiously for the verdict. My dad said it was not a bug, and not to say anything about it to anyone. My siblings and I were not convinced. We thought it was a bug, and the government officials had told him that it was not, and that word of it should not be spread around because they preferred not to have an incident with the Soviets as a result. I am still quite sure of this.

The moon-and-satellite model was kept in the living room. This was unfortunate for the Soviets, because the living room was not where my dad discussed any sensitive government business. I feel sorry for the person who was assigned the task of listening to what was said near the bug. He heard television shows that we watched then, such as *Gomer Pyle* and *Get Smart,* and the phonograph in the family room, not far away, on which the latest Beatles or Beach Boys hit played six times in a row. My brother Steve, the sibling closest to me, would discuss with me the latest events in our school and news of our friends. So the bug picked up such information as who the cutest girls in our classes at high school were, the outcome of our latest sandlot baseball game, and the excitement of the Rolling Stones concert we'd just attended—all no doubt crucial information for our national security and Soviet advantage in the Cold War. Steve and I invented a character we named Don Curtis. Don Curtis was in every imaginable way the epitome of imperfection. We amused ourselves by having one or the other of us take on the role of Don Curtis. The Soviet eavesdropper received an earful of the latest antics of Don Curtis. Recently, my brother and I recalled the bug and joked that the KGB must have had a file on Don Curtis and wondered who he was.

The Soviets were not the only ones who eavesdropped on my father. One day, speaking on the phone with Bill, the man who later became my brother-in-law, I heard a clicking sound, a sound I had heard a few times before on our phone in our Washington house. I mentioned it to Bill, who informed me that it was a bug, probably the FBI. Back then, phone taps apparently made periodic clicking sounds. I assume that they wanted to make sure my father was not a security risk, a spy for an enemy of our government, or some such dastardly person. The FBI agent listening to what the bug recorded mostly heard teenage talk not radically unlike what the Soviets heard, without the TV shows and rock and roll.

There were, of course, good experiences that resulted from being the son of a high government official during the Cold War. I had the opportunity to meet President Johnson at the Smithsonian Institution. Johnson was late, having walked his beagles. When my dad introduced me to him, Johnson was much like a zombie, obviously exhausted due to lack of sleep, with some help from stress and overwork. He stared blankly into space as my father said, "Mr. President, I'd like you to meet my son David." He said, "Good to meet you," as if he were speaking to a wall. At times after this, I wondered about a problem that is seldom discussed in the public arena: the lack of sleep of the nation's commander in chief, and its effect on him when he's called on to make critical decisions that could involve what to do in an international crisis, such as the Cuban missile crisis. Could the exhaustion and stress that are common states for our overworked presidents cause a wrong decision that is fatal to all higher life on the planet?

I was a junior high school student when it was announced that Premier Khrushchev was placing missiles just off our shores, in Cuba. I was quite frightened during this crisis. At the family dinner table we watched the crisis unfold on the television news each evening. It was the major topic of discussion over dinner. A neighbor who played ball with me and my group of friends told me after the ordeal was over that his father, a staunch conservative, had expressed the opinion that we should have bombed Cuba. I asked my dad what he thought would have happened in that event. He said that he thought the Soviets would have felt they had to respond with nuclear weapons, and the final war would have resulted.

My dad never spoke about his talks with Kennedy during the crisis. My most vivid memory is wondering why I should do my homework if the world was about to end. I did decide to do my homework and proceed as usual, but for a teenager that experience was horrible beyond words.

I recall talking with my dad on vacation in Virginia Beach about the Limited Test Ban Treaty, in which the United States, Soviet Union, and Great Britain agreed to cease testing nuclear weapons in the atmosphere, limiting explosions to those underground. My father told me that without his support, there would not have been a treaty. Later, I decided that this was his greatest accomplishment, notwithstanding his discoveries and Nobel Prize, because of the great environmental, peace, and public health benefits of this treaty. It was very important that no more strontium-90 be released into the atmosphere, since it was already at dangerous levels because of the atmospheric testing. I was very pleased and had a feeling of faith in humanity when this treaty was signed. I remember a strong feeling of trust and love for President Kennedy, as if we were all in good hands with a great president who could hardly do wrong. It was a feeling that everything was going to be all right, in contrast to the feeling I had after his assassination.

My dad later told me of his regret concerning the attempted Comprehensive Test Ban Treaty (CTBT). The Americans insisted on having a great number of inspections to assure compliance if we were to have a CTBT, whereas the Soviets insisted on a much smaller number; they feared that the Americans would use the inspection process to gather intelligence. My dad at the time supported a large number of inspections. No CTBT resulted, and the underground tests continued. He wishes, in retrospect, that we had not insisted on so many inspections, and that there had been a CTBT without them. He has lobbied over the years for a CTBT. Finally, after many years, most major nations recently signed a CTBT, much to the joy of both my father and me.

I would like to go to Russia and get a firsthand view of what it is like today. I would like to see how well they are doing with taking care of their nuclear submarines that are sitting around unmaintained, the nuclear material that we hear from time to time mysteriously disappears, the aftermath of Chernobyl, and other such problems. I know they have a museum (perhaps it is more of a repository; I am not sure) that houses preserved bodies of people who were born with mutations and deformations from nuclear weapons testing—victims of radiation exposure. Among these is a baby who was born with only one eye, in the center of his or her head. The child was born alive, but never lived to be very old. It was a cyclops! This is an incredible rarity, something that, as a biologist, I would find extraordinarily interesting to see, even though I have great sympathy for the child, that such a thing happened to a fellow human being.

And I have fantasies of seeing what they picked up from the bug in the model of the moon and satellite they gave my dad. I would love to see the KGB files on Don Curtis.

Imagine a World Without Nuclear Nightmares

MARY LAUFER

*M*y husband was in the Navy for over two years before I understood that the threat of radiation exposure was going to be a part of our lives for a long time, and that, unlike me, he wasn't worried about it at all.

One morning Mark was sitting backward on a kitchen chair between the toilet and bathtub. I was using the fingernail scissors from an old manicure set to trim around his neck and ears for an inspection. The tips of the scissors curved inward, which didn't make the job easy. I found gray hairs in his sideburns. He was twenty-one years old and had gray hairs. I told him I was concerned about him being a reactor operator, that maybe the radiation was affecting him. What about those men who claimed their leukemia was caused by working at naval shipyards or by watching atomic bomb tests in Nevada?

He tried to assure me that nuclear power was *completely* safe. But Mark ate big brown bruises on bananas and never cut the fat off his meat and forgot to wear his seat belt in the car. He'd leave a steak knife on the edge of the kitchen counter and not think twice about little fingers reaching up to grab it. And he used to think condoms were safe, too.

"If it's so safe," I asked, "why are the reactors ninety miles out in the desert? Why does the government continually monitor our air and water to determine radiation levels here in Idaho Falls?"

"Precautions," he answered.

As I snipped away at the curly hair on the back of his neck, I could smell the Clorox Two on his dungaree uniform. I'd washed his clothes separately the night before, measuring three cups of detergent into the machine, running them through the rinse cycle twice. He'd strung his TLD (thermoluminescent dosimeter) back on his belt in the morning, the little black cylinder a constant reminder that he was exposed to radiation.

"Millirems," he said, trying to convince me. "No more than an X-ray."

Snip, snip, I was done. With my hand mirror and the one on the medicine cabinet, he could have seen how jaggedly I cut. Instead, he ran his fingers along the hairline behind his ears and brushed the short hairs onto the floor.

He stood up, gave me a smack on the lips, and said good-bye. I handed him his comb, and he stuck it in his back pocket.

"Aren't you going to look to see how badly I scalped you?"

"That's okay," he said, smiling. "I trust your judgment."

We left behind the reactor prototypes in Idaho when Mark received orders to the USS *Jack* at the Navy Base in Groton, Connecticut. After Sub School, he packed his seabag and climbed down into the fast-attack submarine, our son waving sadly as tugboats pulled the sub away from the pier and started down the river. In the depths of the ocean, without fresh air or sunshine, my husband kept the reactor going for weeks at a time, working with a small group of sailors who called themselves "nukes." They'd all had intensive training in nuclear power, and there was special shielding between them and this new source of radiation. But I was still afraid something might go wrong, and Mark would get an overdose. Or even worse than that—what if his boat didn't come back?

In the Sub Museum, I saw the painting of the *Jack*'s sister ship, the *Thresher,* and the roster of the 129 men who were lost with her. Next to each crew member's name was his rate and rank, and one of them on the list immediately caught my attention: "ET2" (Electronics Technician, Petty Officer Second Class). It was the abbreviation I wrote next to my husband's name when I cashed a check on the base. Mark said they'd learned from malfunctions in the past; there was no cause for worry.

Sure. And the *Thresher*, which sank somewhere off the New England coast with its radioactive fuel—there was no cause for worry about that either? Wouldn't the wreckage eventually release radiation into the ocean? The ocean we swim in, the ocean where fish live before they end up on our plates?

Those concerns somehow shrank in importance the minute I learned that Groton is downwind of Millstone, two civilian nuclear power plants. One day a little booklet called *What to Do in an Emergency* came in the mail. Distributed by the Connecticut Office of Civil Preparedness, it instructed readers that in the event we heard a three-to-five-minute, single-tone siren, we should go inside, close all doors and windows, and turn off fans, air conditioners, furnaces—anything that draws in outside air. The next step was to tune the radio to the emergency broadcast system. If advised to leave, we must "proceed in an orderly fashion along evacuation routes to designated reception centers," where we'd be assigned a shelter. Our reception center was a small community college in Norwich that would have taken days to process those of us who lived in Navy housing, much less half the citizens of Groton.

The booklet addressed only possible instability at the utility reactors that generated the area's electricity. Yet we who lived in Polaris Park brushed our teeth and went to bed about a mile down the road from the Sub Base, where at any one time quite a few submarines sat in port, each with its own reactor. It didn't take a nuclear physicist to figure out that if we were in the evacuation radius for Millstone, we were certainly in the evacuation radius for the Sub Base, and our families were at a high risk of being contaminated if we didn't get out of there fast.

My friend Sue was the only one I knew who did what the booklet told us to do: she kept a suitcase packed with canned food and a change of clothes and little games for her kids to play in the car. Just in case. Just in case there was a nuclear accident and we had to drop everything and take off for Norwich.

I never packed a suitcase. I made a mental list of all the things I would pack: a jar of peanut butter and a box of crackers, a flashlight, and a first aid kit. I even went to the hall closet and pulled out my old red suitcase to see how much it could hold. But something stopped me. It would be too much like packing an overnight bag when you're expecting a baby and being ready on a moment's notice to jump in the car when the inevitable happened. I wanted to trust that the men who were operating the reactors knew what they were doing. Once a year, the nukes on each submarine had to pass a meticulous Reactor Safeguards Exam. The Navy's safety record was exemplary, except for the *Thresher*, of course, and another sub that was rusting on the ocean floor. I guess there's a first time for everything.

The accident at Three Mile Island in Pennsylvania made me more alarmed about Millstone than about the Sub Base. I tried to forget what happened there the way I'd forget about plane crashes when I flew. But there was no forgetting the scared looks on the nukes' faces when they found out that the reactor core was partially exposed at Three Mile Island. I heard the word "meltdown" mentioned, the "uh-ohs" and the "oh-nos" exchanged between them, then their jokes about glowing in the dark. Maybe that's why I kept my gas tank full. If there ever was a leak, I'd be out the door and on my way while everyone who stopped to get gas or grab a suitcase would be caught in the traffic jam at the first signal.

I couldn't understand why people I talked to thought I was paranoid. Didn't they get the booklet in the mail? Didn't they see the danger of living in a city where the threat of radiation looms over everyone? But as time went by, something strange happened: I became one of them. I got used to it. I'd been sitting in the middle of a landfill so long that I didn't smell it anymore.

Slowly I let my gas tank get down to empty with no urgent need to fill it "just in case." The reactors at Millstone became an ordinary part of the scenery, and we even considered buying a house within a short distance of them. Mark's boat appeared less and less hazardous every time I went aboard. Swans swam in circles nearby, and schools of fish darted in the water. We ate Thanksgiving dinner in the sub's mess hall and watched movies together there. Nothing bad happened, so it seemed that nothing ever would.

While I let the perils of nuclear reactors slip from my memory, I wasn't yet aware of other radiation connected to submarines. Many things went on around me that I didn't understand. Our country wasn't at war, yet everyone acted as though it were. The command reminded us Navy wives that departure and arrival dates were not to be discussed over the phone or in public places, as if the Soviets were always listening. Secrecy like this during peacetime mystified me.

One night when Mark was out to sea, I was invited to supper by some friends we'd known in Idaho, Steve and his wife, Julie. We were sitting cross-legged on the carpet while we waited for the fondue to get hot, and I asked Steve why he was able to spend more time at home than Mark. Why was his sub stationed in Holy Loch, Scotland? How come it had two alternating crews that relieved one another every three months, while Mark's boat had a single crew and an unpredictable itinerary? Steve took a sip of his wine, and then in a singsong voice he made the distinction for me between "fast attacks" and "boomers": There were "daddy killers" like Mark's sub, and there were "mommy and baby killers" like his sub. I didn't know him well enough to tell if he was getting drunk or if he was joking.

When I asked him if he was serious, he shrugged his shoulders, then got up and left the room without answering. Julie explained what he'd meant: fast attacks hunted down an enemy's subs and surface ships; their torpedoes could annihilate the men who worked on them. Boomers made regular patrols and carried nuclear-tipped ballistic missiles. These could wipe out entire populations on other continents; women and children would not be spared.

Steve was in the kitchen refilling his glass, and Julie said that she worried when he drank; she wished he wouldn't, but he was under so much pressure. She told me about the simulation drills on the subs and how the guys never know if it's a drill or not; the first thing that runs through their heads is their families—they wonder whether they'll ever see them again. Then they must let go of that and focus on why they are there, no matter how awful it is. She whispered, "Steve almost went crazy on his first patrol. He kept thinking that the boat was carrying 'death,' that it was a 'death ship,' and he stayed in his bunk, sick to his stomach with the thought of it, everyone trying to comfort him. After three days they talked him out of it, and he went back to work."

As I listened to this story, I realized how naive I'd been. I'd still thought of nuclear bombs as being dropped by airplanes or carried by missiles that were housed in underground silos. What had I thought subs were for? Spying. I imagined the boat silently maneuvering into places other vessels couldn't go, the captain putting up that nifty periscope, and a camera clicking. Once their true mission became clear to me, I saw the whole world in a different light. Within a short time I was forced to think more about it, because Mark was transferred to a Trident submarine.

When my husband was assigned to the *Georgia*, it was under construction at General Dynamics' Electric Boat Shipyard. I remember our arrival in Groton, when we drove across the Gold Star Bridge and Mark pointed out Electric Boat, near the edge of the Thames River. It looked to me like a giant version of our son's Play-Doh factory, pumping out a 560-foot submarine, with another one following behind. Now I saw those boats as "boomers" even bigger than Steve's boat, neither safe nor nontoxic. The warheads on just one of their twenty-four missiles had more destructive power than all of the bombs dropped in human history.

There were homes down there near Electric Boat, and I wondered how the locals felt about having nuclear technology proliferate in their backyards. Was it something they learned to live with, like the Millstone power plants? I knew civilians who had jobs as welders; the economy must have revolved around EB's government defense contracts. It appeared that everyone here accepted the mass production of submarines without question. Everyone but me.

Months later, when the *Georgia* rolled off the building platform and was launched into the water, seven hundred antinuclear protesters showed up for the big splash. They picketed with signs that pleaded for disarmament, sang peace songs, and linked hands and prayed during the ceremony. Some lay down on the sidewalk and prevented anyone from entering Electric Boat Shipyard. There were no welders in this bunch! Among those arrested were seminary students, a Franciscan monk, and a blind woman. They came from nearby towns and faraway cities.

A week after the *Georgia* was launched, seven demonstrators cut through the chain-link fence surrounding EB in the middle of the night. I eagerly read the newspaper articles about what the men and women had done. They spray-painted the words "Disarm" and "Stop Trident" on the hull of the boat, and hung a banner that said "Swords into

Plowshares." They brought baby bottles filled with their own blood, poured the blood over the missile hatches, then pounded the hatch covers with hammers until security guards heard the banging. The paper listed their occupations as teacher, nurse, church worker, laborer, companion to an elderly woman, auto mechanic, and pizza deliverer. What they were trying to say stirred my emotions. Half of me openly admitted that I felt nuclear weapons were terribly wrong, and that they should all be dismantled. The other half had a husband stationed on that submarine.

Mark voiced no doubts about what he was doing. He believed that the Soviet Union's recent buildup of submarines was a real threat, and deterrence was necessary to maintain peace. From his point of view, he and others like him protected the demonstrators' butts, allowing them the freedom to demonstrate. After hearing his side of it, I still thought that the demonstrators were noble because they risked jail sentences for their beliefs. But Mark's reasoning seemed more practical, and he was, in fact, risking his life.

One day when I was on my way to the commissary, protesters were blocking the main gate of the Sub Base, parading back and forth in front of it, waving huge posters. As I got closer, I could see they were displaying enlarged photographs of Hiroshima victims. Many of the pictures were of children, and the skin on their faces and arms looked like it had been burned in a fire. After I drove past, I couldn't stop seeing them in my mind. It helped to remember that atomic bombs ended World War II and brought my father home so he could marry my mother and raise a family. But it gave me a chill to think that Mark's submarine would have first-strike capability.

When the new sub started sea trials to test-fire its missiles, Mark stood watches in front of an instrument panel and monitored it for hours at a time, turning a sign that hung from the clock back and forth between A.M. and P.M. I told myself that he didn't work directly with the weapons, so if they were launched in a war, he was blameless. He was a reactor operator, not a killer. I knew a woman whose husband was the weapons officer on the boat. That would get to me, I thought. But over time, even being married to a reactor operator troubled my conscience. Mark's job with the propulsion system made it possible for the "death ship" to lurk in the ocean. What bothered me most was that it didn't seem to bother him.

All the nukes had been the cream of the crop at their high schools, excelling in both math and science. They were men who could do difficult calculations quickly in their heads, who in fact had to depend on their wits, because if they couldn't fix an important piece of equipment, they didn't come home. Yet I began to wonder about their morals. If they had any. Did they realize the enormity of their responsibility? Were there any more Steves out there?

At boat picnics and other get-togethers, I heard the same thing over and over: They wished there was no need for their jobs. They'd rejoice to be suddenly unemployed if it meant the end of the arms race and there was no use for them. But the reality was that the Soviets had missiles aimed at U.S. cities, and we either had to defend ourselves or else let them destroy us. One nuke told me he would rather have lived a hundred years ago than today, that he would gladly trade the chance of catching tetanus or diphtheria for the fear of getting irradiated or irradiating others. Another said that he got depressed hearing world news. He confided, "I don't read the paper or watch the news anymore. If the man tells me to push the button, I'll push the button."

Their resignation scared me. They'd learned to live with a nightmare! How would anything ever change if we all ignored the resistance we felt? The moment you accept nuclear warfare as a permanent solution, you stop searching for an alternative; you lose sight of the way things ought to be. The inventors of the atomic bomb didn't have an ounce of imagination left to ask, "Where will this lead?" No wonder there was public outcry at Trident launchings! The protesters could see where this was going to lead and were tired of waiting for the diplomats to get their act together.

On a rainy afternoon I was sitting in my car with another Navy wife, waiting for the sub to return, our kids making a ruckus in the backseat. I'd parked alongside the EB fence between two "No Parking" signs, and when a policeman stopped nearby, my heart sank. As he got out and walked toward us, I rolled down my window. I felt intimidated by his uniform, his badge, his authority. Surely I wasn't as brave as those men and women who damaged my husband's boat.

The cop inspected the sticker on my windshield that allowed us access to the Navy Base. Then he bent over and looked inside the vehicle.

"Dependents?" he asked.

It didn't matter that I was parked illegally! He would give me a ticket only if I were a demonstrator! I was on the right side—his side. Yet in one way weren't we all on the same side—demonstrators, nukes, Navy wives? We all wanted peace, didn't we?

I think Steve knew that even the Soviets wanted peace. He told me when we first met that he'd learned Russian in college before he went into the Navy. You can't learn a language without learning something about the people who speak it. He must have had some knowledge of their land, their culture, their literature. Strip the country of its leaders, and what would be left but families like ours? They didn't want to live in terror any more than we did.

When the USS *Georgia* was commissioned as the nation's fourth Trident submarine, I did not attend the ceremony with my husband. It was a cold and windy day in February, and Mark said he'd understand if I stayed home. But he couldn't have understood my real reasons for not going, because I was just beginning to understand them myself. It would have been unbearable to sit in the audience and listen to bigwigs give inflated speeches about how this 1.2 billion-dollar vessel was an instrument of peace, not war. I belonged with the activists outside the gates who were being dragged away by police wearing riot gear.

Before Mark had to leave for the Trident's permanent port in Bangor, Washington, I walked on its deck with him. The slogans that the protesters had spray-painted on the steel hull were gone; the hatch covers that they'd dented with their hammers had been repaired or replaced. I was filled with despair as I counted the twenty-four rings that outlined the missile hatches and imagined what waited in the huge tubes beneath them. It was just a matter of time. Sooner or later there would be a reason to use them.

Nothing looked the way it used to after that. Whatever I'd once found beautiful was spoiled now by thoughts of how nuclear war could take it away. Would there be a future for my little boy? Mark talked about the two of us having another baby when his sea duty in Bangor was done. How could he face his work every day, much less think about bringing another baby into this mess?

One night after Mark left, I took a hike along the Thames River with some friends. We were enjoying the peaceful scene until we spotted the red lights of the EB cranes blinking on and off across the water. We stopped walking and stared in silence. Finally one of us held out his arm and said, "We're looking at the end of the world." He'd put all my fears into eight words.

Whether the entire planet would be destroyed was debatable, but deep down I knew that Groton would be a primary target with the Sub Base and EB there. The emergency booklet didn't say to pack a suitcase in the event of a nuclear attack. Unlike a power plant accident, there would be no escape; we'd be incinerated instantly in the heat of a fire-ball. All my worrying over Mark, and he might survive us! The sub-mariners could be the *only* ones to survive! What would it be like to know that the civilization they'd left wasn't there anymore? That lethal fallout was in the air, the water, the soil? Mark took tape recordings with him of the sounds of crickets and frogs and songbirds. What if, when they resurfaced, those recordings were all that remained of nature?

On a Saturday morning I heard a long, droning siren that I recognized as a nuclear attack warning. From an upstairs window I looked out over the slanted rooftops of base housing. No mushroom cloud. Below, my neighbor continued to wash his car in his driveway. I turned on a radio and kept changing the station to be sure only music was playing. A few minutes later, the siren stopped. It was only a test, the man's voice on the loudspeaker said. If it had been an actual nuclear attack, we would have been instructed to seek shelter, he said.

I yelled out the window, "Where? Where could we possibly go?" The guy washing his car glanced up at me and smiled.

A reprieve came with shore duty. My husband returned from Bangor, and we moved to upstate New York. There were no submarines or

Saturday morning drills, just a couple of nuclear power plants about ten minutes away in West Milton, prototypes where Mark trained naval students to work with submarine reactors. The plants were similar to the ones in Idaho, but hadn't been built in the desert because the originals had been determined safe. They were hidden away in the woods so well that our neighbors weren't aware of their existence until Mark told them where he worked.

In the beginning, doomsday was still on my mind. One April morning I saw a flash in the sky, and I thought it was a nuclear explosion before common sense told me it was just the first lightning of spring. My son informed his new friends that the world was going to blow up, and I had to step in and calm his fears even as my own were ebbing. It took months, but slowly I stopped thinking about it. My husband was home every night, not patrolling the ocean with "death." Having another baby didn't seem to be such an awful thing to do anymore.

Now, if the newspaper carried a story about nuclear weapons, I skimmed over it as I ate my breakfast. How many we had, how many the Soviets had, it all seemed to be happening a million miles away from us. The lid blew off a nuclear power plant in Chernobyl and massive radiation spewed out, but that was far away from us, too. If I didn't have to look at it, I didn't have to think about it. This lesson in distancing myself from what was too overwhelming to imagine helped later, when Mark was assigned to submarines in Charleston, South Carolina, and Kings Bay, Georgia. We lived in nice neighborhoods far from the bases.

Mark advanced to Master Chief, and after more than twenty years of active duty, he retired from the Navy. His "brag wall" shows off all of the subs he was stationed on, each wooden plaque having the dates of his service engraved below an emblem. When I dust the plaques, I can't help feeling a little pride for the part that he had in protecting our country. But then I see the photo of a missile that he framed and hung on the wall with his plaque collection. The long, pointed cylinder is shooting up from the water, fiery clouds trailing behind it. A test missile, of course. But it is somehow out of place here; it contradicts Mark's argument that a submarine's true mission is deterrence. If a missile is fired, then deterrence has failed, hasn't it? Anyone looking at this wall must think that a fired missile would be something to brag about.

The commanding officer of Mark's last boat sent me a formal certificate saying I made my husband's career possible by "providing support." It was suitable for framing, but I didn't hang it on the wall. My daughter received a certificate also; it said that her father left her so many times in order to ensure that she inherited "a safer world." Someday this child of ours will realize how unsafe the world that she inherited is. There are still thousands of warheads on hair-trigger alert, vulnerable to accidental attacks. Insecure countries with unstable governments have followed our example and are testing their own nuclear weapons. Dumps of radioactive waste are scattered over the planet and will remain toxic for thousands of years. How will I explain my "support" of this madness? If I tell my daughter that it all started before I got here, and I didn't think there was anything I could do to change it, I'd be telling her that there's nothing she can do, either.

So I will warn her not to give up hope in the future, but to imagine a world without nuclear nightmares. A world with energy sources that are harmless to the environment. Where arms negotiations don't stop until all weapons of mass destruction are gone. Where children of former enemies chat over the Internet and grow up without ever thinking of aiming missiles at each other. Then she must try her hardest to make it happen. If the Earth is destroyed, it will be because we settled for things as they were. The reactor operator, the Navy wife, even the welder. None of us will be blameless.

It may be the protesters who save our butts. Every time a protester has the courage to cry out, "This is wrong!" a few more people wake up. A young man from Greenpeace came to our door recently and informed us that the government plans to make tritium for nuclear warheads at a commercial nuclear power plant in our area. It jolted me. I promised him I'd send letters to the Department of Energy. Letters! What good will letters do? There was a time I walked on the deck of a Trident submarine, right over the missile tubes. I should have brought along a sledgehammer.

Reciprocal Paranoia

REFLECTIONS ON THE ATOMIC ERA AND THE COLD WAR

PHIL WOODS

> The Cold War has not been a heroic episode, an occasion for triumphs, but the most futile, wasteful, humanly destructive no-through-road in history. It has led to inconceivable investment in weapons with inconceivably destructive powers, which have threatened—and continue to threaten—the very survival of the human species (and other species, perhaps more worthy of survival). It has nourished and reproduced paranoias; enlarged authoritarian powers and the license of over-mighty security services; deadened imagination with a language of worst-case analysis and a definition of half the human race as an enemy Other.—E. P. Thompson

I

*L*ittle did I know my life would begin in the shadow of this reciprocal paranoia.[1] I was born in July 1946—roughly one year after the Bomb was used. My father was a storyteller. I grew up hearing his service tales. He had been an instructor in the Army Air Corps during the war. By funny twists of fate he'd managed to miss his overseas assignments, and this frustrated him. He'd missed his chance to participate in the Big One. My father regretted never having flown a B-17 over Germany.

He believed his children needed to know what sacrifices his generation had endured before they were able to have children, settle down in a home, and have a normal family life as it was being defined in those postwar years. Thus, he insisted the whole family see films like *Twelve*

O'Clock High. I can remember very clearly sitting in the front seat between my parents at a drive-in movie. I always paid close attention to my dad's commentary and asides. He'd say things like "We really didn't have a fighter that was as good as the British Spitfire until the P-51 Mustang came along at the end of the war. We were no match for the German fighter planes, and our fighters, before the P-51, didn't have the fuel capacity to accompany the bombers all the way to Germany and back. The flak [antiaircraft fire] was murder." He said things like that—aviation lore he'd picked up through talking to guys who made it back.

I can see him like it was yesterday, sitting at our kitchen table after breakfast on a weekend, showing the kids flying maneuvers, with his hands as the plane. He seemed to know all the strengths and weaknesses of each plane in use during the war. This balding father, with worry lines already engraving themselves into his forehead, but still youthful and impassioned, would say:

> Now, you take the P-39. It was designed to be our number one fighter, but it wasn't any good at that. Too slow, too much armor. Couldn't hold a candle to the Japanese Zero or a Messerschmitt. But it was a damned good fighter bomber. Really good against tanks. That's what the Russians used the ones we gave them for. Did I ever tell you about the time we flew a squadron of them up to Alaska to give the Russians as part of lend-lease?

He'd be off and running then. We'd be spellbound, and two hours later I'd leave the table having flown with him through some mythic time zone where men did great and noble things, dealt with absurdity, and had lots of laughs and adventures to tell their kids about later on.

I grew up with a heroic sense of what war is. Many boomers I talk to, if their parents missed actual combat, also were instilled with patriotic pride and a Hollywood sense of what modern battle is like. My mother always tells me World War II was a "glamorous war." Even Daniel Ellsberg reports going to Vietnam full of images of John Wayne. This was the American mythology.

My father stayed in the Air National Guard until the Korean War. With child number three about to be born, he realized he had other responsibilities, and resigned from the Guard. Nonetheless, he was an Air Force man. He subscribed to the Air Force Association magazine. Picture a balding man in his mid-thirties who looks much like any other young professional of that era, kind of a gray flannel suit guy. In his imagination he must have still thought of himself as a fighter pilot, a knight in the sky jousting in the modern way, keeping count of his kills. In his dreams he probably said, "Let me have a crack at those jets. If Chuck Yeager can do it, so can I."

Because of his stories and the Air Force Association magazine, I grew up with images of Russia's latest Darth Vader–like hardware. This was balanced out by our shiny new aircraft. Much of it was depicted in glossy advertisements from the defense contractors. In part, it was aimed at building a constituency for continued or expanded funding. The editorial line, however, was somewhat confused. For the most part they wanted you to believe we were consistently technologically ahead of these backward and dastardly Commies. On the other hand, they kept having to generate enough credible threat by the other side to justify expanding the Air Force's budget. Thus, many of the Russian planes, shown in comic book colors of dread, were sketches of prototypes that never went into production, but were useful for generating the proper sense of threat. For men, it all seemed like thrilling adventure. I think that was what really tied my father to it, besides his patriotism.

My pop was also very proud of the Strategic Air Command and its bulldog-tough General Curtis LeMay. My dad respected LeMay's stripping the B-29s of much of their armor and defensive firepower in order to increase their bomb load. This could be done because the Japanese had virtually no fighters left and B-29s flew at thirty thousand feet. Of course, this proved difficult for the precision bombing called for. LeMay then authorized them to fly lower and firebomb whole cities in a vast preview of the new weapon soon to come.[2]

What we now know, thanks to the great investigative reporter Richard Rhodes,[3] is that LeMay was a kind of monster. You may need this type of attack dog in an all-out war. Grant and Sherman certainly would understand LeMay. But you damned well better keep such a beast on a short leash and under full civilian control. I had grown up with the notion that Ike, the old general who played golf all the time and tried to calm the country down, had done just that. As Rhodes notes, however,

By 1954, Curtis LeMay had apparently begun raising the ante with the Soviet Union on his own, *covertly and extralegally*. Reconnaissance over-flights of the Soviet Union had begun no later than 1950. LeMay used these flights not only to gather electronic and photographic intelligence; he also used them to probe Soviet air defenses, knowing as he did so that he might be provoking war. There is testimony that he may have meant to do just that. If he could not initiate preventive war, he seems to have concluded, he might be able to push the Soviets to sufficiently high levels of alert to justify launching a full preemptive attack. . . .

[In fact,] In 1954 LeMay remarked to a reconnaissance pilot whose plane had been damaged by a MiG-17 while over the Soviet Union, "Well, maybe if we do this overflight right, we can get World War III started."[4]

The pilot thought LeMay was joking. I think not!

The 1950s marked the birth of the full-blown military-industrial complex of Ike's farewell speech. LeMay had enough leeway, according to Rhodes, that he did everything in his power to start World War III by constantly attempting to provoke the Russians into a suicidal attack in order to unleash a full-scale fusillade by LeMay's bombers. In the early 1950s, LeMay had propeller-driven B-36s loaded with atomic bombs fly over Moscow, daring the Russians to shoot one down and give him an excuse. Later it was B-52s with U-2s to scout and give warning.

LeMay operated from a simple logic: "War with the Commie Russians is inevitable; let's get it over with while we have overwhelming superiority. This is the best way to minimize our own casualties." Apparently, he operated from this premise up through the Cuban missile crisis. For example, Rhodes somberly summarizes:

During the Cuban missile crisis, the determination of LeMay and some of his subordinates to follow military logic, subverting Presidential authority to do so, nearly led to full-scale nuclear war with the Soviet Union. The United States came much closer to self-inflicted nuclear destruction at that time than most Americans realize.[5]

LeMay—like many other hard-liners—considered Kennedy a coward. The missile crisis was merely the confirmation. Carl Olgesby believes that from such deductions the road led to Dallas.[6] Similar hard-line sentiment is probably behind the "October Surprise" that Reagan and Casey buggered Jimmy Carter with.[7] As they say, even paranoids have real enemies.

My dad became paranoid, but I never heard him question or criticize Curtis LeMay. Like most Air Force guys, he believed that they had really won the war, and LeMay was one of their champions. In this respect he admired LeMay the way some GIs revere Patton—a man my father also admired and told legendary stories about. Yet when the decade ended, my dad and I watched Ike's famous military-industrial complex farewell speech. My dad said, "The president is right about this." By saying this, he conveyed both the speech's significance and the fact that this was deeply troubling for him as a patriot who worked as a civilian in the very bowels of the beast.

For Ike, on the other hand, it is very likely that the origin of his farewell speech grew out of his suspicion that the Francis Gary Powers U-2 incident that killed his peace summit with Khrushchev in Paris was engineered by the CIA to prevent detente. After the incident, Eisenhower told a key aide never to let him be in the same room alone with its director, Allen Dulles.[8]

While we don't know for sure what the implications of Ike's remark are, we do know some things about the career of Secretary of State John Foster Dulles's brother: Allen Dulles was the Bern-based head of the Office of Strategic Services (OSS) European operations, and he held secret meetings with Nazi representatives in Switzerland two weeks before the war ended, in violation of the signed agreements with the Soviets not to seek a separate peace.[9] Second, Dulles was on hand to help plan and endorse the cockeyed Bay of Pigs fiasco, for which JFK summarily dumped him. Ah, but who goes to Dallas? JFK. And who comes back to be a senior member of the Warren Commission? Allen Dulles. The plot thickens. I believe these subterranean vibrations of betrayal, paranoia, and double cross infected my father like a virus. Whether this reflects the collective unconscious, I can't say. I only know we swim in the zeitgeist, and sensitive souls often drown in the deep water.

I remember watching my father's first crackup
Furiously he tore through his dresser drawers
screaming at my mother
while tossing his medals
                              in the trash
His discharge papers
                              His CU diploma
All in a terrible frenzy

(from my unpublished poem "Even When the Cold War and Heredity
Get Your Mama and Papa, in Middle Age You See & Try to Forgive.")

If you look at the photos of Khrushchev in Paris, waiting for Eisenhower's arrival, you see a chunky Russian version—Marshal Rodion Malinosvky—of the LeMay bulldog.[10] This guy is wearing enough bric-a-brac to decorate a bad Hollywood costume drama. As with their war memorials, the Russians had a great tendency to overdo it. His face, however, is tough as nails. This is the kind of tenacity that defeated the Panzers in the arctic cold of the Russian heartland. This is the kind of face that drove the Red Army into Berlin. This face says, with every muscle, "Don't fuck with us, or there'll be Hell to pay!"

Aha! Maybe he's LeMay's doppelganger or brother. Maybe he's why Khrushchev beseeched Eisenhower to give him an out, give him some way to save face after the U-2 incident. Save face and thereby save the summit. But the military-industrial complex had Ike by the short hairs. The poor man who orchestrated D-Day couldn't figure out a way to give the Russians a face-saving gesture that would fly domestically. A golden opportunity was wasted! One that might have prevented the tragedy of Vietnam.

I was seven
He was gone for awhile
He seemed calmed, but not himself
at the sanitarium

.   .   .   .   .   .

I remember one man's brown sickly
puffy face
I don't know if he had electric shock

like my pop did but he looked just
as zombied out

When papa came home
to the rundown house
my mother's father rented for us
he seemed pretty happy

.   .   .   .

But the money wouldn't square
with needs of four kids
& a wife with a penchant
for buying furniture
when her giddy body
was flying with high octane mania

That's when he became a time/motion man
at the bomb storage plant
Inspecting anthrax shells & mustard gas
        canisters in the igloos
to see if the Chicano expendables
        were earning their keep
before the mushroom clouds came
or the sci-fi Nazi weapons
from the igloos
did the big Alchemical Boogie

*(from my unpublished poem "Even When the Cold War & Heredity
Got Your Mama & Papa, in Middle Age You See & Try to Forgive")*

II

It's 1959. The variety show host Arthur Godfrey recites a poem on his
Christmas show in honor of the Strategic Air Command and its brave
commander, General Curtis LeMay. My father is so moved by it that he
vows to write to the show for a copy of the poem, though he never
actually gets around to it. I have to admit that I followed his lead, and
swelled with pride in my country and the brave men who were defend-
ing it.

Earlier in the decade my father spoke in a hotel conference room at the north end of Colorado Springs. From this room one could look out the windows to the north, to where the future Air Force Academy was being built. This was a Toastmasters event. On a visual level my dad looked pretty much like all the other dads in the room—struggling middle management and sales guys hoping improved public speaking would give them a leg up, help them climb the economic totem pole. There was always a strong odor of Willie Loman around these men and their aspirations, which of course I knew nothing about when I was with them as a boy. Today, it seems to me that Arthur Miller would have understood them very well.

My father gave a futuristic speech about how this school under construction was already misnamed; he said it really should be called the Air and Space Academy. There were murmurs in the crowd. My father drew scant applause. They basically thought he was spouting some fairly crackpot notions about the future. A year or two later *Sputnik* was launched, and the rest is history.

Let us now return to the wackiness of the Atomic Fifties. As a child I didn't fully appreciate how history begins in tragedy and ends in farce. I faithfully watched Walter Cronkite take me through World War II every Sunday, swelling with more and more patriotic fervor. I even watched the Army's low-budget propaganda show *The Big Picture*. I saw the GIs digging foxholes in Nevada two miles from ground zero with no more protection than a helmet and a hole. I saw them get up and march toward the mushroom cloud.

When the film *The Atomic Cafe* came out, I saw the true absurdity of this blindness—a blindness most of those men lived out with shortened, cancer-ruined lives. But as Duke Wayne would say, "In any war you're going to have casualties." All through the 1950s we were told about the Peaceful Atom. The booster mentalities went ape shit with that hype. Here in Colorado we got a chance to have Edward Teller experiment on us in what Nelson Rockefeller cheerfully called "a national sacrifice area." They tried a couple of underground blasts on the western slope to melt the oil out of the shale in one of the most expensive subsidies of big oil since Teapot Dome.

Teller also wanted to use nukes to build a new Panama Canal and to bring seawater to the parched interior of Australia by setting off three or four. Oh, that Hungarian scientist under his fur hat! What a Transylvanian jokester! What a great Dadaist sense of humor! This beat walking a lobster on a string by a country mile. Give him more Coors money, I say! Let him suck the National Science Foundation for all it's worth, and the National Endowment for the Arts, too. He's really a performance artist. Out of the way, Christo! Your curtains are a penny-ante game. We're talking about sculpting continents. Real earth conceptual pieces. Out of the way, Faust. Make way for the Mad Hungarian! He believes in the West!

Back in Pueblo my father kept pestering my mother about building a fallout shelter. The poor woman probably thought, "We can't afford basic things we need now; how in the hell are we going to afford to pour concrete to build an underground shelter in our backyard? I'm not sure I'd want to come out of one of those things after two weeks, anyway." They compromised. A corner of the basement was weekly stocked with some Spam and stuff—a few candles and jugs of water.

The threat was part of our daily lives. We practiced for air raids in elementary school by going into the hallway, since all the classrooms were full of glass and facing out. The boys were instructed to stand against the walls and to arrange their hands and arms in such a way as to protect the face and eyes. The girls were to move to the center of the hall and drop to one knee beside the boys. I didn't know much, but I knew enough to know the probability of this protecting us against an atomic bomb was on the order of slim to none. Nonetheless, I faithfully obeyed and took some pride in the protective role given to the boys.

We even practiced an evacuation of the city. It was slow but orderly. Mothers and fathers picking up their kids and driving east, fifteen miles out of town. The only drawback was that this evacuation took us past the airport and next to the Pueblo Army Depot, where my father worked. He believed this base was a likely target because it stored chemical and biological weapons. (Weapons, by the way, that are now beginning to leak and are part of a costly disposal process. The Army wants to burn them in an advanced incinerator that it maintains will not pollute the atmosphere. The city wants the Army to move everything and burn this stuff in Utah. I guess Mormons are thought to have a higher tolerance for carcinogens than Coloradans.)

The most absurd thing about my hometown in those days was that it took a strange pride in the Cold War. Being a city with an endemic inferiority complex, its good citizens swelled with prestige when announcing, as they routinely did, that Pueblo would be one of the first places hit because of its steel mill. The opportunity to die first apparently was a high honor. Even as a little kid, I thought this was nuts! I concluded Pueblo's most likely chance of getting hit consisted of the fact that it was directly south of Colorado Springs. This permanent military city has the North American Air Defense Command situated in rooms carved out of the solid rock of Cheyenne Mountain. This base was portrayed in the film *WarGames*. It is the command central to which the president, by pushing the red button, gives the signal to push all the other buttons. What kind of hit would be required to knock out such a facility for command and control buried beneath all that rock and concrete, I do not know. Also nearby are the Air Force Academy, Fort Carson, and an air base.

I figured an overshot of a Russian missile just might nail our little burg and its huge inferiority complex. Unlike my fellow citizens, this did not cause me to swell with some kind of heightened importance. So, the Russkies are popping real big bombs and spewing all kinds of nasty fallout all over the world. We add our share, and kids find a big sci-fi kind of term has crept into their unconscious. The term is strontium-90. They say it's in the milk. They say it comes from the oddly entrancing mushroom clouds. I'm in high school now. I'm trying to play ball and get a date, but out of the corner of my eye I see Khrushchev jerking us around in Berlin. Yes, sir, Mr. K is taking the measure of young Jack in Vienna and not being impressed. Hence Jack feels compelled to flex his macho. Hey, look at this, you fat Russian fart! Cooler heads intervene. Harriman gets the Russkies to go along with a test ban treaty. Things are looking up.

Then, damned if it isn't showdown at the Havana OK Corral. But Jack's a cool customer, even though he may well have provoked the showdown. He asks all the best and the brightest, who later take us right into the Southeast Asian quagmire, what to do. Curtis is hot to drop. He's loading bombs and picking targets. Jack says, "What will the Russian response be?" Curtis doesn't give a rat's ass! He's kicking ass and taking names so fast in his mind, the Russkies won't know what hit them! They won't have enough left to respond with, to even worry about. "What a Harvard pimple! What a wimp! *PT 109,* my ass!"

When you're in a tight spot, you turn to your brother. From a knee-jerk Cold Warrior trained at Cardinal Spellman's feet, Bobby Kennedy has matured. Bobby stays calm; counsels caution; urges Jack to do what Ike didn't do for Mr. K. Give Nikita a way to save his windbag face. Give them an out—a face-saving gesture. Cut a deal. Promise no more Cuban invasions for no more misplaced Russian missiles.

They never forgave JFK. Not the hard-liners. They don't like weakness. If you're the last man standing, it doesn't matter! You don't shake the devil's hand.

The fact is that, in retrospect, all this fear of the Russians can now be seen as being largely delusional: "Well, it seemed real at the time. So screw you, you candy-assed sob sisters, appeasement-loving, pinko-liberal bastards. We're the real Americans. I don't know what you are; probably some kind of Stevenson closet fairy. What's the point spread on tomorrow's game? Tomorrow's war?"

I think that scary week when the Russians blinked, as the parlance goes, aged my father, took something out of him. I remember conversations at the dinner table that suggested a deep fatalism on his part. I think, in his heart of hearts, he thought we were doomed. We'd come a long way from Gregory Peck's magnetic smile in *Twelve O'Clock High* to a feeling that something terrifyingly lethal was really outstripping the human capacity for restraint.

III

But the deal is, Stalin was not Hitler. The Russian threat was never the same as the Nazi one. Stalin was the latest czar with a modern ideology for window dressing. He cautiously followed traditional Russian expansionist notions and buffer zone defense strategies, but his paranoid nationalism crippled any genuine international Communist movement. This was not a demonic threat to the West. Hell, they didn't even regain prewar levels of steel production until 1955.[11] By now, with their economic collapse and fundamental weaknesses all too apparent, the whole nasty business looks unconscionably perverse.

But we are now talking about what Jung calls the collective shadow that each culture inherently contains. Just as individuals carry their private darkness, so do whole societies. Hawthorne knew about our Puritan paranoia, witch-hunts, and sexual repression. In fact, he describes it with clinical precision. Furthermore, during the Cold War, before the big buildup in Vietnam, Graham Greene laid it out with utmost prescience. Apparently American officialdom never read books like *The Quiet American*.

Equally prophetically, especially in the light of Rhodes's revelations regarding LeMay, Stanley Kubrick expressed quite hilariously, in *Dr. Strangelove*, the moth-to-flame addiction of the "deterrence crowd." Alas, our decision makers are largely tone-deaf. They don't get IT! After reading Rhodes, I'm inclined to think of Kubrick's 1964 film as a documentary, with scarcely a whiff of exaggeration.

IV

Phil is at football practice circa 1962. Everyone is uptight! It's the week of the Cuban missile crisis. Somehow, beating Central doesn't seem too damned important at the moment. Next week and being alive long enough to get laid—now that seems important. Our somewhat dinosaur coaches, possibly Korean War veterans, but probably just Cold War draftees, are speculating on whether they'll be called back into the service. I'm sixteen years old. I don't know beans, but I know enough to know these two guys are badly out of touch. When the mushroom clouds bloom, boys, you don't have to worry about getting recalled for KP; you can kiss your keisters good-bye.

Two years later, after the Vietnam teach-ins and the Fulbright hearings, I discover Bob Dylan by way of Joan Baez. Eventually I get the original version of "A Hard Rain's A-Gonna Fall."[12] It knocks me out and changes my life. Dylan says that the song is so long because he didn't know if we were going to be around, so he felt like he had to put everything he was feeling into that song. We made it through the Cuban missile crisis by a gnat's ass. Luck and serendipity played a large role.

My father used to say, "When will they end the war?" He intuited that World War II had never really ended—Germany was defeated and fascism won—the military-industrial complex and the Cold War dance clouded all life in the postwar period.[13] My father's question—"When will they end the war?"—is all too similar to Ginsberg's line: "America . . . / when will we end the human war?"[14]

My father was a casualty of the Cold War. In this he is not alone. His working life concluded at a weapons depot where thousands of aging chemical and biological weapons are stored. His job was to do time/motion studies on the efficiency of the largely Chicano workforce servicing the hideous stores kept in the prairie igloos. His job: cut jobs!

It's really not such a great surprise that he went crackers; more like a question of what does this say about the "sane" who don't? Before his retirement, he would say at moments when he felt the stings of invisible persecution: "They look at me." God knows how he was looking at them as his sickness progressed; he may well have provoked the very hostility he complained of. But it was also structural, inherent in the occupation he took out of desperation to provide for his family. In the course of trying to find the secure career path to support his family, he ran into the underground reefs of the dark side of American life. His personal contradictions intersected with the culture's. He never could reconcile a rather selfless belief in New Deal–style public service with the ethos of the entrepreneur and the drive to "make it."

The Cold War impacted his life. Van der Post is helpful here:

[Schizophrenia] is so difficult to heal, I believe, because it was supported by a similar tendency of dichotomy in the spirit of an entire civilization backed up, as it were, by all that was negative in the twentieth-century Zeitgeist, and so was in a sense incapable of cure without healing at the same time the mass of humanity and cultural pressures rallied unconsciously behind it.[15]

The culture's schizophrenia either triggered or enhanced my father's. He started to develop a paranoid sense of reality worthy of a Thomas Pynchon novel. "Even paranoids have real enemies," as the saying goes. By his last years, he was a sad, prematurely aged, broken man. He used to call God "Freddie." He'd say all the time, "Freddie, I'm ready."

After his funeral, my sister told a story. She found him in the backyard, staring up at the stars. She said, "Dad, what are you doing?" "I'm talking to God," he said. I believe he truly was, because his life journey forced him to wrestle with so much about human existence that stubbornly remains somehow unfathomable. I was thinking of such things when I wrote:

> A child of the Depression
>> he died bewildered
>> in the 80s,
>> asking,
>> asking his eldest son
>> for comprehension,
>> for some . . . Sense.

> I gave him so little,
> His hands were so cold in the coffin.

> He had no desire to live further
> In a world he found crazy
>> & lethal.

> . . . .

> I wanted at one time, to
>> vindicate his tortured life.
> I wanted to ease my own guilt.

> To live
>> I give these angels
>> away.[16]

A huge gulf opened between us. He was unreliable for emotional support and guidance. I felt incredible distance between us.

When he was forced to retire at age forty-eight, he was a broken man—a victim of incompetent Freudian psychiatry and electric shock. I would have conversations with him during which I'd say, "Dad, remember when we did such and such?" He'd say, "Son, I can't remember those years." In their misguided attempt to cure his depression and hallucinations, they deprived him of memory, will, and motivation. As far as I could tell, he never gained a shred of insight from any of his stays in the sanitarium, and each stay eroded the qualities that had given him the capacity to overcome his background.

He thought the phone was tapped, that the church across the street was zapping him from the basement, that the Army and Air Force were engaged in civil war, that the TV was photographing him. It is very difficult to be around a person in such severe pain and delusion. His paranoia has reminded me of the scene in Doris Lessing's *The Golden Notebook* where her chief protagonist is conducting an affair with an exiled American screenwriter who's fled the McCarthy-inspired witch-hunts. This woman is so obsessed with the prospects for another world war that she compulsively clips the most horrific news stories confirming her worst suspicions, and tacks them to her walls.

Well, the truth is the Cold War was written on the walls of all our skulls, and we haven't yet performed the necessary exorcism because first we'd have to tell the truth. And all the Orwellian creatures that profited by this disaster, such as the Yale redneck George Bush, are congenitally incapable of doing so. But then he was once directly in charge of the Spooks. And as Richard Helms once admitted to Congress, they sometimes lie.[17] Is this an occupational hazard? Can a democracy survive such an occupation?

V

What is apparent now is that without nuclear weapons, World War III would have happened already. It would probably have been a conventional, though nonetheless devastating, war. There was enough hatred, animosity, and misperception to have started one quite easily.

Two Japanese cities were sacrificed so that we could see what would actually happen. By luck and pluck, we didn't do the dance that many, many people were drawn to do, much as many of us find ourselves drawn to want to dive into airy voids from high places. A strange enticement. We live under its psychological shadow.

Michael Meade says that ever since Hiroshima, there has been an inner doubt in the whole human race about whether we really want to keep the human journey going.[18] This doubt has entered youth with their first breath because it is endemic to the culture. Every generation since World War II has been afflicted with it. Among the most sensitive youth, on the threshold of the millennium, it is pervasive. They find it in

Christian videos about the Apocalypse and the videos purporting to confirm Nostradamus' most dire predictions.

If not nuclear destruction, then they are well aware of the growing potential for ecological disaster. These two horsemen of gloom gallop with the horses of violence and social breakdown that children live with in their neighborhoods. They sense the racing horse of overpopulation sprinting ahead of these steeds, and it causes such youth to succumb to a devastating despair and resignation. They say with their eyes: "You have not given us a livable future. The utopian Sixties failed; we feel a bitter disappointment. The people in charge lie about everything and will compromise us into hell. We have no heroes, no one and nothing to believe in. We huddle together, piercing our flesh, for warmth. We admire Tupac with his stomach tattoo: 'Thug for Life.' At least he never lied to us."

They live in the psychological fallout of atomic brinkmanship and the Cold War. They have been Isaac staring up at Abraham's gleaming knife. They have defiantly chosen their own culture, even when it affirms little more than the thin notion of commercialized dress, music, makeup, and attitude. They do not trust the fathers because the fathers have not been there as mentors and protectors. Whatever they do can be viewed as no more than a symptom of a much deeper illness—a sickness of the soul.[19]

Most of these weapons are still with us. The military-industrial complex groans on, the only form of Keynesian pump priming allowed in the land of the rugged individual. Those sitting in their Roman villa-like trophy homes while electronic bread and circuses are being fed to the plebs—they, too, don't really believe in a future! Therefore, it's okay to cannibalize the assets. It's okay to live on casino capitalism[20] in the last orgy of conspicuous consumption before Mother Nature steps in and says, "It's time to pay up! Your Faustian bargain is over!"

I think my father intuitively knew where planet Earth and its human creatures seem hell-bent on going. I think that's why he walked out into the backyard to talk to the stars. Though his family was not ready for him to go, he clearly had had enough.

But I cannot end this way. When recently asked why "there's little bad news" in his poetry—"no Bhopals, no Chernobyls"—Gary Snyder responded:

I feel that the condition of our social and ecological life is so serious that we'd better have a sense of humor. That it's too serious just to be angry and despairing. Also, frankly, the environmental movement in the last twenty years has never done well when it threw out excessive doom scenarios. Doom scenarios, even though they might be true, are not politically or psychologically effective. The first step, I think, and that's why it's in my poetry, is to make us love the world rather than to make us fear for the end of the world. Make us love the world, which means the nonhuman as well as the human, and then begin to take better care of it.[21]

NOTES

The epigraph is from E. P. Thompson, "Ends and Histories," in *Europe from Below: An East–West Dialogue,* ed. Mary Kaldor (London: Verso, 1991), 21. Thompson continues: "[The Cold War's] refraction into internal ideological and political life, on both sides, has been malign. I need not document the offenses against human rights on the other side. On this side we have had absurd spy games, McCarthyism and Red baiting, the purging of trade unions and academies, the inhibition or closure of many intellectual areas. . . . I could even regard those forty-five years of waste and ideological terror with distaste and a sense of personal grievance. How much of our lives went into restraining that Coldness from becoming Hot!"

1. Alexander Hammond, "God's Nation Interprets the Bomb: A Collage from the Early Years," in *Warnings: An Anthology on the Nuclear Peril,* ed. John Witte et al. (Eugene, OR: Northwest Review, 1984).

2. Richard Rhodes, "The General and World War III," *New Yorker,* 19 June 1997, 48. Rhodes notes: "LeMay laid on firebombings night after night until the end of the war, by which time sixty-three Japanese cities had been totally or partially burned out and more than a million Japanese civilians killed. Hiroshima and Nagasaki survived to be atomic-bombed only because Washington had removed them from Curtis LeMay's target list."

3. Ibid., 54.

4. Ibid. Emphasis added.

5. Ibid., 48.

6. Carl Oglesby, *The Yankee and Cowboy War: Conspiracies from Dallas to Watergate* (Mission, KN: Sheed, Andrews, and McMeel, 1976).

7. Gary Sick, *The October Surprise: America's Hostages in Iran and the Election of Ronald Reagan* (New York: Times Books, 1991).

8. Michael R. Beschloss, "Ike's Nightmare Summit at Paris," *U.S. News & World Report,* 31 March 1986.

9. Carl Oglesby, "Reinhard Gehlen: The Secret Treaty of Fort Hunt," *Covert Action* 35 (Fall 1990).

10. Beschloss, 35.

11. Seweryn Bialer states this somewhat differently in *The Soviet Paradox: External Expansion, Internal Decline* (New York: Vintage, 1986), 346–347: "The most important difference between the contemporary Soviet Union and Nazi Germany lies in the two countries' international behavior. Unlike the Nazis, the Soviets do not war with their adversaries. They do not propagandize or glorify offensive military action as the means by which to achieve their international goals. The foreign adventures they undertake are in fact low-risk and low-cost affairs, and not the 'go-for-broke' gambles of the Nazis. . . . Soviet international behavior . . . differs from that of the Nazis in its pragmatism, gradualism, and caution. The Nazi regime was a racist and extraordinarily uninhibited personal dictatorship with an enormous nationalistic appetite for conquest, whereas the Soviet Union is an oligarchical system that takes advantage of the weak, is fearful of the strong, and adverse to taking risks in situations where it may lose everything. This was true even before the advent of nuclear weapons".

12. Bob Dylan, "A Hard Rain's A-Gonna Fall," on *Freewheelin' Bob Dylan* (Columbia).

13. Bertram Gross, *Friendly Fascism: The New Face of Power in America* (New York: Evans, 1980).

14. Allen Ginsberg, "America," in his *Howl and Other Poems* (San Francisco: City Lights, 1956), 31.

15. Laurens van der Post, *Jung and the Life of Our Time* (New York: Random House, 1975), 134.

16. Phil Woods, "The Old Pilot," in *The Good Journey* (Chicago: Mesilla Press 1996), 20–21.

17. Thomas Powers, *The Man Who Kept the Secrets: Richard Helms and the CIA* (New York: Pocket Books, 1981).

18. Michael Meade, *Throw Yourself Like Seed: Youth, Elders & the Work of Change,* talk delivered at San Rafael, CA, 25 September 1995 (Pacific Grove, CA: Oral Tradition, 1996), audiocassette.

19. Michael Ventura, "The Age of Endarkenment," *Whole Earth Review* (Winter 1989).

20. Noam Chomsky, *Class Warfare: Interviews with David Barsamian* (Monroe, ME: Common Courage, 1996).

21. "Gary Snyder: The Art of Poetry LXXIV," interview with Eliot Weinberger, *Paris Review* (Winter 1996): 113–14. For a final chill from Curtis LeMay, see Edward Sanders, *1968: A History in Verse* (Santa Rosa, CA: Black Sparrow, 1997), 49–50: " 'Toward the end of our visit,' wrote Fischer/'I happened to mention that I was going to/Bobby Kennedy's for his wife's telethon.'//'Bobby Kennedy?' LeMay said without expression. 'He's going to be assassinated.' "

Cold Fear and the Real Dr. Strangelove

CRAIG McGRATH

*L*ike anyone my age, October 1962 is imprinted quite clearly in my mind. As a nine-year-old, I remember going from my second floor classroom down into the basement of our grade school during that fourth week of October for a nuclear air raid drill. I remember being told by the well-meaning nuns to get down on hands and knees along with my classmates, as we stood in obedient rows beside our school lunch tables. Then the nuns called out in frayed voices, "You see the flash at the windows," and we were told to turn away from the long line of basement windows and "Duck and cover, quickly, children!" The sisters swirled like black-and-white dervishes as they, too, threw themselves to the floor.

We were not told about missile flight times or that there would likely be no warning at all of a bomb or missile. We had thrown ourselves into little fetal balls during the mock attack to protect ourselves, but were never told the truth of radiation poisoning and nuclear attack. The adults, I learned later, in truth did not know either.

The ones who kept the truth from us were led by Air Force General Curtis LeMay. The cigar-chomping LeMay, a man of great roving paranoia, had been the driving force behind the building of the U.S. nuclear bomber force, the Strategic Air Command. I learned the truth of his life on a recent investigative cable television program.

The program showed declassified papers from the early 1950s that laid out a plan developed by the Air Force. This secret plan, drafted independently of any civilian authority, was called Project Final Control. The idea of the scheme was to overfly Soviet territory constantly with Strategic Air Command (SAC) planes as the initial move in a plan to intimidate the Soviets into giving up their Eastern European satellites, break their new alliance with China, and, finally, dissolve their country. It was a kind of crazed, provocative bullying conducted from the air. It was unlikely to succeed, and it could have ignited a nuclear war. It turned out this was what LeMay, our own Dr. Strangelove, wanted—and he told his pilots that in no uncertain terms.

In 1954 LeMay began to implement the plan, directing his pilots to make flights over the Soviet Union. He was expecting this to draw a Soviet response and, over time, cause an uncontrollable military chain reaction on both sides, the beginning of World War III. He believed that war was desirable and that the United States would "win" a nuclear war. Dozens of these flights took place during the mid-1950s. All were made without the president's knowledge. During his second term, Dwight Eisenhower apparently learned of the overflights and ended them. These events, aides believed, were the motive behind his farewell address to the nation in January 1961, in which he warned against the growing throttlehold that the military-industrial complex was gaining over the U.S. government.

The threshold of nuclear annihilation was reached less than two years later, in October 1962. During the Cuban missile crisis, LeMay, now head of the entire Air Force, pushed President Kennedy to begin air strikes against Cuba as a prelude to all-out nuclear war with the Soviets. LeMay believed the United States would "prevail" in the "nation-killing" operation against the Russians. At the height of the crisis, on October 26, SAC, without authorization, fired an unarmed missile from a southern California air base across the Pacific, toward Russia. At the same time SAC bombers deliberately flew beyond their fail-safe points, closer to Soviet territory, another direct provocation. Cooler heads prevailed within both U.S. and Soviet governments that October, and the confrontation ended peacefully. The Soviets removed their missiles from Cuba, and we would remove a handful of our missiles from Turkey.

In their day LeMay and his sidekicks helped make the idea of the destruction of civilization and the poisoning of the biosphere acceptable. He, and his accompanying nuclear weapons, ended the distinction between military and civilian casualties for all time and made instant global annihilation not only a live option but a winnable, desirable goal. They had, in truth, made a suicide pact with the technology they were obsessed with and worshiped.

It was scary and infuriating to see the previously hidden history of the secret Air Force flights, and how the military flirted with annihilation because of the deranged ramblings of a real-life Dr. Strangelove. I also thought of how people, over time, stood up in their own ways to that kind of indifferent armed madness. As adults, some of us refused to cooperate with those people who shook dice with the life of the Earth. Their secret and not so secret schemes had cheapened all life in the years since 1945, and made much of our economy and public life a servant to a military that was focused on global annihilation.

By 1989 I was working on the staff of the Minnesota Nuclear Weapons Freeze Campaign. The Cold War was nearly over, but few of our leaders seemed to take notice that the house of high-technology cards was crumbling because of its own dangerous and deadly processes. The plutonium and uranium processing factories—the bomb factories—at Rocky Flats, Colorado, near Denver; at Savannah River, South Carolina; and at Fernald, Ohio, were shutting down one after the other because of environmental contamination.

With each passing month it was learned that the local environmental damage around these plants was much more devastating than anyone had imagined. At Rocky Flats, hundreds of thousands of gallons of highly radioactive waste had been dumped and mixed over decades with pesticides, rocket fuel, and a wheat-destroying virus to create a demon's brew of Earth-killing toxins. This dump site would eventually be under study for designation as a "national sacrifice area" by the Department of Energy, a piece of land so poisonous that it will be deadly for hundreds, if not thousands, of years. At the first bomb factory at Hanford, Washington, plutonium contaminated hundreds of acres. At this site, 150 underground tanks were holding millions of gallons of toxins and highly radioactive nuclear waste. Since the plant had been shut down, it was discovered that nearly half of the tanks were leaking, sending plumes of radioactive waste into the surrounding ground and water, moving toward the Columbia River.

Yet strangely, in macabre fashion, military leaders and politicians in 1989 were still obsessed with the building of plutonium bombs. The MX missile, with ten plutonium warheads, each warhead with an explosive equivalent of five hundred Hiroshima-type bombs, was coming on-line, its numbers reduced by citizen pressure from one hundred to forty, as were the B-1 bomber and the cruise missile.

At the Minnesota Freeze we had learned near the end of 1988 that the railway system of the United States was being considered by the Pentagon as a way to move the MX missile around on secret rail cars in a kind of nuclear shell game. One of these rail schemes involved sending missile-laden trains through the Dakotas and part of western Minnesota. That brought it close to home. Minnesotans would be put under the gun. We started calling and publicizing around the Twin Cities and greater Minnesota, letting people know about the railroad plan.

During the spring of 1989, the Minnesota Freeze had decided to try lobbying our local congressman. He was on the Appropriations Committee and had the power of the purse. Even though the bomb factories were officially off-line, there was talk that they might reopen at some point in the future, when new nukes were demanded. We wanted him to cut off funding for further plutonium production at the bomb factories and at laboratories around the country. The meeting with the Minneapolis congressman was instructive about the power of the Cold War mentality on liberals.

Ten of us, a cross section of the community, went to his downtown office and were seated around an oak conference table by one of his aides. The congressman arrived and strode to his seat at the head of the table. We made our pitch, citing the closure of bomb factories in Russia, the long half-life of the bomb materials, and the dangers of the bomb plants themselves. He looked around us and then through us. It was as though we were not there—or our presence was making him visibly uncomfortable. At first he didn't respond. After some minutes and more advocacy and small talk, he drew a cigar out from a jacket pocket and nervously began chewing the end of it. Finally, he lit it and spewed smoke into the room for us to imbibe with him. He was feeling tough and edgy that day. We were talked to like simple children. We didn't know the realities of politics in Washington. There was nothing he could do for us. Even though he was sure of his tenure, he would not consider a bill to defund and permanently close the bomb factories.

Finally he said, "No, no, talk to some of the other congressmen, like the guy down in Iowa. What's his name?"

We left frustrated but enlightened.

With one avenue blocked, we tried another. Citizen diplomacy was another means we used that year to counter the Strangelove doctrine. Instead of objectifying the "enemy," we would put a real face on our opponents. The International Freeze office in New York had called after our encounter with the congressman and wanted to know if Minnesota Freeze could set up five days of events for two visiting Soviet writers. They were coming to the United States as part of a ten-member delegation that included a wide range of people. The opportunity had arisen because Freeze people from other parts of the United States had visited Russia the year before to observe missiles being destroyed under an earlier nuclear weapons treaty, and now a Soviet delegation was coming as a gesture of reciprocity.

With only a few weeks' notice, and no budget set aside for such a visit, we decided within a few hours that our answer was yes. The Minnesota Freeze would organize events and receptions, and get our Soviet visitors around. Our two guests would be an Azeri screenwriter and novelist, Maksud Ibragimbekov, and a Moscow poet and journalist, Larissa Vasilieva.

I began calling Twin Cities officials to set up a schedule of meetings. The St. Paul mayor's office called back quickly, and after a brief conversation with the chief of staff, she said they would be very happy to receive Larissa and Maksud. The mayor would meet them and might have a surprise for them. Despite repeated calls, it was be nearly two weeks before I heard back from the Minneapolis mayor's office. In the meantime, I had asked a Russian-language student from the University of Minnesota who was volunteering in our office to see what he could find out about our two guests.

My follow-up calls to the International Freeze coordinator in New York netted me the further information that Larissa was fluent in English but Maksud was not, and he would need a translator. I immediately asked around for referrals to a translator. Being a university town, Minneapolis had a network of émigrés and translators. Through the grapevine, I learned of a Hungarian–American translator. She was clearly fluent in Russian, but hesitant.

"I don't know if I can do this," she patiently repeated, first over the phone and then in person. She wanted to know if Maksud and Larissa were from the Soviet government. I replied that Maksud was a member of a regional parliament. I was unaware of any government connections beyond that. She was concerned about being seen working with Russians, even in a translating capacity. Finally she recommended someone else, who didn't return my phone calls.

Exasperated, I called another prospect who had been recommended through a university source. He asked me who the people were that were coming from Russia. I recited the four-sentence bios I had about Maksud and Larissa: basically their ages, where they lived, and what their occupations were. Then he wanted to know where he would be translating; I ran off some of the list I had put together and a couple of receptions I had set up. One was at the Unitarian Society, just behind and above the Walker Art Museum. He gasped, appalled.

"No, never," he sputtered.

I thought the guy was going to have apoplexy right on the phone.

"Why?" I asked.

"They are a Communist organization."

"What?"

"The FBI has told me they are a communism organization, the Unitarian Society. I will have nothing to do with them."

He slammed down the receiver, and I was left staring at the phone in my hand, a dial tone buzzing up at me.

The third time was the charm with translators. As luck would have it, the Hungarian–American woman called back, feeling guilty, and gave me another name. I was put on to a person who had translated for some Russians who had previously visited Minnesota. A day later a rumpled guy of medium-short height with a Russian-style mustache and strong, happy eyes was sitting in my office. His name was Basil. He was thirty-five and finishing his master's degree in Russian at the University of Minnesota. His parents had immigrated from the Ukraine at some point in the past. He had none of the political nervousness that the previous candidates had shown.

Knowing little Russian, I asked him to read to me a Freeze document in Russian that I had on my desk. After three sentences, I knew he was the man we needed. He was fast and fluent, and had good inflections, as well as an accent, probably Ukrainian. We talked about price; his going rate was twenty-five dollars per hour. I asked if, in the interests of world peace, he would be willing to work for twenty. He grinned, half-rolled his eyes, and said yes.

The following day I learned from our student volunteer that Maksud was indeed a screenwriter and filmmaker of some repute, but that his movies, not surprisingly, had never been shown outside the Soviet Union—and probably not outside Azerbaijan. Digging through the stacks in the libraries across the river on the main campus, he found that one of Maksud's movies was called *The Door*. It was a film about Azeris in conflict with the Russian legal system. Also, Maksud apparently had been banned for a while during the Brezhnev era, and been allowed to come back after Gorbachev had taken over, during the Glasnost era.

As the arrival date grew closer, I began hearing on the staff grapevine that some board members were getting nervous about the visit. There were fears of political retribution against the Freeze for dealing with Soviet writers. I decided to act preemptively, and met with the board. At the meeting, I noted that the larger list of Soviets, although they wouldn't be visiting Minnesota, included a Russian who had suffered in Stalin's concentration camps before and during World War II, and further noted that a Ukrainian Orthodox archbishop was part of the entourage. In addition, a Russian environmentalist, not particularly popular with the government, from what I could find, was on the list. I turned to the older board member who worked for one of the large defense contractors in the city and was the most concerned. His eyes darted furtively, as though someone might be listening. His high-strung tension was palpable in the small room as his hands moved softly in front of him, smoothing out a piece of nonexistent paper. He tightened his lips, looked at me, lowered his chin an inch, and moved it back up. His eyes asked, "Do you know what you're doing?" I said I thought we should take a chance. And we did.

At the airport on arrival day, six of us—four staff and two board members—waited at the end of the accordion walkway as the jet from New

York landed and taxied. Near the end of the line of passengers, a bald, wide man of medium height in a silvery silk suit, with square glasses branded across his face, and short, stumplike arms, trundled into the waiting area, followed by a woman of fifty. She was trim, with dark eyes and hair. They saw our makeshift sign welcoming them in Russian. They smiled as they approached, and I walked forward with a bunch of red and yellow tulips crooked in my left arm. I extended my hand and introduced myself.

"Maksud Ibragimbekov." He introduced himself in a thick Caspian accent. His friendly, dark eyes scanned the group. He gingerly stepped aside for his companion to come forward. I shook her hand.

"Larissa Vasilieva, from Moscow."

Her voice was distinct and rich. I handed her the flowers and let the rest of the crew introduce themselves.

After checking in and having dinner, we left Maksud and Larissa at the hotel. Tomorrow would be a busy day with a visit to St. Paul and a reception in the evening.

The next day the St. Paul mayor met us in his inner office at City Hall. He was gracious, and spoke part of the time to Maksud and Larissa in Russian. They asked if he had been to the Soviet Union. He said no, but that he was going in a few weeks. His itinerary was going to include Novosibirsk, the sister city of the Twin Cities. Maksud recommended parts of Novosibirsk that he might enjoy during his upcoming trip. I asked him about the U.S. Conference of Mayors' resolution currently circulating that called for a bilateral ban on nuclear testing between the United States and the Soviet Union. The mayor emphasized that he had signed the document and that he considered this a milestone in relations between the two nations. Maksud also spoke of the test ban and its importance. Eventually the conversation turned more prosaic, and the mayor offered to get Maksud and Larissa two seats for a touring Russian play from Leningrad that was in St. Paul.

The meeting the next day with the Minneapolis mayor was different. He had been a congressman for a number of years before becoming mayor. During a U.S. Senate bid, he had been tarred by the Moonies as politically unreliable or unpatriotic. He had lost that Senate primary. When he showed, the mayor was fifteen minutes late and sat at a table on the other side of the room from us. An aide quickly handed him the file I had sent weeks earlier to his office. He began talking about his recent trip to the Philippines.

Instead of support for the Conference of Mayors' proposal for a test ban, he began with talk of how we might all prevent a Communist takeover of the Philippines. After a couple of minutes, I had to intervene and remind him of who Larissa and Maksud were, that they were not military people, and why they were in the country. Basil was translating rapidly through these uneasy moments, leaning over Maksud's shoulder. That seemed to confuse the mayor further. I finally got him to wish both of them a happy stay, and he proceeded to angle around the crowded table arrangement to present Maksud and Larissa with a wooden key to the city.

The next morning, after a long sleep and a leisurely breakfast, we toured the Meridel LeSueur Center in the West Bank area of Minneapolis, where the Freeze and a number of other organizations are headquartered. In the central conference room, the Freeze made a commitment that we would continue to work for a ban on nuclear weapons testing in our own country and would try to keep our bomb-making facilities closed. Larissa appreciated our work and hoped that the Soviet government would initiate another unilateral ban on testing that the United States could join.

Despite the paranoia about Russians in Minnesota, and the approach/avoidance mentality that a number of people had evidenced, the visit went well and included several receptions and speaking engagements. The tour ended with a final slice-of-the-Twin-Cities night in St. Paul. We had a round table discussion at Macalester College and then a farewell celebration at O'Gara's restaurant, a famed St. Paul nightspot. Afterward, when we walked out into the cool, crisp Minnesota spring night, there were eight of us left, including Maksud, Larissa, myself, and other Freeze people.

It had been a long day, with many tough questions about whether the openness and changes in the Soviet Union would hold and take root. They both agreed they would. There was no going back. Larissa moved to my side, gently hooking her arm around mine and walking with me the way a couple would. Maksud, already next to me, moved slightly closer, holding my elbow, and the three of us walked together across the parking lot. As I walked with Larissa and Maksud, I looked up. In the crisp black sky hung a brilliantly clear full moon.

I thanked Maksud and Larissa again for coming so far to see us. Basil had peeled off a few minutes earlier to go home, exhausted. Larissa quietly translated across me for Maksud and answered for both. They were happy to be here, she said a bit wistfully, as though a connection broken long ago was being reestablished. I looked up again at the moon, pointing slightly with a raised hand.

"We have a saying in our country that when the moon is full, people often behave crazy or go loony. Do you have a saying like that in your country?"

Larissa translated. They both smiled. Larissa said with a gentle gravity, "Yes, we do also in Russia," and leaned her head against my shoulder. "No more," she said.

We kept walking. Maksud gave me a squeeze on the elbow like a handshake. His silver silk suit was lit by the moon, almost aglow, reflecting the light back and out into space.

It was possible, after all, to say no to the lunatics in any country who would howl at the full moon. The ones who would break the moon and its cycle of life, and make us barren. If we took a chance, our children might not have to hide frightened under tables during air raid drills, believing that by ducking and covering, they would somehow survive radiation with a half-life of thousands of years. The gigantic cruel hoax might be stopped.

Looking back on these hopeful days at the end of the Cold War, it's clear that the peace movement made a major contribution to ending the arms race. We had a profound effect on the dialogue of the time and helped alter the course of acceptable debate. Even though the Freeze issue failed in Congress, the peace movement, along with many others who labored independently, went on to work against each major weapons system as it came down the line, often with great success.

Within a few weeks of Maksud and Larissa's departure, the MX missile railway scheme was dropped due to public outrage. Star Wars, the seamless fantasy in the skies with its particle beam weapons and giant mirrors, was never built. Nuclear weapons testing was stopped in both the United States and Russia in 1992, and the ban was made official policy in 1993. Our citizen diplomacy effort to keep the American and Soviet/Russian bomb-making plants closed helped in a public way to focus the seriousness of the issue. And while talk of new tritium production was bandied about in Congress, the bomb factories in the United States remain mostly closed except for cleanup purposes.

We also changed the sterile, bloodless military language used to lull people into compliance with the building of weapons of mass destruction. Human beings are no longer easily referred to as "assets" by military and political leaders, at least in public. Civilian casualties are not routinely called "collateral damage" with a dismissive tone and military swagger in the Pentagon voice. We forced a human face not only on perceived enemies but on all people, and in doing so, we took away some of the military's ability to define, reduce, and destroy human beings. I felt involved at a very visceral level with the fight for the fate of the Earth, and still do. It was a human responsibility we shouldered in spite of the fear that fed the deadly processes of the Strangelove doctrine.

All in the Family

SONYA HUBER

*L*ike most kids of the early 1980s, I was terrified about the threat of nuclear war. Unlike most kids, though, I was as familiar with a Geiger counter as with a typewriter by age ten. So I considered myself lucky; in the event of a nuclear holocaust, I would know what to do. I knew about lead shielding and what iodine pills were for.

My parents' business helps industries and hospitals around the country dispose of nuclear waste. My mother still runs the office end of things, and my father has driven all over the country, pulling a Geiger counter out of the trunk of his car as he visits his clients, making sure the X-ray machines and industrial gauges in small towns across middle and southern America are running properly, attending to accidents, arranging licenses, and routing trucks filled with barrels of nuclear waste.

We traveled with my father as he visited hospitals. We put the small radioactive sources used to test hospital devices underneath the van seat, covered with formed lead semicircles and flexible lead shielding, and then threw our duffel bags and sleeping bags on top. My father is employed in the nuclear waste trade, and it is a lucrative business for the companies whose employees scoop "hot" or contaminated waste into barrels and ship the barrels to a disposal site.

A career in the radiation field wasn't my father's lifelong dream. He wanted to go to medical school but couldn't afford it. His parents emigrated from a farming community in Germany to Arkansas, with nothing but children in tow. My grandfather was a butcher and my grandmother a nurse, who also knew how to use a shotgun to destroy the rattlesnakes that slithered into their log house. My father's sisters all entered the convent, and his brother enlisted in the Air Force. My father wanted to go to medical school from the time he was a teenager, and he certainly was bright and devoted enough, but there was no money to send him.

My father's list of jobs looks like a crazy quilt. After helping my grandfather butcher cows, he sold pots and pans door-to-door and worked in a pill factory. He moved north, hoping for a construction job on the Sears Tower. He took correspondence courses in cartooning and was trained as a locksmith. Now he is a highly intelligent scientist, a successful businessman with just the slightest trace of Southern twang in certain words and a hell-bent work ethic.

My mother emigrated from Germany to Arkansas, alone, when she was sixteen. After earning her GED, she attended night courses in accounting and business management while working full-time in my father's office and raising three kids. Through floods and computer hard-drive meltdowns and coworker insanity, she has been the heart of the business and kept it running smoothly. She would never brag about jumping cultures and languages or learning accounting in her spare time, even when forced. The most she'd aspire to is to being "good people."

Now my parents are working hard, because there's a lot of nuclear waste waiting to be shipped that no one wants to touch. Since this waste and the money it produced kept us fed, and since the office was in a wing of the house that we all roamed through, nuclear waste was the primary topic of conversation at the dinner table. As with most family businesses, we were all employees. I remember, when I was four or five, stamping our return address onto envelopes and peeling apart the carbon-smelling sheets of colored invoices. I stapled together Leak Test Kits, which are used to detect contamination, for a nickel apiece from when I was in third grade, and made coffee for the office before going to school. I learned to type in the office, and eventually typed reports detailing the consultants' visits to hospitals. When I got older, I answered phone calls, copied and collated endless radiation safety training manuals, cleaned the office on weekends, and filed during the summers. I remember the procession of secretaries and consultants like family members: they baby-sat us, we played with their kids, and we watched soap operas together in our living room during their lunch break.

My brother went to college to study business and marketing, but he's back with the family business and has just received a license for a new kind of waste barrel he designed. It's funny for me to imagine the father and son "decon" jobs that happen nowadays. A "decon" is a contract to decontaminate a large area, usually industrial, where a spill has occurred, where the cleanup staff has to wear protective suits that cover them from head to toe and need to be changed regularly. I imagine them stomping around in white suits that make them look like spacemen, growling at each other, both using the exact same phrases and gestures to argue about how to approach an unwieldy air shaft or a tricky regulatory requirement.

The work of "the office" consumed us. We traveled with my father as he visited hospital radiation departments, and the names of the cities and the hospitals and factories bring me a strange sort of nostalgia. With my mother's ingenuity, we entertained ourselves in hot hospital parking lots, air-conditioned hospital cafeterias, and small town gift shops and parks. Toward the end of the day, we'd be so bored that we could only sit and stare at the hospital entrance, waiting for my father to emerge with his briefcase in one hand and a survey meter in the other. The scientific terms of radiation work arouse in me a pride at seeing my parents acting with confidence, knowing things and making decisions: pica, rad, curies, millirem, dosimeter. I wonder, now, if this complete absorption with "the office" was a product only of financial need. Did we pull together because it takes a lot of teamwork for a small business to survive? Something tells me that there might not have been such an undertone of stress if we had been marketing pet food. At least for me, the feeling of tension around the office, the sense of urgency, was intensified because of my fear about the power of radiation.

Like many children my age, I was brought to near hysterics on a nightly basis, thinking about whether nuclear war would break out while I was sleeping. The prayer "If I should die before I wake . . ." always seemed foreboding and chancy, so I rarely ever said it. It's hard for me to know which came first, my morbid imagination or the cleanup training videos that seemed to play in an endless loop in our living room. The first short stories I wrote were all set on a postapocalyptic desert landscape populated with genetically altered life-forms. The Cold War rhetoric on TV provided more than enough fodder for my imagination. On top of that, I was exposed to the ways that people in our nuclear culture make their jobs and day-to-day existence possible. My father stored sources of radioactivity in a cement-lined closet in our house. When I asked whether it was dangerous, he consoled me with graphs about exposure and drawings that proved that sitting near a shielded source was safer than sitting too close to the television. When I asked about accidents and Three Mile Island, there was always a reassuring scientific answer to soothe my worry.

Paul Loeb described a United Nuclear employee who explained to a fourth grade class, "You know when you come home, kids, you're all dirty and your mother says you have to take off your shoes and sweatshirt? Well, nuclear safety is the same sort of thing."[1] In the same way, my father visited my fourth grade class to talk about his job. He wanted to make radiation safety a part of our lives, and he passed out little party favors that the Nuclear Regulatory Commission must have produced—a cardboard holder containing a black pellet inside a clear plastic shell. The cardboard was printed with a nature scene and an explanation of how, in the future, our nuclear waste would all be stored in glass and would be safe. Ironically, most of the kids had pulled the pellets out of their plastic coverings by the end of the school day. The pellets rolled across the scuffed linoleum during spelling class, lodged under the radiator, or waited to trip a stumbler with untied shoes.

From about fifth grade on, my main argument against the safety of nuclear power was that no person, no technology is perfect. But the scientific evidence seemed to prove me wrong, although it left me unconvinced. I think now that this excess of scientific evidence lulls many nuclear workers into a denial that is necessary for them to function. At my house, we never once discussed the threat of nuclear terrorism, nuclear attack, or meltdown as we sat around the kitchen table, even though we talked about nuclear waste every single day.

When I began to reflect on my family, I thought that this silence was a sign of family dysfunction, but quite a few well-researched projects have shown it to be a nationwide act of denial. Paul Loeb's description of Hanford, Washington, in *Nuclear Culture* could be a model for many towns across the United States. Hanford was a nuclear company town built to construct nuclear weapons and, later, to generate nuclear power. Loeb described a city full of citizens who were aware of corruption, errors, and real danger at work, yet functioned and made a living.

Despite the abstract training materials, statistics, and trinkets for schoolchildren, reality became clearer during my sophomore year of high school, when a core meltdown at Chernobyl spewed fallout across Eastern Europe and into the world's jet stream. The contamination was classified as "low level" merely because it was not material used to make a nuclear bomb. I began to pay more attention to my father's business and the mistakes that were made in the industry. I remember calls we received in the middle of the night about a spill—Could my father come right away or send some of his "guys" out in the morning? A truck had been leaking waste all over the road from St. Louis to Kentucky.

One of my jobs at the office around this time was to reorganize the library. The training brochures and medical journals I leafed through described routine accidents where unsuspecting people were contaminated and suffered horrible radiation burns, cancer, and death, and how to treat these disasters. I read about the latest technology for soaking up liquid contaminant and the rate at which barrels began to leak when placed in the ground. I remember a colorful laminated booklet that depicted an apparently common scenario: a radioactive source is encased in shielding, becoming a gauge for use in a factory, maybe to check the level of soup in a can. The gauge is sent to a developing country in Latin America, where there may or may not be adequate nuclear regulations. Years later, the equipment is dismantled, its function unknown, and poor children scavenging for food at the dump find the source and break it open to play with the brightly colored powder, thus contaminating themselves and an entire village.

At the dinner table, we discussed the trucking company whose secretaries went on strike and informed all the area newspapers that explosives were being stored next to the nuclear waste in their warehouse—a story that never made it to the state or national news. I remember hearing about another poor community in central Illinois; a developer so badly wanted a waste dump in the town that he erased a water table on a geologic map of the area and submitted that documentation as part of his proposal. He hoped to get a piece of the nuclear promise, which had offered an endless supply of clean energy, enough to fuel the American lifestyle forever.

Maybe it was worry about these stories that led me to send a part of every one of my Pizza Hut paychecks to Greenpeace, an activist environmental organization. But I was shocked when, during high school, I was informed that a truck of Greenpeace activists was following my father's truck on a decontamination job on the East Coast, and even more surprised when I was asked if I had played any part in sending Greenpeace to spy on my father. I had never considered doing such a thing—I knew that radioactive waste was what put food on the table and what was sending me to college.

I went to a private wannabe-Ivy in Minnesota, an overwhelming and challenging resocialization. Talking with students from Nigeria and the Upper West Side, hearing about how other kids had grown up, what they liked to do and where they were from, I learned about difference. Standing among a group of freshmen at an ice cream social or some other forced bonding experience, someone asked, inevitably, what my folks did for a living. "They dispose of nuclear waste," I answered. What I had expected was a reflection of my own feelings about the matter at that point: concern, questions about the problems related to waste disposal, a discussion about the raging debate on the proposed long-term storage site at Yucca Mountain. Instead, there was a silence in which the other kids looked at each other, followed by laughter.

I had stunned them with something unique, I guess. I wanted laughs, and I wanted to be liked. I forgot about the flash of unease and laughed along with them. "My father disposes of nuclear waste" became a party gag I yanked out for show-and-tell, a conversation. Now I wonder why it was funny. Maybe the idea of actually disposing of waste somewhere in the Midwest fit with someone's vision of backwardness. None of my New York friends' parents had jobs that placed them in bodily danger. Was nuclear waste some modern hyperbolic poop joke, a messy thing that nobody wanted to talk about?

I never thought too much about the ironic laughter, although I sent away for an application to the state school back home, thinking I might like to go home and fade into the woodwork. But by that time, I'd discovered the campus environmental groups, and became immersed in campaigns to fight toxic exposure and exploitation of workers in that sleepy Minnesota town. When I helped organize protests against the "temporary" storage of nuclear waste on the floodplains of the Mississippi River, right across the road from the Prairie Island Native American reservation north of Minneapolis, I learned about the nuclear industry.

I began to read more about the links between nuclear power propaganda ("It's safe and economical, and provides jobs") and nuclear arms propaganda ("It's safe and provides jobs, and we have no choice"). The basic connection had been clear to me for a long time—Could I trust someone in charge of the button more than I could trust someone not to fall asleep at a nuke plant's control panel? I learned that despite evidence that mistakes could and did happen, and despite proof that nuclear energy was amazingly costly, 175 new reactors are planned for construction in the United States by 2030, and the nuclear industry is aggressively marketing its wares abroad.[2] And other exciting trivia: the United States has a stockpile of around 13,570 nuclear warheads, but that doesn't seem to be enough. The 1997 military budget is a quarter-trillion dollars, and 10 percent of this will go toward nuclear weapons. There's a symbiotic relationship of sorts between nuclear plants and nuclear arms: a thousand-megawatt reactor produces five hundred pounds of plutonium per year. To make an atomic bomb, you need ten pounds of plutonium. I created a glowing "waste" barrel with a flashlight stuck inside to be used in a street theater protest, meant to symbolize the ninety-two million gallons of liquid nuclear waste sitting in corroding, often leaking storage tanks. Learning about the nuclear industry from the outside, I saw my parents as cogs in this huge machine, and felt guilty for going to college on a "nuclear scholarship."

I learned about my parents' being exposed to radiation while standing at a pay phone outside a sushi restaurant in the early summer of 1994. I'd moved to the East Coast after graduation, wanting to explore the country and put some distance between myself and home. I had been working an overnight shift six days a week at a residential home for teenagers. I'd heard nothing from my mother for two weeks.

When I reached her at the office, she had an edge to her voice, a well-controlled hysteria. I asked if she was okay, and she said she hadn't slept in a few nights. I asked her why, and she said that she and my father had been exposed. As in "exposed to radiation."

I think I answered with a yell and a rapid fire of questions. I asked what it meant, and why she hadn't called. It had happened two days ago.

"It's fine. We've just been really busy."

I was hurt and stunned that something this serious would happen and I would hear nothing about it. She described what had happened, and I asked her repeatedly, "Aren't you scared?"

She said, "We didn't have time to be scared."

A monitoring device didn't register any contamination as my father left a job site. He drove home in the pickup, came into the office, and walked around, touching carpeting, desks, files, and walls. Next he drove home, touched the kitchen counter, and hugged my mother. Then he went back to work to help recalibrate a survey meter. When he turned the meter on, it went crazy, clicking up in the high ranges. The first assumption was that it was broken or needed a new battery. When they removed it from the vicinity of my father, the clicking slowed. The meter had been working fine, they figured out, and he was contaminated. My parents were immediately working day and night to rip up the carpeting, test and retest the areas where my father had been, scrubbing their skin, and being evaluated. They had to have someone haul away part of the seat of the pickup truck, as well as the kitchen counter. State employees working for the Nuclear Regulatory Commission had to come in over the weekend to survey the office and supervise the disposal of everything that had been "crapped up."

After hearing the news, I hung up and sat on the curb, stunned that something like this could have happened and she had not called. She had been trying to protect me, or trying to convince herself that everything was fine. Or maybe, to her, everything was fine and I was over-reacting. I walked home, dazed, and called a close friend. There was concern in his voice, but I could tell that it wasn't something he could be empathetic about; it was too unreal. He mentioned the movie *Silkwood* and asked if my parents had to go through something like the decontamination scenes. I didn't know, but what was important to me was that it was not a movie. I felt like I had made so many nuclear waste jokes to my friends that there was no way to talk seriously about my fears. I called my sister and found that there was almost nothing to say, besides a feeling of guilt that I wasn't around to help out with the latest crisis.

To me, the doubts I had about radiation had always been abstract. With this information, I became enraged but didn't know whom to be angry at. The worker who surveyed my father? A faulty film badge? I imagined their deaths, even though my mother had said that there weren't going to be any long-term effects. How could there not be? Despite being skeptical about the science and security of radiation, I had somehow hoped that the industry was right and competent, and that there was nothing to worry about.

I wondered how it would feel to be married to the atom, to be so deeply ingrained in a business like that, for both of them to have this occupation as opposed to whatever else fate might have handed them. But they would not think like that. Maybe they weren't concerned about the risk of cancer down the line. And if there was fear, they'll never tell me. They have always assured me that there was nothing to worry about.

I recently edited a training manual about radiation safety for my mother, and saw the way that government agency-produced materials attempt to downplay the risks of radiation. According to the statistics, drinking coffee will take six days off the average life expectancy. Working with nuclear waste will take off forty. So I assume you can either drink double espressos and eat an occasional hot fudge sundae, or work in a reactor. And, as the guide says, "Nuclear industry ranks below mining, construction, agriculture, transportation, all industries, and government in number of deaths for 10,000 workers for forty years." But I haven't ever heard of a farm having a core meltdown, which I don't think is included in these statistics. And, as one of Paul Loeb's interviewees said, "Coal miners at least realize they're risking their lives . . .," but the average nuclear worker or community member is not given the information necessary to question the nuclear industry, and we can't feel, smell, or see radiation, so we have no choice but to trust government reports.[3]

I admit that I still laugh with everyone who cracks up when I tell them about my family's business. "Just like *The Simpsons!*" they yell. But I realize that it's gallows humor, and the laughter is something that people use to hide their fear. And I try to tell people that somebody has to clean up the waste and that the industry is run dangerously, undemocratically, and with twisted priorities. Since my parents got exposed, I've realized that they *are* in a sense cogs in a huge machine, and don't have input about where the industry is headed. Anyone who is steering it isn't at risk for getting exposed, doesn't have to deal with the waste on a day-to-day basis, and doesn't have to get their hands dirty or risk having their car seats and kitchen counters shredded. I'm not sure how my parents feel about the nuclear industry these days; I imagine they are focused on the details that affect their business rather than the overarching nuclear agenda. These days, I have come to understand that they are not responsible for that agenda. I only feel resentful that the industry itself is so shrouded in secrecy while it threatens so many people's lives.

NOTES

1. Paul Loeb, *Nuclear Culture: Living and Working in the World's Largest Atomic Complex* (Philadelphia: New Society, 1986), 185.

2. Helen Caldicott, "Nuclear Shadow: The Weapons, the Power, the Waste," *The Nation,* 29 April 1996, 11–16.

3. Loeb, 89.

In the Belly of the Beast

BARBARA KINGSOLVER

The Titans, in the stories of the ancient Greeks, were unearthly giants with heroic strength who ruled the universe from the dawn of time. Their parents were heaven and earth, and their children were the gods. These children squabbled and started a horrific, fiery war to take over ruling the universe.

A more modern legend goes this way: The Titans were giant missiles with atomic warheads. The Pentagon set them in neat circles around chosen American cities, and there they kept us safe and free for twenty-two years.

In the 1980s they were decommissioned. But one of the mummified giants, at least, was enshrined for public inspection. A Titan silo—a hole in the ground where an atomic bomb waited all its life to be launched— is now a missile museum just south of Tucson. When I first heard of it I was dismayed, then curious. What could a person possibly learn from driving down the interstate on a sunny afternoon and descending into the ground to peruse the technology of nuclear warfare?

Eventually I went. And now I know.

The Titan who sleeps in his sleek, deep burrow is surrounded with ugliness. The museum compound, enclosed by an unkind-looking fence, is set against a lifeless backdrop of mine tailings. The grounds are gravel flatlands. The front office is blank except for a glass display case of souvenirs: plastic hard hats, model missile kits for the kids, a Titan-missile golf shirt. I bought my ticket and was ushered with a few dozen others into a carpeted auditorium. The walls bore mementoes of this silo's years of active duty, including a missile-shaped silver trophy for special achievement at a Strategic Air Command combat competition. The lights dimmed and a gargly voice rose up against high-drama music as the film projector stuttered, then found its stride and began our orientation. A ring of Titan II missiles, we were told, encircled Tucson from 1962 until 1984. The Titan II was "conceived" in 1960 and hammered together in very short order with the help of General Motors, General Electric, Martin Marietta, and other contractors. The launch sites are below ground—"safely protected from a nuclear blast." The missile stands 103 feet tall, 10 feet in diameter, and weighs 150 tons. A fatherly sounding narrator informed us, "Titan II can be up and out of its silo in less than a minute, hurling its payload at speeds of over 15,000 miles per hour nearly halfway around the world. This ICBM waits quietly underground, its retaliatory potential available on a moment's notice."

The film went on to describe the typical day of a missile crew, and the many tasks required to keep a Titan in a state of constant readiness. Finally we were told sternly, "Little remains to remind people that for 22 years a select group of men stood guard 24 hours a day, seven days a week, protecting the rights and freedom we enjoy in these United States." Day and night the vigilant crew monitored calls from their command post, "Waiting . . ." (a theatrical pause) "for a message that never came."

We filed out of the auditorium and stood in the hostile light of the gravel compound. Dave, our volunteer guide, explained about reinforced antennas that could go on transmitting during an attack (nuclear war disturbs radio transmissions, among other things). One small, cone-shaped antenna sat out in the open where anyone could trip over it. Dave told us a joke: they used to tell the rookies to watch out, this was the warhead. My mind roamed. What sort of person would volunteer to be a bomb-museum docent? The answer: he used to be a commander here. Now, semiretired, he trained cruise-missile operators.

It was still inconceivable that a missile stood erect under our feet, but there was its lid, an enormous concrete door on sliding tracks. Grate-covered holes in the ground bore a stenciled warning: TOXIC VAPORS. During accidents or miscalculations, deadly fuel would escape through those vents. I wondered if the folks living in the retirement community just downhill, with the excruciatingly ironic name of Green Valley, ever knew about this. Dave pointed to a government-issue weathervane, explaining that it would predict which way the poisonous gases would blow. What a relief.

We waited by the silo entry port while a Boy Scout troop emerged. I scanned the little boys' faces for signs of what I might be in for. Astonishment? Boredom? Our group then descended the cool stairwell into the silo. Just like a real missile crew, we put on hard hats to protect ourselves from low-hanging conduits and sharp edges. Signs warned us to watch for rattlesnakes. The hazards of snakes and bumped heads struck me as nearly comic against the steel-reinforced backdrop of potential holocaust. Or, put another way, being protected against these lesser hazards made the larger one seem improbable.

A series of blast doors, each thicker than my body, were all propped open to let us pass. In the old days, you would have had to wait for security clearance at every door in turn before it would admit you and then heave shut, locking behind you. If you turned out to be an unauthorized intruder, Dave explained, you'd get a quick tour of the complex with your face very near the gravel.

Some forty steps down in the silo's bowels, we entered the "No Lone Zone," where at least two people stood guard at all times. This was the control room. Compared with my expectations, undoubtedly influenced by Hollywood, it seemed unsophisticated. The Titan control room was run on cathode-ray tubes and transistor technology. For all the world, it had the look of those fifties spaceship movies, where men in crewcuts and skinny ties dash around trying to figure out what went wrong. No modern computers here, no special effects. The Titan system was built, Dave said, with "we-need-it-now technology." I tried to get my mind around the notion of slapping together some little old thing that could blow up a city.

Dave was already moving on, showing us the chair where the missile commander sat. It looks exactly like a La-Z-Boy recliner. The commander and one designated enlisted man would have the responsibility of simultaneously turning two keys and engaging the missile, if that call came through. All of us stared mutely at the little holes where those keys would go in.

A changeable wooden sign—similar to the ones the Forest Service uses to warn that the fire danger today is MEDIUM—hung above the controls to announce the day's STRATEGIC FORCES READINESS

CONDITION. You might suppose it went to ultimate-red-alert (or whatever it's called) only a few times in history. Not since the Cuban missile crisis, maybe. You would be wrong. Our guide explained that red-alerts come up all the time, sometimes triggered by a false blip on a radar, and sometimes (unbeknownst to crew members) as a test, checking their mental steadiness. Are they truly sane enough to turn that key and strike up a nuclear holocaust? For twenty-two years, every activity and every dollar spent here was aimed toward that exact end, and no other.

"But only the President can issue that order," Dave said. I believe he meant this to be reassuring.

We walked deeper into the artificially lit cave of the silo, down a long green catwalk suspended from above. The entire control chamber hangs on springs like huge shock absorbers. No matter what rocked and raged above, the men here would not be jostled.

On the catwalk we passed an eyewash facility, an outfit resembling a space suit, and a shower in case of mishaps involving toxic missile-fuel vapors. At its terminus the catwalk circled the immense cylindrical hole where the missile stood. We peered through a window into the shaft. Sure enough it was in there, hulking like a huge, dumb killer dog waiting for orders.

This particular missile, of course, is impotent. It has been relieved of its nuclear warhead. Now that the Titans have been decommissioned, they're being used as launch missiles for satellites. A man in our group piped up, "Wasn't it a Titan that blew up a few weeks ago, when they were trying to launch a weather satellite?"

Dave said yes, it was, and he made an interesting face. No one pursued this line of thought, although questions certainly hammered against the roof of my mouth. "What if it'd been headed out of here carrying a payload of death and destruction, Dave, for keeping Tucson safe and free? What then?"

Like compliant children on a field trip, all of us silently examined a metal hatch opening into the missile shaft, through which service mechanics would gain access to the missile itself. A sign on the hatch reminds mechanics not to use their walkie-talkies while inside. I asked what would happen if they did, and Dave said it would totally screw up the missile's guidance system. Again, I felt strangely inhibited from asking very obvious questions: What does this mean, to "totally screw up the missile's guidance system"? That the bomb might then land, for example, on Seattle?

The Pentagon has never discussed it, but the Titan missiles surrounding Tucson were decommissioned, ostensibly, because of technical obsolescence. This announcement came in 1980, almost a decade before the fall of the Berlin Wall; it had nothing to do with letting down the nation's nuclear guard. Make no mistake about this: in 1994 the U.S. sank $11.9 billion into the production and maintenance of nuclear missiles, submarines, and warheads. A separately allocated $2.8 billion was spent on the so-called Star Wars weapons research system. The U.S. government document providing budget authority for fiscal year 1996 states, "Although nuclear forces no longer play as prominent a role in our defense capability as they once did, they remain an important part of our overall defense posture." It's hard to see exactly how these forces are on the wane, as the same document goes on to project outlays of roughly $10 billion for the nuclear war enterprise again the following year, and more than $9 billion every year after that, on through the end of the century. In Nevada, New Mexico, Utah, Texas, the Great Plains, and many places we aren't allowed to know about, real live atomic bombs stand ready. Our leaders are hard-pressed to pretend some foreign power might invade us, but we are investing furiously in the tools of invasion.

The Pentagon was forced to decommission the Titans because, in plain English, the Titans may have presented one of the most stupendous hazards to the U.S. public we've ever had visited upon us. In the 1960s a group of civilian physicists at the University of Arizona worked out that an explosion at any one of the silos surrounding Tucson would set up a chain reaction among the other Titans that would instantly cremate the city. I learned about this in the late seventies, through one of the scientists who authored the extremely unpopular Titan report. I had months of bad dreams. It was not the first or last time I was floored by our great American capacity for denying objective reality in favor of defense mythology. When I was a child in grade school we had "duck and cover" drills, fully trusting that leaping into a ditch and throwing an Orlon sweater over our heads would save us from nuclear fallout.

The Extension Service produced cheerful illustrated pamphlets for our mothers, showing exactly how to stash away in the basement enough canned goods to see the family through the inhospitable aftermath of nuclear war. Now we can pass these pamphlets around at parties, or see the quaint documentary *Atomic Cafe*, and laugh at the antique charm of such naivete. And still we go on living in towns surrounded by nuclear choke chains. It is our persistent willingness to believe in ludicrous safety measures that is probably going to kill us.

I tried to exorcise my nightmare in a poem about the Titans, which began:

When God was a child
and the vampire fled from the sign of the cross,
belief was possible.
Survival was this simple.
But the savior clutched in the pocket
encouraged vampires to prosper
in the forest.

The mistake
was to carry the cross,
the rabbit's foot,
the spare tire,
St. Christopher who presides
over the wrecks:
steel cauliflowers
proliferating in junkyard gardens.
And finally
to believe in the fallout shelter.

Now we are left in cities ringed with giants.

Our tour finished, we clattered up the metal stairs and stood once again in the reassuring Arizona sun. Mine tailings on one side of the valley, the pine-crowned Santa Rita mountains on the other side, all still there; beneath us, the specter of hell.

Dave opened the floor for questions. Someone asked about the accident at a Titan silo in Little Rock, Arkansas, where some guy dropped a wrench on the missile and it blew up. Dave wished to point out several things. First, it wasn't a wrench, it was a ratchet. Second, it was a crew of rookies who had been sent in to service the missile. But yes, the unfortunate rookie did drop a tool. It bounced and hit the missile's sheet-metal skin, which is only a quarter of an inch thick. And which doesn't *house* the fuel tank—it *is* the fuel tank. The Titan silo's "blast-proof" concrete lid weighs 740 tons. It was blown 300 yards through the air into a Little Rock cornfield.

Dave wanted us to know something else about this accident: the guys in the shock-absorber-suspended control room had been evacuated prior to the ill-fated servicing. One of them had been drinking a Coke. When they returned they were amazed to see how well the suspension system had worked. The Coke didn't spill.

We crossed the compound to a window where we could look straight down on the missile's nose from above. A woman near me gasped a little. A man asked where this particular missile had been headed for, back in the days when it was loaded, and Dave explained that it varied, and would depend on how much fuel it contained at any given time. Somewhere in the Soviet Union is all he could say for sure. The sight of these two people calmly discussing the specifics of fuel load and destination suddenly scared the living daylights out of me. Discussing that event like something that could really happen. They almost seemed disappointed that it never had.

For years I have wondered how anyone could willingly compete in a hundred-yard dash toward oblivion, and I believe I caught sight of an answer in the Titan museum—in faces that lit up when they discussed targets and suspension systems and megatons. I saw it in eyes and minds so enraptured with technology that they saw before them an engineering spectacle, not a machine designed for the sole purpose of reducing civilizations to rubble.

Throughout the tour I kept looking, foolishly I suppose, for what was missing in this picture: some evidence that the people who ran this outfit were aware of the potential effects of their 150-ton cause. A hint of reluctance, a suggestion of death. In the absence of this, it's easy to get caught up in the internal logic of fuel capacities, circuitry, and chemical reactions. One could even develop an itch to see if this amazing equipment really works, and to measure success in purely technical terms.

The Coke didn't spill.

Outside the silo after the tour, I sat and listened to a young man regaling his girlfriend with further details about the Little Rock disaster. She asked him, "But that guy who dropped the, whatever it was. Did he die?"

The man laughed. "Are you kidding? That door on top was built to withstand a nuclear attack, and it got blown sky-high. Seven hundred and forty tons. That should tell you what happened to the guys inside."

She was quiet for a while, and then asked him, "You really get into that, don't you?"

"Well, sure," he said. "I love machines. It fascinates me what man is capable of designing."

Since that day, I've had the chance to visit another bomb museum of a different kind: the one that stands in Hiroshima. A serene building set in a garden, it is strangely quiet inside, with hushed viewers and hushed exhibits. Neither ideological nor histrionic, the display stands entirely without editorial comment. They are simply artifacts, labeled: china saki cups melted together in a stack. A brass Buddha with his hands relaxed into molten pools and a hole where his face used to be. Dozens of melted watches, all stopped at exactly eight-fifteen. A white eyelet petticoat with great, brown-rimmed holes burned in the left side, stained with black rain, worn by a schoolgirl named Oshita-chan. She was a half mile from the hypocenter of the nuclear blast, wearing also a blue short-sleeved blouse, which incinerated except for its collar, and a blue metal pin with a small white heart, which melted. Oshita-chan lived for approximately twelve hours after the bomb.

On that August morning, more than six thousand schoolchildren were working or playing in the immediate vicinity of the blast. Of most of them not even shreds of clothing remain. Everyone within a kilometer of the hypocenter received more than 1,000 rads and died quickly—though for most of them it was surely not quick enough. Hundreds of thousands of others died slower deaths; many would not know they were dying until two years later, when keloid scars would begin to creep across their bodies.

Every wooden building within two kilometers was annihilated, along with most of the earthquake-proof concrete ones, and within sixteen kilometers every window was smashed. Only concrete chimneys and other cylindrical things were left standing. Fire storms burned all day, creating howling winds and immeasurable heat. Black rain fell, bringing down radioactive ash, staining walls with long black streaks, poisoning the water, killing fish. I can recite this story but I didn't, somehow, believe it until I looked at things a human being can understand: great handfuls of hair that fell from the head of Hiroko Yamashita, while she sat in her house eight hundred meters from the hypocenter. The pink dress of a girl named Egi-chan, whose blackened pocket held a train ticket out of the city. The charred apron of Mrs. Sato, who was nursing her baby.

The one bizarre, incongruous thing in the museum at Hiroshima, it seemed to me, was a replica of the bomb itself. Dark green, longer than a man, strangely knobbed and finned—it looks like some invention that has nothing to do with people. Nothing at all.

What they left out of the Titan Missile Museum was in plain sight at Hiroshima. Not a sound track with a politically balanced point of view. Just the rest of the facts, those that lie beyond suspension systems and fuel capacity. A missile museum, it seems to me, ought to be horrifying. It had better shake us, if only for a day, out of the illusion of predictability and control that cradles the whole of our quotidian lives. Most of us—nearly all, I would say—live by this illusion. We walk through our days with our minds on schedule—work, kids, getting the roof patched before the rainy season. We do not live as though literally everything we have, including a history and a future, could be erased by two keys turning simultaneously in a lock.

How could we? How even to pay our monthly bills, if we held in mind the fact that we are camped on top of a technological powder keg? Or to use Carl Sagan's more eloquent analogy: we are all locked together in a room filled with gasoline vapors, insisting that because *they* have two hundred matches, *we* won't be safe unless we have *three* hundred.

The Cold War is widely supposed to have ended. But preparations for nuclear war have not ended. The Titan museum's orientation film is still telling the story we have heard so many times that it sounds, like all ultra-familiar stories, true. The story is that *they* would gladly drop bombs on us, if they weren't so scared by the sheer toughness of our big missiles. *They* are the aggressors. *We* are practicing "a commitment to deterrence."

Imagine you have never heard that story before. Look it in the eye and see what it is. How do strategic-games trophies and Titan-missile golf shirts stack up against a charred eyelet petticoat and handfuls of hair? The United States is the only nation that has ever used an atomic bomb. Dropped it, on men and women and schoolchildren and gardens and pets and museums, two whole cities of quotidian life. We did it, the story goes, to hasten the end of the war and bring our soldiers home. Not such an obvious choice for Oshita-chan. "To protect the rights and freedom we enjoy" is a grotesque euphemism. Every nuclear weapon ever constructed was built for the purpose of ending life, in a manner so horrific it is nearly impossible to contemplate. And U.S. nuclear science has moved steadily and firmly, from the moment of its birth, toward first-strike capacity.

If the Titan in Green Valley had ever been allowed to do the job for which it was designed, the fire storm wouldn't have ended a world away. Surely all of us, even missile docent Dave, understand that. Why, then, were we all so polite about avoiding the obvious questions? How is it that a waving flag can create an electromagnetic no-back-talk zone? In 1994, half a century after the bombing of Hiroshima, we spent $150 billion on the business and technology of war—nearly a tenth of it specifically on nuclear-weapons systems. Any talk of closing down a military base raises defensive and reverent ire, no matter how wasteful an installment it might be. And yet, public debate dickers and rages over our obligation to fund the welfare system—a contribution of about $25 a year from each taxpayer on average, for keeping the poorest among us alive. How can we haggle over the size of this meager life preserver, while shiploads of money for death sail by unchallenged? What religion of humankind could bless the travesty that is the U.S. federal budget?

Why did I not scream at the top of my lungs down in that hole?

I didn't, so I'll have to do it now, to anyone with the power to legislate or listen: one match in a gasoline-filled room is too many. I don't care a fig who is holding it.

I donned the hard hat and entered the belly of the beast, and I came away with the feeling of something poisonous on my skin. The specter of that beast could paralyze a person with despair. But only if you accept it as inevitable. And it's only inevitable if you are too paralyzed with despair to talk back. If a missile museum can do no more than stop up our mouths, with either patriotic silence or desperation, it's a monument the living can't afford. I say slam its doors for good. Tip a cement truck to the silo's gullet and seal in the evil pharaoh. If humanity survives long enough to understand what he really was, they can dig him up and put on display the grandiose depravity of the twentieth century.

I left, drove down into the innocent palm-shaded condominiums of Green Valley, and then, unexpectedly, headed up the other side of the valley into the mountains. When I reached the plateau of junipers and oaks, I pulled off the road, hiked into the woods, and sat for a long time on a boulder in the middle of a creek. Water flowed away from me on either side. A canopy of sycamore leaves whispered above my head, while they waited for night, the close of one more day in which the world did not end.

In a poem called "Trinity," Sy Margaret Baldwin explained why she would never go down to the site of the first atomic-bomb explosion, which is opened to the public every year:

> . . . I would come face to face with my sorrow, I
> would feel hope slipping from me and be afraid
> the changed earth would turn over and speak
> the truth to the thin black ribbons of my ribs.

PART II

Coyote Learns to Glow

The Society of
the Living Dead

CATHERINE QUIGG

*F*or more than two generations, hundreds of young women came from surrounding farms and nearby small towns to work with radioactive materials in downtown Ottawa, Illinois, about eighty miles southwest of Chicago. They painted luminous watch and clock dials and hands at the Radium Dial and Luminous Processes factories from 1920 to 1978. Exposed to radioactive radium and tritium, many of these workers developed cancers, tumors, and other radiation-related illnesses. Some died premature and painful deaths. As an antinuclear activist, researcher, and writer in the 1970s, I began hearing stories about these unfortunate women and their tragic lives. I investigated their claims in the early 1980s with a small grant from the Center for Investigative Journalism in Washington, D.C.

During the early spring of 1984, I spent two weeks in the rural town of Ottawa, near the junction of the Illinois and Fox rivers, interviewing as many survivors as I could find. I met with these women in their homes, on the phone, or over coffee in the comfortable living room of a longtime resident. Most seemed anxious to tell of their experiences; a few were shy and fearful of the stigma of having cancer. Next I reviewed pertinent records and documents at the regional office of the U.S. Nuclear Regulatory Commission (NRC) in Glen Ellyn, Illinois, and the Illinois Department of Nuclear Safety (IDNS) in Springfield. The state of Illinois authorized the use of radium in Ottawa in 1957, and the NRC licensed the use of tritium there from 1961 to 1978. I also talked with scientists from Argonne National Laboratory near Darien, Illinois, who measured the radioactivity in the workers' bodies, and I spoke with appropriate federal government officials. In the process, I discovered how state, federal, and corporate negligence allowed radiation contamination and overexposure to affect the health of workers.

Even today, despite recent revelations about radiation victims by the U.S. Department of Energy, this large group of victims and families has gone unnoticed and uncompensated for their work-related illnesses or untimely deaths. Emphasis on businesses' profits in the 1980s fostered public apathy toward environmental and health investigations, making it difficult to publish articles raising questions of corporate negligence or malfeasance in these areas. My numerous queries to the media proposing an article about these women were rejected. Discouraged, I set my notes aside and moved on to other concerns. Now I look back in sadness at Ottawa radiation victims never recognized for the injustice nor compensated for the pain they suffered. I wish I had been more persistent in bringing their plight to public attention. Most of them are dead today. Their story should concern us all. With assistance from early notes, I would like to share the highlights of their painful ordeal.

Radium Dial Company, a subsidiary of U.S. Standard Chemical Company of New York, employed the first wave of dial painters from 1920 until December 1936 at Ottawa; there were smaller plants in Chicago, Streator, and Peru, Illinois. Supervisors at the early Radium Dial plant allowed workers to place camel's hair brushes between their lips to get a fine point for painting luminous numbers on timepieces. With each lick of her brush, a dial painter swallowed a little radium and added forever to the deadly burden carried in her bones. Within a few years, some workers became seriously ill.

"They said it was all right, nothing wrong, to put the brush in your mouth and paint numbers and then dip the brush in again," recalled Charlotte Purcell, who started at Radium Dial in 1922, at age sixteen. She stopped working in 1932, when her arm was amputated to halt the spread of cancer. When I met her at her home in Chicago, Purcell walked slowly, with a cane.

I spoke on the phone with Marie Rossiter Hunter, a dial painter from 1923 to 1930. She said, "We used to paint our eyebrows, our lips, and our eyelashes, and then look at ourselves in the darkroom—just for fun." Rossiter remembered eating her lunch at her desk. "They never said anything; they never stopped you," she said, sounding angry at the recollection. At the time of our conversation, she had had six leg operations, and her bloated legs were turning black. She said doctors told her that her bones were honeycombed with radium.

Besides radium ingestion, workers were exposed to radioactive dust and to penetrating external gamma radiation from workplace surfaces contaminated by the decay products of radium.

For many women, the first symptoms of radium poisoning were tumors and pain in their feet, probably caused by years of standing on radium-contaminated floors. Bone cancers often came with slow-healing spontaneous fractures; leg and arm bones weakened, and snapped. Some workers became anemic when radium continuously bombarded their bone marrow, where blood cells are produced. Many had breast tumors, leading to mastectomies. Others had serious problems with their teeth. Because of their myriad deadly diseases, local newspapers referred to the early Ottawa dial painters as "The Society of the Living Dead."

In 1935 Catherine Wolf Donahue petitioned the Illinois Industrial Commission for workers' compensation for permanent disability, medical care, and hospital care. A dial painter at Radium Dial from 1922 to 1931, she suffered from radium poisoning with disintegration of the jaw and malignancy of her hips. At the time of the trial, she weighed only seventy-one pounds, half her normal weight, and had to be carried into the courtroom. Donahue's attorney contended that Radium Dial's New York–based executives should have known the hazards of brush licking and stopped this practice, especially after the highly publicized 1927 New Jersey dial painters' lawsuit against U.S. Radium Corporation. In the fiercely contested court battle, Radium Dial argued that radium was an abrasive, not a poison. The court ruled in favor of Donahue, awarding her $5,561. Donahue died three months later, leaving her young husband and two small children.

To avoid further claims, Radium Dial shut its doors in December 1936. By that time, at least twenty-four of its workers had died horrible, lingering deaths from radium poisoning.

The second wave of Illinois dial painters were employed by Radium Dial's successor company in Ottawa, Luminous Processes, Inc., from 1938 until 1978. The new company, a closed corporation, had the same president as Radium Dial—Joseph Kelly, Sr.—the same equipment, and many of the same workers as the old company. It was located in a two-story brick building just two blocks from the old site. The women I interviewed were mainly "second wave" workers who had worked at the "new" Luminous Processes, although some had worked solely at Radium Dial, and others at both factories.

Former Radium Dial workers took jobs at Luminous thinking the new operation safe. Their supervisors informed them that earlier dial painters had died because they put brushes in their mouths, and since brush licking was no longer permitted, exposure to radium would not be harmful. The supervisors didn't know, or neglected to mention, that the decay products of radium emit powerful gamma external radiation that, like X-rays, can penetrate the body without being ingested. That's why exposure to radium, primarily from some of the daughter products along the decay chain, can cause a wide range of diseases, including cancer of the breast, bone, bone marrow, and skin.

At first, workers called "screeners" used wood spatulas to spread radium paint on screens placed over watch dials. The excess paint was removed with hand-held sponges. They painted clock hands with fine-tipped brushes dipped in open jars of radium paint. Smocks were their only protective clothing. Beginning in 1948, workers applied radium paint with hand-held sponges as watch and clock dials revolved on a table in front of them. Clock hands continued to be painted manually. On average, workers processed three million dials each year.

There was no state registration for the use of radium in Illinois until 1957, when the Radiation Installation Act was passed. And it took the State Radiation Protection Act of 1974 to give Illinois power to license companies and to set upper limits on worker radiation exposure. The lack of either state or federal oversight was especially reprehensible during the 1940s, when the war effort swamped Luminous with orders from the federal government for military items such as aircraft instrumentation, compasses, and other equipment. The U.S. armed forces became a regular Luminous customer through its contractor, the Bendix Corporation of Southfield, Michigan. State inspection reports from

July and September 1965 tell of work areas contaminated with radium and its daughter decay products. Inspectors stated that safety precautions were ineffective; ultraviolet light did not identify radium contamination on workers' hands as intended; and "waterless" hand cleaners were not effective in removing radioactivity from employees' hands or from under their fingernails.

"You couldn't work in that plant without getting covered with the stuff," said Pearl Schott, a dial painter from 1946 to 1977. "Only paint thinner would remove the luminous paint from our bodies." She complained that "Company officials took our film badges [to record external radiation exposure] in a dark room and dusted them off before they sent them out for readings."

In May 1973 a state inspector found gross radioactive contamination in work areas, offices, the lunchroom, and the rest room. There was radioactivity on at least six employees' hands, and radioactive waste in unmarked containers. Despite these negative findings, Illinois continued to authorize radium use at Luminous, and permitted the gradual introduction of radioactive tritium beginning in 1957. During the late 1960s and early 1970s, most dial painters alternated between radium and tritium work. "If we changed material, it was like going from Lux to Camay," said one former worker. "No one spoke of the dangers of either."

By 1975, the company had switched from state-licensed radium to exclusive use of the now federally licensed tritium. Federal documents show tritium use skyrocketed; hundreds of thousands of timepieces containing thousands of curies of tritium were produced and shipped each month from Luminous to the Westclox factory in Peru, Illinois, for further assembly. The process for tritium work at Luminous was much like that for radium work. Workers spread luminous tritium paint with hand-held sponges over clock dials placed under screens, and removed the excess. These screeners had exhaust fans to vent gaseous tritium, but other painters, who applied tritium manually to watch dials with artist brushes or glass rods, had no exhaust fans.

Company officials told the women that tritium was harmless. But tritium gives off mainly internal radiation. Tritiated water vapor can be absorbed through the lungs or diffused through the skin. Scientists say tritium, which replaces ordinary hydrogen, incorporates into all body tissues, including ovaries and testes, which contain the genetic DNA. Bone marrow is one of its most important targets.

In my long conversation with Debra Mooney Smith, a radium and tritium screener from 1973 to 1975, she blamed her many health problems on her work at Luminous Processes. She said, "They told me there was really nothing that was going to hurt us with tritium—that you had to have a high amount of it before it could do anything to you." According to Smith, "There was no ventilation, no windows you could open, no air conditioning—only a few fans. A lot of times I was working right over the screen; my face was just inches away." She said many workers griped about the terrible smell of tritium paint and its fumes, "which rose right up to our faces, causing constant headaches."

Another screener, Mary Kapsul Hougas, confirmed Smith's observations: "We'd work right over the screen with our noses practically in it. There was nothing between us, the material on our hands, and our breathing." When told to go upstairs to work with tritium, her sister-in-law, Lee Chiovatero Hougas, objected because "I didn't want any more tumors." Nonetheless, the manager told her tritium was harmless, and assigned her to wash tritium screens in a small, isolated room that had no fans.

After complaints about the smell of tritium and an outbreak of skin rashes, Luminous's vice president, Warren N. Holm, flew in from New York to reassure workers. He told them: "If you could measure worm particles in tomato juice, like you measure radiation in the air, you would never want to drink tomato juice again."

Tritium handlers were required to take monthly urine tests, the results of which were sent to the NRC. Test results indicated a range up to almost double the amount allowed by federal regulations. From 1975 to 1977, at least twenty-nine women had tritium readings over the federal limit. In April 1976, an NRC inspection showed widespread tritium surface contamination, worker overexposure, and excessive radioactive releases to the outside environment. Things only got worse. Radium contamination continued to be a problem, even after Luminous's license to use it had expired. As late as 1977, state inspectors found radium-contaminated desktops, unsecured jars of radium paint, and radioactive waste emptied down toilets, into the local sewage system. In January 1978, federal inspectors again confirmed excessive tritium levels in the plant's atmosphere—up to 170 times the NRC's permissible limit. Four months later, the situation had not improved.

Finally, because of the company's repeated disregard for regulations, the NRC ordered immediate suspension of its license on February 17, 1978. Luminous immediately shut down its Ottawa plant. At that time, the company had thirty-five employees working with tritium in timepiece production, as well as others in shipping and receiving.

By 1980, seven former Luminous workers had jointly filed for workers' compensation with the Illinois Industrial Commission, claiming that their cancers, blood disorders, tumors, and other ailments were caused by occupational radiation exposure. The women said safety precautions at the plant were almost nonexistent, and they were constantly being contaminated by radioactive materials they used and by debris thrown in open bins. Company officials continued to assure them radium and tritium were safe to handle, they reported.

The women asserted in their lawsuit that their survey of one hundred former Luminous painters showed that at least sixty-five had died since the 1960s; of this group, twenty-eight died of cancer, well over twice the expected cancer rate. Their fatal illnesses included radium poisoning and cancers of the lungs, breasts, lymph glands, bowels, throat, and brain. As years went on, more former workers were added to the list of those with cancers, tumors, and other radiation-related ailments.

Since 1980, nothing has been done to compensate Luminous workers for their pain and distress. Their workers' compensation legal case has fallen through bureaucratic cracks. The state, the federal government, and the corporations involved with "The Society of the Living Dead" have all washed their hands of any responsibility to these women.

I remember having coffee one morning in a ranch-style house on a hill overlooking the village of Ottawa with Lee and Mary Hougas. They showed me their voluminous scrapbook with death notices and photos of their fellow radium dial painters. As they turned each page, I could tell they knew each woman intimately—her kind of work, her family, her illnesses, her hospitalizations, and the unusually early date of her death.

Their litany began: "Died of breast cancer, died of cancer, leg amputated, died of bone cancer, brain cancer, died of . . . ," and it went on and on as they pointed out one woman after another. In a group photo of former workers, their fingers lingered on a slim, sweet-faced young woman. I was told, "She had a horrible death. There was nothing left of her; her bones disintegrated. She was such a doll. Such a shame." I finished my coffee, thankful it was strong.

Reflecting on her own work at Luminous, Mary Hougas said: "We were very naive. We were innocent victims of the times, victims of ignorance, and victims of our state officials and inspectors. The only reason I speak out now is for my two grandchildren. I think we're going into an era when a lot of radioactive materials are going to be used. It may happen again, and if I can prevent it by talking about it, I will."

We should listen.

Voiceless Victims

JIM CARRIER

*T*he animals were always the first to know.

Spadefoot toads that came out to breed in the rain early July 16, 1945, were evaporated by the Trinity explosion. Shadows of carbonized lizards pockmarked the sand of the Jornada del Muerto Desert. Partly eviscerated jackrabbits were found 800 yards from ground zero, while dozens of cattle thirty miles away were burned and blistered from radioactive fallout.

When the Cold War began, sheep in Utah died after eating fallout-dusted sagebrush. Ducks landing on Idaho waste ponds flew off with a human's limit of radioactive iodine. Salmon in the Columbia River became radioactive from eating "hot" insects.

In laboratories, animals too numerous to count—dogs, monkeys, hamsters, mice—were injected, fed, and made to inhale plutonium and other radionuclides. And as the bomb was perfected, pigs were caged and dogs suspended nearby to burn their flesh. Rabbits and monkeys were strapped in drone planes and flown through fallout to zap their organs.

The history of the atom bomb is accompanied by an untold story of animal contributors. Many were important test animals—six dogs and several hundred rats and mice, for example, first established the bone-seeking and deadly properties of plutonium. Beagles still are used today to grow tumors at Albuquerque's Inhalation Toxicology Research Lab. In many cases, animals were shock troops, bellwethers of the Atomic Age, absorbing the first waves of radiation.

"Everything close to the ground died. My dog Shep went blind and had tumors hanging all over. We didn't even have any birds around here," said Joe Fallini, whose ranch downwind from the Nevada Test Site repeatedly was enveloped in fallout dust. As a boy, he had to shoot his dog. As early as 1949, the lowly jackrabbit was recognized by the Atomic Energy Commission as a "reliable indicator" of radioactive contaminants.

Rocky Flats plutonium was noticed on the fur of rabbits hopping among leaking barrels. Researchers at the Idaho National Engineering Lab checked the accuracy of downwind maps by hunting jackrabbits from a chair strapped to the fender of a Land Rover. The jacks' livers showed radioactivity in proportion to the distance from emitting reactors.

In the Columbia River downstream from the nuclear reactors of Hanford, Washington, algae, plankton, and insects began accumulating radionuclides at the rate of two to three curies per mile of riverbed. As a result, birds and fish accumulated radioactive concentrations thousands of times that of the river. Swallows that fed on radioactive mosquitoes were the hottest; shorebirds were next, followed by diving ducks. One study showed duck eggs 1.5 million times as radioactive as the river, with reproduction unaffected. Salmon, whitefish, and shellfish became radioactive.

Despite heavy radiation, there is no record of mass deaths among fish and wildlife. Indians along the Columbia did report odd growths on fish. Alaskan Eskimos became radioactive because of a food chain that began with lichens. Lichens snared fallout. Caribou ate lichens. Eskimos ate caribou and became the most radioactive humans on Earth by 1960.

Western plants, especially sagebrush, served as fallout collectors for animals. Radioactivity that collected on leaves showed up in organs of wildlife a day or two after a bomb test in Nevada. Hanford researchers found that tumbleweed, the Russian thistle, could become an "aerial radiation hazard" by sucking up radiation from the ground. Alfalfa also was efficient at collecting fallout, especially strontium-90 and iodine-131, which cows passed on in milk. This finding in the late 1950s went unheeded until children were discovered poisoned a decade later.

From 1955 until 1962, when atmospheric testing ended, dozens of Western ranchers from Taos, New Mexico, to Adel, Oregon, lost cattle and sheep to mysterious maladies. The Atomic Energy Commission denied their claims as "not possible." The most famous case was the loss of 1,400 ewes and 2,900 lambs in southern Utah in 1953. Grazed on pastures next to the Nevada Test Site, they had been trailed twenty to thirty days across the heaviest fallout area to lambing sheds near Cedar City, Utah.

Upon arrival, McRae Bulloch and other sheepmen noticed lips and ears covered with sores, lost wool, and many newborns malformed or stillborn. "We lost most of our lambs. We got the county agent," said Bulloch, now seventy-five. Suspecting fallout, government veterinarians performed tests showing sheep thyroids with significant levels of iodine-131. After lambing, supposedly healthy ewes were pushed toward summer pastures in the mountains to the east. "They'd hang back. We'd lift them into the truck. When we got to the ranch, we had a truckload and every sheep was dead."

The government blamed malnutrition or disease. The Bullochs, who had to sell water rights and property to pay debts, sued the government and lost. Although a federal judge later labeled the government case a "fraud," the sheepmen never were paid.

By today's standards, animal exposure to nuclear explosions was the most horrific experiment of the Atomic Age. Pigs, cows, burros, sheep, rabbits, mice, and monkeys were caged at close range. They often were killed or torn apart. The very first experiment, at Trinity, was a failure. A box of white test mice strung by their tails on signal wires never lived to see the shot. They died of thirst before the detonation.

In a November 1951 bomb test at the Nevada Test Site, mongrels were anesthetized, placed in "semi-form fitting" jackets with holes cut out, and suspended upside down at various distances from ground zero. According to a declassified document, dogs had been extensively burned and irradiated in the lab at the Virginia Medical College. But the Nevada test "offered the first opportunity for us to carry out field tests using dogs exposed to an actual atomic bomb explosion." The dogs were burned "because of our belief that a large proportion of the thermal casualties [in an atomic war] would arise from secondary fires produced by the initial blast and thermal radiation," the government document says. To test the efficacy of fabrics, the dogs were draped in various kinds—olive drab cotton sateen, serge, and DuPont Orlon.

Before the test, the dogs were exercised to maintain optimum health and given Purina Dog Chow and water. But the first two test dogs died in their slings (designed to swing with the bomb blast) from overexposure to cold and rain after the shot was delayed. After the "Dog Shot," researchers found "dogs five and nine were living. Dog eleven at the seven-thousand-foot station was dead but still very warm; death had apparently occurred after the burning and shockwave phase. The animal's skin was burned. . . . the burned areas were coagulated on the surface. . . . Dog twelve was dead at the nine-thousand-foot station and burns received were similar."

A similar fabric test used pigs dressed in little uniforms. Unfortunately, the pigs gained weight while waiting, and the too-tight uniforms had to be retailored. In the 1956 series of tests called Plumbbob, one thousand pigs were used to "study medical handling and treatment of mass casualties." Color films show them squealing and squirming as the blast overtook and roasted them.

Lab use of animals has been wide-ranging and in many cases was crucial to safeguarding nuclear workers and the public. Wright Langham, a pioneer health physicist, warned in 1950 of a "drastic weakness in our knowledge of the toxicity of plutonium as applied to man." He suggested experiments on dogs because their skeletons resemble humans', they excrete plutonium as people do, and they live long enough to allow tumors to develop.

Foxhounds were used initially, but beagles became the test animal of choice because of their gentle disposition. Thousands were injected or made to inhale plutonium at the Albuquerque lab, Los Alamos, Hanford, and at Colorado State University, the University of Utah, and the University of California at Davis.

Using bone cancer rates from watch-dial painters—poisoned in the 1920s when they licked their radium-laden brushes—researchers injected dogs with radium and plutonium and learned that plutonium is more toxic in producing skeletal cancer. Unlike radium, plutonium deposits on the surface of bones, where the bone-growing cells are. As a result, the standard exposure allowed for plutonium workers was lowered dramatically in the 1950s. Test dogs also inhaled the "maximum permissible lung burden" for nuclear workers, sixteen nanocuries of plutonium, and rarely developed cancer.

"They are still alive. To me, that would be reassuring [to a worker]," said Charles Hobbs, associate director of the inhalation lab, known as the "puppy palace." "Many times we will observe increased cancer but no real shortening of the lifespan." The beagles rarely were dosed to death, he said, and tumors came late in their lives, after ten to twelve years for dogs, which live an average of fourteen and a half years.

The beagles were the tip of a huge body of experimental work that assumed the worst: nuclear war and its aftermath. Given the gruesome possibilities, researchers got AEC money for a vast body of work that now seems Strangelovian. Oak Ridge scientists, for example, exposed pigs to 966 rads, twice the fatal human dose, to test whether they would remain safe to eat. They found that the loin and shoulders developed less bacteria than the hams. At Colorado State University, chickens were zapped with up to one thousand rads. If they survived, egg production remained the same, but chick size decreased dramatically. At Texas A&M, goats were irradiated to check the effect on their hearing. Several experiments suggest animals can detect ionizing radiation and try to avoid it—bobcats, deer mice, and ants, for example.

North of Nunn, Colorado, between Greeley and Cheyenne, a fenced short-grass prairie was irradiated for nine years with 8,750 curies of cesium 137, a deadly amount. It killed the grass up to eight or nine meters away, said Leslie Fraley Jr., whose doctorate at CSU was based on the Armageddon study.

One consistent conclusion of the tests: Nature is very resistant to radiation and resilient when it disappears. The slow rate of radionuclide movement through the ecosystem and into the food chain makes human poisoning nearly impossible at such places as Rocky Flats, said Fraley. In a sense, nature binds up the poison. Animals also deposit less radiation in their muscles than in bones or other organs, so people can eat a lot before reaching federal limits.

Lastly, animals lower on the evolutionary ladder, such as lizards and insects, survive higher doses. But even they drift toward extinction if high doses continue, said Frederick Turner of the University of California at Los Angeles, who zapped lizards in the Nevada desert for eight years.

Mutations caused by radiation don't seem to survive. "Nuclear facilities may get higher mutations. But if deleterious, chances are they will be selected out," said Dr. Ward Whicker, a radiation ecologist at CSU. "We're not going to see two-headed giraffes popping up." But writer Terry Tempest Williams says she saw a two-headed snake once while trespassing to stop a nuclear blast in Nevada. Near Rocky Flats, the story of "Scooter," a farm piglet with stunted rear legs, never was linked with radiation but led to widespread suspicion about radiation leaks from the bomb manufacturing plant.

The use of animals was always a touchy issue. In August 1951, prior to the "Dog Shot" test, one official urged Washington not to show test animals to reporters. In a 1955 memo, Richard Elliott, the Nevada Test Site's public relations director, noted that use of monkeys had been downplayed by not announcing monkey conditions after blasts and refusing requests for photos—"which we got by with and which most certainly helped avoid criticism."

Today, only fifty beagles live at the Albuquerque lab. Studies are concluding, long-term funding is out of favor, and "there's also the question of using dogs in biomedical research," said veterinarian Hobbs. "We've used [beagles] very seriously. If you disagree with using dogs for biomedical research, then you wouldn't like what we do. But we do it within laws and regulations."

The work that seemed so important during the Cuban Missile Crisis has "outlived its relevance," said Turner, whose tests on lizards continued until 1972. "In ten years, the fear of atomic war abated, and society entered another stage where nuclear energy was the principal concern, and what nuclear power plants might emit. They don't emit much. We were supposed to emulate a postnuclear attack."

Meanwhile, across the West, critters slowly are retaking the territory. The prairie zapped dead in Nunn is growing back. Antelope in Idaho show tiny amounts of radioactivity in their bones, as do trout in Colorado mountain lakes. But scientists say neither shows any lasting effects. At the Nevada Test Site, old ground zeros are inhabited again by coyotes, jackrabbits, ground squirrels, and mice. While their body radionuclides often rank as low as those of off-site animals, plutonium is common in their fur, bellies, and muscle.

Yet memories of animal victims remain vivid. Ray Winn, a former test site worker responsible for recovering equipment after A-blasts in the 1950s, still is stopped cold by one. The year was 1958, just before the test ban, when the AEC was rushing to set off as many bombs as possible. The devices were suspended from balloons and set off, sometimes as often as one per day. Under pressure to collect data from the latest blast, Winn was lowered by helicopter into a detonation area. He was wearing a full "bunny" protective suit.

"There was debris, wreckage and craters. I looked over and I saw...."

He paused in the telling and began to weep.

"This is stupid after twenty-five years . . . I looked over and saw a mother coyote with her baby. The baby was dead. The mother had her paws around it, and she was blind.

"I said, 'I've got to go.' There was a Marine chopper above me. He was in a 200-rad area. He was screaming at me.

"I said, 'That's it,' and I left. I walked off. I left weapons. I was simply emotionally and physically exhausted. I had nothing left to give."

Downwinders All

MARY DICKSON

*G*rowing up in Salt Lake City in the 1960s, I don't remember hearing about nuclear testing. We had bomb drills in grade school that sent us scurrying under our desks as part of the "duck and cover" defense which supposedly would keep us safe in the event of a real-life nuclear attack. Or we shuffled off to the school's dark basement, toting our Clorox jugs of water, laughing about what we'd eat and where we'd pee if we were ever really trapped there. Such drills were eagerly anticipated exercises that were more like unannounced recesses than serious preparation for potential disaster. We heard about the Communist menace and atomic bombs, but we didn't hear anything about cancers or strange tumors or fallout. We drank our milk and ate our vegetables, assuming that, as the Mormon hymn told us, all was well.

The first time I heard about testing was at a Saturday matinee; the movie was *Crack in the World*. It was about scientists who exploded a nuclear bomb underground to stop a crack in the Earth. The explosion doubled the speed at which the crack spread, nearly wiping out life on Earth. It made me nervous. I was only seven, but it made perfect sense to me that if you exploded a bomb underground, the Earth would shift. But that was just a movie.

The Earth shifted for me in the spring before my thirtieth birthday, when I was diagnosed with thyroid cancer. I had no symptoms other than the corn-sized nodule on my neck. The "Big C," as my uncle called it, was growing inside me for no apparent reason. The dreaded cancer had quietly crawled up behind me and grabbed me around the throat. My world lost its predictability with two words: "It's malignant." Facing surgery and radiation treatment, I didn't think it mattered how I got it. The only thing that mattered was to get rid of it. Friends and family gave me long, sad looks, as though they expected the worst. Unable to face me, my sister left her cherished Madame Alexander doll on my desk at work with a note I knew she had written in tears. Did she think I wasn't coming back? I overheard a friend at the office whisper, "She's so brave," as I pounded away at the keys of my typewriter, trying not to think about my surgery the next day. Was there something the doctors weren't telling me?

The surgeon cut out my thyroid and the lymph nodes around it. A few days later they gave me radioactive iodine to drink. They euphemistically called it a "cocktail." After I swallowed it, a nurse wheeled me back to my room in a high-backed wheelchair made of lead to protect her from me. On the door of my room was a sign: "Caution! Radioactive Material." Stamped on my hospital bracelet was the symbol for radiation. I was the radioactive material.

Every day, a radiologist opened the door to my room and pointed his Geiger counter at me to see how "hot" I was. Knowing it wasn't safe to enter the room, the nurses shoved trays of food under my door. I did nothing but drink water to flush out the radiation. I was isolated in that small white room for four days until the reading on the Geiger counter was low enough that I could be around people again. When I left the hospital, they destroyed my clothes and everything I had touched. The doctors cautioned that it would be best for me not to be around babies or pregnant women for a few more days. Frightened by their warnings, my husband took to sleeping in the back room.

Like him, some people felt it best to avoid me, whether out of fear of the radiation or because I was now a reminder of the randomness with which misfortune strikes. If it could happen to me, it could happen to them. When I ran into an old acquaintance and told her why I'd been out of the office for three months, she backed away from me as if my bad luck might be contagious. She wasn't the only one I made nervous. My husband scolded me when, months after surgery, my hand instinctively went to my neck, feeling for more lumps. "Stop looking for more," he cried, as if my vigilance would bring the disease back. I'll never stop feeling for more. "Since I've had thyroid cancer, does that mean I've had my bout with cancer and I won't get any other kind?" I naively asked my doctor, desperate for reassurance. He smiled and said there are no guarantees of anything.

After I recovered, I went back to editing the *Desert Sun,* a newspaper that monitored the Nevada Test Site and carried stories about nuclear tests, leaks, and radiation. A radiobiologist I met told me thyroid cancer was common among those exposed to radiation as children. Even then, I didn't think of my own cancer as anything but bad luck in a random universe. Like so many of us, I assumed radiation was something that affected only people in southern Utah who were directly downwind of the blasts.

Then I met Carole Gallagher. It was 1989. She was a New York photographer who moved to Utah to document the effects of nuclear testing on people living downwind of the Nevada Test Site. She interviewed and photographed hundreds of people, collecting one horror story after another.

The first time I interviewed Gallagher for an article I was writing, I mentioned my cancer. She latched onto the story of my disease, and started grilling me about my life—when I was born, where I was raised, and if I drank milk.

"Testing," she cried, "you got cancer from the testing!"

"But I grew up in Salt Lake," I protested.

She shook her head. "You people are so naive. You think it stopped at Richfield. It went everywhere."

She showed me a map of the fallout. Utah and Nevada were blotted out, and the black ink spread as far north as Minnesota and Canada. She told me how contaminated hay, milk, wool, and meat from Utah and Nevada had been shipped all over the country. That was when Carole Gallagher asked to interview me.

When Gallagher's book *American Ground Zero: The Secret Nuclear War* was released nationwide, I reluctantly opened my copy. I read two stories before bursting into tears. I saw my face among the photographs of ranchers, teachers, and scientists, all of us victims of nuclear testing. I really was a downwinder. But I had been lucky. Doctors pronounced me fully recovered. Other people in Gallagher's book were not so fortunate. Many have already died.

I waited a few days before opening the book again. I read the list of other diseases possibly related to fallout: diabetes . . . heart disease . . .

birth defects . . . severe allergies . . . arthritis . . . auto-immune diseases like lupus and MS. My older sister had just been diagnosed with lupus; a good friend, with MS.

In her book, Gallagher reports the circumstantial evidence linking nuclear fallout to those diseases. She contends that the government knew the facts—about fallout, about contaminated milk, about the susceptibility of children—and that they lied to the people. People like me, my sister, and my friend. Could we all have been poisoned by the deadly winds of the Cold War? The world suddenly seemed far more sinister. The damage was done, and there was nowhere to hide. A friend of mine says that she is always comforted by the sound of sirens because "it means that me and mine are safe"; the sirens scream for someone else. When the pink clouds of fallout drifted across the skies in all directions, no sirens rang out to signal the danger. We blithely went about our lives, assuming we were safe. We trusted our government when they assured us we had nothing to worry about. Are any of us safe?

Reports keep coming out, revealing more of the truth. An article in the *Bulletin of the Atomic Scientists* claiming that the government warned the film manufacturer Eastman Kodak about expected areas of heavy fallout during the 1950s, so it could protect unexposed film. People living downwind never received the same courtesy. A fourteen-year study by the National Cancer Institute showing that virtually all Americans in the 1950s were exposed to fallout, and that as early as 1953 our government knew that drinking milk from cows that had eaten contaminated foliage could cause thyroid cancer. Each time I read a new piece of evidence, I start to cry.

I have no proof that I got my cancer from breathing the air or drinking the milk. No one can tell me for certain. All these years later, scientists and statisticians are still arguing. Meanwhile, I've started a list of people I know who have had cancer: eighteen childhood friends and neighbors who grew up with me on the rim of Parleys Canyon. My Utah grandmother, grandfather, cousin, aunt, and another cousin's husband. Neighbors, friends, and coworkers, including my coeditor at the *Desert Sun*. Even Carole Gallagher. The list keeps growing. If I add to it auto-immune diseases like my sister's lupus, its size doubles. The only thing we all have in common is the years we lived downwind. A young mother living across the street from me recently came to my door in tears to tell me she had been diagnosed with aggressive leukemia. The first thing the doctor asked her was "Did you grow up in Utah?"

Before I got cancer, I always thought I led a charmed life, that things always went my way. I eased my dark fears by convincing myself that the really terrible things always happen to other people in other places. I would be spared. I still feel lucky. But after being labeled "radioactive material," I realize that I and all those I love are just as vulnerable as everyone else. We all live . . . after all . . . downwind.

The Clan of One-Breasted Women

TERRY TEMPEST WILLIAMS

I belong to a Clan of One-Breasted Women. My mother, my grandmothers, and six aunts have all had mastectomies. Seven are dead. The two who survive have just completed rounds of chemotherapy and radiation.

I've had my own problems: two biopsies for breast cancer and a small tumor between my ribs diagnosed as a "borderline malignancy."

This is my family history.

Most statistics tell us breast cancer is genetic, hereditary, with rising percentages attached to fatty diets, childlessness, or becoming pregnant after thirty. What they don't say is living in Utah may be the greatest hazard of all.

We are a Mormon family with roots in Utah since 1847. The "word of wisdom" in my family aligned us with good foods—no coffee, no tea, tobacco, or alcohol. For the most part, our women finished having their babies by the time they were thirty. And only one faced breast cancer prior to 1960. Traditionally, as a group of people, Mormons have a low rate of cancer.

Is our family a cultural anomaly? The truth is, we didn't think about it. Those who did, usually the men, simply said, "bad genes." The women's attitude was stoic. Cancer was part of life. On February 16, 1971, the eve of my mother's surgery, I accidentally picked up the telephone and overheard her ask my grandmother what she could expect.

"Diane, it is one of the most spiritual experiences you will ever encounter."

I quietly put down the receiver.

Two days later, my father took my brothers and me to the hospital to visit her. She met us in the lobby in a wheelchair. No bandages were visible. I'll never forget her radiance, the way she held herself in a purple velvet robe, and how she gathered us around her.

"Children, I am fine. I want you to know I felt the arms of God around me."

We believed her. My father cried. Our mother, his wife, was thirty-eight years old.

A little over a year after Mother's death, Dad and I were having dinner together. He had just returned from St. George, where the Tempest Company was completing the gas lines that would service southern Utah. He spoke of his love for the country, the sandstone landscape, bare-boned and beautiful. He had just finished hiking the Kolob trail in Zion National Park. We got caught up in reminiscing, recalling with fondness our walk up Angel's Landing on his fiftieth birthday and the years our family had vacationed there.

Over dessert, I shared a recurring dream of mine. I told my father that for years, as long as I could remember, I saw this flash of light in the night in the desert—that this image had so permeated my being that I could not venture south without seeing it again, on the horizon, illuminating buttes and mesas.

"You did see it," he said.

"Saw what?"

"The bomb. The cloud. We were driving home from Riverside, California. You were sitting in Diane's lap. She was pregnant. In fact, I remember the day, September 7, 1957. We had just gotten out of the Service. We were driving north, past Las Vegas. It was an hour or so before dawn, when this explosion went off. We not only heard it, but felt it. I thought the oil tanker in front of us had blown up. We pulled over and suddenly, rising from the desert floor, we saw it, clearly, this golden-stemmed cloud, the mushroom. The sky seemed to vibrate with an eerie pink glow. Within a few minutes, a light ash was raining on the car."

I stared at my father.

"I thought you knew that," he said. "It was a common occurrence in the fifties."

It was at this moment that I realized the deceit I had been living under. Children growing up in the American Southwest, drinking contaminated milk from contaminated cows, even from the contaminated breasts of their mothers, my mother—members, years later, of the Clan of One-Breasted Women.

It is a well-known story in the Desert West, "The Day We Bombed Utah," or more accurately, the years we bombed Utah: aboveground atomic testing in Nevada took place from January 27, 1951, through July 11, 1962. Not only were the winds blowing north, covering "low-use segments of the population" with fallout and leaving sheep dead in their tracks, but the climate was right. The United States of the 1950s was red, white, and blue. The Korean War was raging. McCarthyism was rampant. Ike was it, and the cold war was hot. If you were against nuclear testing, you were for a communist regime.

Much has been written about this "American nuclear tragedy." Public health was secondary to national security. The Atomic Energy Commissioner, Thomas Murray, said, "Gentlemen, we must not let anything interfere with this series of tests, nothing."

Again and again, the American public was told by its government, in spite of burns, blisters, and nausea, "It has been found that the tests may be conducted with adequate assurance of safety under conditions prevailing at the bombing reservations." Assuaging public fears was simply a matter of public relations. "Your best action," an Atomic Energy Commission booklet read, "is not to be worried about fallout." A news release typical of the times stated, "We find no basis for concluding that harm to any individual has resulted from radioactive fallout."

On August 30, 1979, during Jimmy Carter's presidency, a suit was filed, *Irene Allen* v. *The United States of America*. Mrs. Allen's case was the first on an alphabetical list of twenty-four cases, representative of nearly twelve hundred plaintiffs seeking compensation from the United States government for cancers caused by nuclear testing in Nevada.

Irene Allen lived in Hurricane, Utah. She was the mother of five children and had been widowed twice. Her first husband, with their two oldest boys, had watched the tests from the roof of the local high school.

He died of leukemia in 1956. Her second husband died of pancreatic cancer in 1978.

In a town meeting conducted by Utah Senator Orrin Hatch, shortly before the suit was filed, Mrs. Allen said, "I am not blaming the government, I want you to know that, Senator Hatch. But I thought if my testimony could help in any way so this wouldn't happen again to any of the generations coming up after us . . . I am happy to be here this day to bear testimony of this."

God-fearing people. This is just one story in an anthology of thousands.

On May 10, 1984, Judge Bruce S. Jenkins handed down his opinion. Ten of the plaintiffs were awarded damages. It was the first time a federal court had determined that nuclear tests had been the cause of cancers. For the remaining fourteen test cases, the proof of causation was not sufficient. In spite of the split decision, it was considered a landmark ruling. It was not to remain so for long.

In April 1987, the Tenth Circuit Court of Appeals overturned Judge Jenkins's ruling on the ground that the United States was protected from suit by the legal doctrine of sovereign immunity, a centuries-old idea from England in the days of absolute monarchs.

In January 1988, the Supreme Court refused to review the Appeals Court decision. To our court system it does not matter whether the United States government was irresponsible, whether it lied to its citizens, or even that citizens died from the fallout of nuclear testing. What matters is that our government is immune: "The King can do no wrong."

In Mormon culture, authority is respected, obedience is revered, and independent thinking is not. I was taught as a young girl not to "make waves" or "rock the boat."

"Just let it go," Mother would say. "You know how you feel, that's what counts."

For many years, I have done just that—listened, observed, and quietly formed my own opinions, in a culture that rarely asks questions because it has all the answers. But one by one I have watched the women in my family die common, heroic deaths. We sat in waiting rooms hoping for good news, but always receiving the bad. I cared for them, bathed their scarred bodies, and kept their secrets. I watched beautiful women become bald as Cytoxan, cisplatin, and Adriamycin were injected into their veins. I held their foreheads as they vomited green-black bile, and I shot them with morphine when the pain became inhuman. In the end, I witnessed their last peaceful breaths, becoming a midwife to the rebirth of their souls.

The price of obedience has become too high.

The fear and inability to question authority that ultimately killed rural communities in Utah during atmospheric testing of atomic weapons is the same fear I saw in my mother's body. Sheep. Dead sheep. The evidence is buried.

I cannot prove that my mother, Diane Dixon Tempest, or my grandmothers, Lettie Romney Dixon and Kathryn Blackett Tempest, along with my aunts developed cancer from nuclear fallout in Utah. But I can't prove they didn't.

My father's memory was correct. The September blast we drove through in 1957 was part of Operation Plumbbob, one of the most intensive series of bomb tests to be initiated. The flash of light in the night in the desert, which I had always thought was a dream, developed into a family nightmare. It took fourteen years, from 1957 to 1971, for cancer to manifest in my mother—the same time, Howard L. Andrews, an authority in radioactive fallout at the National Institutes of Health, says radiation cancer requires to become evident. The more I learn about what it means to be a "downwinder," the more questions I drown in.

What I do know, however, is that as a Mormon woman of the fifth generation of Latter-day Saints, I must question everything, even if it means losing my faith, even if it means becoming a member of a border tribe among my own people. Tolerating blind obedience in the name of patriotism or religion ultimately takes our lives.

When the Atomic Energy Commission described the country north of the Nevada Test Site as "virtually uninhabited desert terrain," my family and the birds at Great Salt Lake were some of the "virtual uninhabitants."

One night, I dreamed women from all over the world circled a blazing fire in the desert. They spoke of change, how they hold the moon in their bellies and wax and wane with its phases. They mocked the presumption of even-tempered beings and made promises that they would never fear the witch inside themselves. The women danced wildly as sparks broke away from the flames and entered the night sky as stars.

And they sang a song given to them by Shoshone grandmothers:

Ah ne nah, nah	Consider the rabbits
nin na nah—	How gently they walk on the earth—
ah ne nah, nah	Consider the rabbits
nin na nah—	How gently they walk on the earth—
Nyaga mutzi	We remember them
oh ne nay—	We can walk gently also—
Nyaga mutzi	We remember them
oh ne nay—	We can walk gently also—

The women danced and drummed and sang for weeks, preparing themselves for what was to come. They would reclaim the desert for the sake of their children, for the sake of the land.

A few miles downwind from the fire circle, bombs were being tested. Rabbits felt the tremors. Their soft leather pads on paws and feet recognized the shaking sands, while the roots of mesquite and sage were smoldering. Rocks were hot from the inside out and dust devils hummed unnaturally. And each time there was another nuclear test, ravens watched the desert heave. Stretch marks appeared. The land was losing its muscle.

The women couldn't bear it any longer. They were mothers. They had suffered labor pains but always under the promise of birth. The red-hot pains beneath the desert promised death only, as each bomb became a stillborn. A contract had been made and broken between human beings and the land. A new contract was being drawn by the women, who understood the fate of the earth as their own.

Under the cover of darkness, ten women slipped under a barbed-wire fence and entered the contaminated country. They were trespassing. They walked toward the town of Mercury, in moonlight, taking their cues from coyote, kit fox, antelope, squirrel, and quail. They moved quietly and deliberately through the maze of Joshua trees. When a hint of daylight appeared they rested, drinking tea and sharing their rations of food. The women closed their eyes. The time had come to protest with the heart, that to deny one's genealogy with the earth was to commit treason against one's soul.

At dawn, the women draped themselves in Mylar, wrapping long streamers of silver plastic around their arms to blow in the breeze. They wore clear masks, that became the faces of humanity. And when they arrived at the edge of Mercury, they carried all the butterflies of a summer day in their wombs. They paused to allow their courage to settle.

The town that forbids pregnant women and children to enter because of radiation risks was asleep. The women moved through the streets as winged messengers, twirling around each other in slow motion, peeking inside homes, and watching the easy sleep of men and women. They were astonished by such stillness and periodically would utter a shrill note or low cry just to verify life.

The residents finally awoke to these strange apparitions. Some simply stared. Others called authorities, and in time, the women were apprehended by wary soldiers dressed in desert fatigues. They were taken to a white, square building on the other edge of Mercury. When asked who they were and why they were there, the women replied, "We are mothers and we have come to reclaim the desert for our children."

The soldiers arrested them. As the ten women were blindfolded and handcuffed, they began singing:

You can't forbid us everything
You can't forbid us to think—
You can't forbid our tears to flow
And you can't stop the songs that we sing.

The women continued to sing louder and louder, until they heard the voices of their sisters moving across the mesa:

Ah ne nah, nah
nin na nah—
ah ne nah, nah
nin na nah—
Nyaga mutzi
oh ne nay—
Nyaga mutzi
oh ne nay—

"Call for reinforcements," one soldier said.

"We have," interrupted one woman, "we have—and you have no idea of our numbers."

I crossed the line at the Nevada Test Site and was arrested with nine other Utahns for trespassing on military lands. They are still conducting nuclear tests in the desert. Ours was an act of civil disobedience. But as I walked toward the town of Mercury, it was more than a gesture of peace. It was a gesture on behalf of the Clan of One-Breasted Women.

As one officer cinched the handcuffs around my wrists, another frisked my body. She found a pen and a pad of paper tucked inside my left boot.

"And these?" she asked sternly.

"Weapons," I replied.

Our eyes met. I smiled. She pulled the leg of my trousers back over my boot.

"Step forward, please," she said as she took my arm.

We were booked under an afternoon sun and bused to Tonopah, Nevada. It was a two-hour ride. This was familiar country. The Joshua trees standing their ground had been named by my ancestors, who believed they looked like prophets pointing west to the Promised Land. These were the same trees that bloomed each spring, flowers appearing like white flames in the Mojave. And I recalled a full moon in May, when Mother and I had walked among them, flushing out mourning doves and owls.

The bus stopped short of town. We were released.

The officials thought it was a cruel joke to leave us stranded in the desert with no way to get home. What they didn't realize was that we were home, soul-centered and strong, women who recognized the sweet smell of sage as fuel for our spirits.

Tragedy at the Center of the Universe

VALERIE KULETZ

THE URANIUM STORY

On a crisp autumn afternoon in 1995 my husband and I drove west from Albuquerque to the Laguna Pueblo and then to the small village of Paguate to interview Mrs. Dorothy Purley, a Laguna Pueblo woman who had worked in New Mexico's Grants uranium district when its mines were viable. Paguate is an old village, the requisite Catholic church at its center, with dirt roads winding around clusters of small, earth-colored adobe dwellings. To get to Paguate we had to drive through the recently capped-off Jackpile–Paguate uranium mine. The disrupted landscape appeared endless; one could not see where the mine began and where it ended—it was everywhere. From Mrs. Purley's kitchen, its walls painted a brilliant turquoise blue, I could see the massive mine stretching out in all directions. I could also see the enlarged thyroid on Dorothy's neck. She later confirmed she was suffering from cancer, which is not uncommon in this section of the nuclear landscape. As she told me:

> My mother died of it . . . my brother died of it! My aunt! How many aunts and how many uncles have died? And you know it's just a shame that the DOE doesn't believe what's going on. . . .
>
> I'm in that same situation right now. This cancer has really ruined my health. . . . You know, it really hurts, and I'm standing here living on borrowed life right now. I don't know when

my time is going to expire, but all I do is keep praying that God will continue to give me my strength. . . . I'm too young to die. I'm not ready to die. That's why I'm up and about, going here and there [speaking on behalf of radiation victims]. When they call me, I go![1]

At first Dorothy stayed home because she felt ashamed of her sickness, but her sister persuaded her to make her story public, even within her own community, to break the unspoken code of silence. As her sister said: "People have to *know* what's wrong, people have to *see* what's wrong, maybe that way our people will understand what is going on, on the Laguna Reservation, mainly in Paguate."[2]

Dorothy said that a nineteen-year-old had recently passed away because of prostate cancer, as had a fifteen-year-old with leukemia; that her brother-in-law had skin cancer; and that the number of miscarriages on the reservation had increased radically since the uranium mining began, as well as birth defects and serious respiratory and allergy ailments. The list of radiation-related incidents was not unlike that enumerated by the Moapa Paiute women living near the Nevada Test Site. Only the Laguna landscape was pitted with uranium mines instead of bomb craters.

Those who have attempted to inform the public about uranium mining and milling in the Four Corners area refer to the postwar period as a "hidden holocaust," a tragic legacy of the Cold War. Still, today, few Americans are aware of this particular story of national sacrifice. Most tourists speak about the Four Corners area with admiration for its beauty and share the Anglo colonist's fascination with its "picturesque" Indian cultures. Uranium fields aren't on the AAA road map of Indian Country.

The Four Corners area, where New Mexico, Arizona, Utah, and Colorado meet, contains two-thirds of U.S. uranium deposits, most within reservation boundaries. Located within much of the Navajoan Desert, or Painted Desert (also regarded as an extension of the Great Basin), this uranium-rich area of the Colorado Plateau is known as the Grants Uranium Belt. It is the first node on the network of pollution sites stretching out across the map of the nuclear landscape.

Arid-ecosystems geologists who promote hazardous waste disposal in desert regions describe the region this way:

[The Navajoan Desert] is located in northeastern Arizona, southeastern Utah, and the northwestern corner of New Mexico and is best correlated with the exposure of the Chinle Formation, which contains variously colored clay shales. Most of the area is composed of valley slopes, plains, and badlands, located between sandstone hogbacks. *The Chinle Formation is of interest to the energy industry because of the naturally occurring deposits of uranium in the interbedded sandstone and conglomerate strata and the clays of the deep shale beds, as well as oil and gas deposits in deeper formations* [emphasis added]. The clays were formed in swamplands and frequently have high concentrations of smectite [a swelling clay] that may reduce the hydraulic conductivity of the soil, an important consideration in waste disposal facility siting.[3]

This geologic discourse is typical of those that, while noting the importance of these formations for "the energy industry," leave out the existence of its human inhabitants, many of whom are Indian. What first appears as a purely objective scientific account upon closer inspection is little of the sort; it is an account for use by the energy industry. However, living on the "Chinle Formation" is one of the largest concentrations of Indians in North America, as well as a significant number of Spanish-speaking people.

THE SCALE OF THE URANIUM OPERATIONS

Because of the density of uranium deposits in this area and because a cheap and expendable labor force could be quickly mobilized there, "as much as *ninety percent* of the country's uranium mining and milling have been undertaken on or immediately adjacent to Indian land since the mineral became a profitable commodity in the early '50s."[4] Indeed, Indian activists and their supporters cite just this kind of information when accusing the United States of nuclear colonialism.

In 1941 uranium was discovered by the U.S. Bureau of Indian Affairs in Monument Valley and the Carrizo Mountains on the Navajo reservation in Arizona. "From 1942 to 1945 over 11,000 tons of uranium-bearing ore were mined at Monument Valley by the Vanadium Corporation of

America."[5] The yellow cake processed from this uranium was used by the scientists at Los Alamos to make the original atomic bombs, the first of which was exploded in 1945 at New Mexico's Alamogordo Bombing and Gunnery Range (now White Sands Missile Range).[6] From 1946 to 1968, more than thirteen million tons of uranium ore were mined on the Navajo Reservation alone—all for use in nuclear weapons and nuclear reactors.[7]

The acreage designated for uranium development was immense. The *Southwest Indigenous Uranium Forum Newsletter* gives an idea of the monumental scale of these operations:

> In 1958, the Bureau of Indian Affairs reported that over 900,000 acres of tribal land were leased for uranium exploration and unreclaimed open-pit and underground mines on the former nuclear reservation.
>
> The heaviest uranium exploration, mining and milling activity occurred on predominately [*sic*] Indian lands in the Grants Mineral Belt and San Juan Basin in New Mexico. In 1976, the Department of the Interior called the New Mexican portion of the Grants Mineral Belt "the hottest uranium exploration area in the country." Two years later, 740,000 acres of Indian land in this region were leased for uranium exploration and development.[8]

At the height of the second uranium boom in the late 1970s, the Bureau of Indian Affairs "approved 303 uranium leases covering 250,000 Indian acres in the region, and the federal government estimated a total of 3.5 million acres, including federal uranium, were going to be developed."[9] Near the Navajo Reservation, at the Laguna Pueblo, more uranium mining and milling occurred, most notably the Jackpile–Paguate mine—until 1980 the largest uranium mine in the world (and the largest ever in the U.S.), covering approximately 2,800 acres. During its thirty-year operation, the mine produced twenty-two million tons of ore and removed forty-four million tons of materials from three open pits and several underground mines.[10] This was the mine I gazed out upon from the window of Dorothy Purley's kitchen.

Fifty percent of the residents of the state of New Mexico live within a fifty-mile radius of the Jackpile–Paguate mine, including those living within the Albuquerque metropolitan area and the city of Grants. The mine itself is larger than downtown Albuquerque. Two rivers run through it, the Rio Paguate and the Rio Moquino, which eventually run into the Rio Puerco and the Rio Grande.[11] The Jackpile–Paguate mine was owned by the Anaconda Copper Company, a subsidiary of the Atlantic Richfield Company. In fact, scattered over much of this portion of the nuclear map are the names of transnational corporations and federal government agencies. Some of the companies that contracted with the U.S. Department of Energy were: Kerr-McGee, Vanadium Corporation of America, Foote Mineral, AMEX, United Nuclear Corporation, Exxon, Mobil Oil, and Gulf. In addition to the big corporate mines, between three hundred and five hundred shallow uranium mines were opened by "independent" Native Americans with the encouragement of the U.S. Small Business Administration. Uranium ore from these mines was sold to the Atomic Energy Commission at the Kerr-McGee milling plant (by the 1970s the largest in the world) near Shiprock, New Mexico.

THE TOLL ON THE PEOPLE

Indian lands under uranium mining and milling development were extensive, with the Navajo Reservation, Laguna Pueblo, and Acoma Pueblo carrying some of the heaviest burden and consequently suffering some of the most severe health repercussions. Though the uranium booms helped the destitute Indian economy to some extent and for a brief time, they also transformed these Indian lands (almost overnight) from a pastoral to a mining-industrial economy, resulting in a mining-dependent population. Indians did not get rich off the uranium development on their lands because they lacked the capital and the technical knowledge to develop them and, at least initially, they were kept ignorant of the value of their land. Instead, development was contracted out to large energy companies. Because "national security" and energy consumption needs (read "national competitiveness") were at stake, Indians were not given the right to stipulate conditions for development and reclamation for decades—and then the right was never sufficient. Unchecked and unmonitored production was excused during World War II and the

Cold War on the grounds of national security and, in the 1970s, on the basis of the energy crisis and the ongoing arms escalation that mushroomed in the 1980s.[12] Throughout the postwar period, American Indian populations were exploited as a cheap source of labor. For example, Indian miners were paid at a rate two-thirds that of off-reservation employees.[13] In addition, Indians were not compensated adequately for the uranium taken from their lands. "As of 1984, stateside Indians were receiving only an average of 3.4 percent of the market value of the uranium extracted from their land."[14] The median income reported in 1970 (at a boom time for uranium mining) at the Laguna Pueblo was only $2,661 per year—a little more than $220 a month, or $50 per week. And Indians paid a high price for the right to work the mines. Uranium development's legacy has been one of a severely polluted environment, human and nonhuman radiation contamination, cancers, birth defects, sickness, and death. Health risks associated with uranium mining and milling have been identified and examined by different investigators, and reported in a variety of sources including the Southwest Research and Information Center publications and the *New England Journal of Medicine* as well as others.[15]

Since large amounts of water are used in the mining process and mountains of uranium tailings are produced as a by-product, uranium pollution poisons the earth, air, and water. Radioactive particulates (dust particles containing uranium-238, radium-226, and thorium-230) blow in the desert winds, and radioactive elements travel in both surface and ground water. Radioactive materials from the mining of uranium produce radon and thoron gases, which combine with the molecular structure of human cells and decay into radioactive polonium and thorium. The dust irritates cells in the lining of the respiratory tract, causing cancer. Radioactive materials can also damage sex cells, causing such birth defects as cleft palate and Down's syndrome.[16]

In seeking federal assistance to study the effect of low-level radiation on the health of their children, Navajo health officials called attention to at least two preliminary studies—one conducted by the March of Dimes (principal investigator Dr. L. Shields) and the other by the Navajo Health Authority (principal investigator Dr. D. Calloway). Calloway's study suggested that Navajo children may have a five times greater rate of bone cancer and a fifteen times greater rate of ovarian and testicular cancer than the U.S. average.[17] However, despite these preliminary findings, no funding was granted for extended epidemiological studies of the impact on Navajos living near uranium tailings and mines.[18]

Further extending the nuclear landscape and causing harm to those who live there, millions of gallons of water in the Four Corners area were subjected to radiation pollution by the extractive processes of uranium mining. Accidents, such as the Rio Puerco incident, cause serious water pollution in an already water-scarce environment.

RIO PUERCO

On July 16, 1979, at Church Rock, New Mexico, the United Nuclear Corporation's tailings dam broke, sending at least ninety-four million gallons of radioactive water into the nearby Rio Puerco.[19] Said one resident of the Navajo Reservation:

> It had a terrible odor and a dark chocolaty color. Right away, we could tell it was unusual. It was a day later that it came over the radio about the spill, telling people to stay away from the river. A week later they put up signs saying it was dangerous.[20]

The Rio Puerco accident has been called the worst single nuclear accident in U.S. history, far outweighing the well-reported Three Mile Island accident. Why wasn't this massive radioactive pollution reported in the national press? The Navajo people in the surrounding area were unable safely to use their single source of water, nor could they sell or eat the livestock that drank from this water. Acute toxicity caused by increased acidity of the water resulted in burns leading to infections that required amputations. No serious study of possible radiation contamination of soil sediment was ever conducted, and no large-scale study of exposure was ever initiated. Only an out-of-court settlement totaling $525,000 was offered as a collective payment to victims of the Rio Puerco disaster.

But, then, the Rio Puerco was not a clean river prior to this accident. As noted by one groundwater protection researcher: "Between 1969 and February of 1986, the Puerco flowed year-round, fed by millions of gallons of contaminant-laden water that poured daily into one of its tributaries (called the North Fork) from three underground uranium mines. . . . No one bothered to tell the Navajos that the water that poured from the mines during the uranium boom years of 1952–1964 and 1969–1981 was not safe for man or beast."[21] And the Rio Puerco disaster was not the only one. "Between 1955 and 1977, fifteen tailings dams broke, releasing their contents into the wider watershed areas."[22]

SCIENCE AS A MECHANISM OF EXCLUSION

Today—seemingly as invisible as the Rio Puerco accident—the uranium mines and tailings are, for the most part, left unreclaimed. Although a 1983 Environmental Protection Study confirmed that the Navajo Reservation alone had approximately 1,000 significant nuclear waste sites, the Environmental Protection Agency (EPA) deemed them all "too remote" to be of "significant national concern."[23] A 1978 study by Los Alamos National Laboratory (LANL) concerning rehabilitation of land and water contaminated by uranium mining and milling offered one solution: to zone such areas as forbidden to human habitation.[24] A report in 1972 by the National Academy of Sciences suggested that the Four Corners area be designated a "national sacrifice area."[25] Other scientific accounts, as noted below, were completely contrary to these findings and denied that any significant pollution problems existed or that adverse health effects could be associated with living in the region. Though seemingly different in content, all these reports belie the same prejudice: The land and by implication the people living on the land were better left ignored. That is, neither was worth saving.

To understand how an entire society could ignore an environmental disaster on the scale of the Rio Puerco incident or the open-pit uranium mines, it is necessary to examine some of the ways scientific discourse can be used as a mechanism of exclusion, particularly when it is marshaled against anecdotal evidence presented by nonscientists (evidence like that offered by Dorothy Purley, quoted at the beginning of this essay). In the case of the Grants uranium district, anecdotal statements from Native speakers may be in themselves incontestable—but they carry no weight in establishing a causal link between the reported illnesses and the existence of radioactive mine tailings or unreclaimed pits. Although anecdotal testimony has sometimes been accepted in court cases regarding other issues, the history of anecdotal statements in this region is one marked by what social scientists call *delegitimation*. Anecdotal statements about the health risks associated with unreclaimed uranium mines and tailings are gathered in preliminary studies or as testimony in open hearings and may be incorporated into draft environmental impact statements but do not constitute scientific evidence. They are simply reported; any claim they may have on the truth can be—and in some cases has been—diminished by the overwhelming weight of contrary "scientific" evidence. The statements are, in effect, excluded from consideration, and the people who speak them are, by extension, excluded from any decision-making process bearing on their welfare.

Many "preliminary studies" suggested serious health risks to children in communities near abandoned uranium districts. One "preliminary" study showed "a twofold excess of miscarriages, infant deaths, congenital or genetic abnormalities, and learning disabilities among uranium-area families,"[26] compared with Navajo families in nonuranium areas. Even after being informed of these and other findings, no federal or state agencies provided funding for further study. In fact, in 1983, one agency, the Indian Health Service (a division of the U.S. Department of Health and Human Services) had sent a report to Congress ("Health Hazards Related to Nuclear Resources Development on Indian Land," 1983) stating that there was "no evidence of adverse health effects in Indians in uranium development areas and that there is no need for additional studies or funding for such studies."[27] The one "official" scientific investigation of birth defects that was funded, primarily by the March of Dimes Birth Defects Foundation, was too "small" to render "significant" results. Its conclusion states: "It was unlikely that our small study population would have demonstrated a real effect in terms of statistical significance."[28] Since statistical significance in epidemiological studies generally requires large study populations, Indian communities are disadvantaged because they are usually quite small.

Thus, inadequate funding and the shortcomings of statistical analyses for small populations can result not only in a lack of "official" documentation to support the "preliminary" and "anecdotal" knowledge of health risks, but also in the production of official documentation that is contrary to the preliminary studies. For the communities living in uranium districts, a little (underfunded) science is *not* better than no science at all. What gets circulated, and what has credibility, is the "official" report—even if that report is based on inadequate foundations.

Scientific knowledge in this contested terrain is deeply influenced by state and federal agencies, by funding, as well as many other nonscientific factors. Epidemiological studies are costly, as are the "experts" who administer them. Poor communities do what they can, but their findings have little purchase when it comes to lawsuits against state agencies or private companies. In the end, we must look seriously at the discrepancies between community-sponsored "preliminary" studies and federally funded "expert" accounts of health risks.

In the 1986 open hearings concerning the environmental and human impact of the unreclaimed Jackpile–Paguate mine, a radiation scientist representing Anaconda argued that the individual lifetime risk of cancer in the most exposed individuals at Paguate (the village overlooking the 2,800-acre mine) under the no-action alternative (the proposal that Anaconda need not engage any reclamation of the massive mine) is far less than the lifetime risk of dying due to excess cosmic rays received by living in Denver, Colorado.[29] In his testimony, this specialist does not tell the audience how he arrives at this analogy, nor what the standards are for such a statement. He does not tell the audience that standards on the hazards of radiation exposure have changed drastically over time, such that smaller and smaller doses are recognized as sufficient to cause cancer. Since he is an "expert" in this field, his analysis overrides the anecdotal statements of the residents claiming to be adversely affected.

Public hearings for the environmental impact draft statement for the Jackpile–Paguate mine's reclamation project began with no fewer than ten PhDs and other "technical" experts in a variety of scientific disciplines, including a mining engineer, a plant ecologist, a radiation ecologist, an expert in biomedicine, and others. All testified in obfuscating technical language that America's largest uranium mine could be safely left unreclaimed. All were under contract with Anaconda.

Even if we ignore the fact that these testimonies are paid for by the uranium mining company, the discrepancy between these statements and earlier studies of the general area made by Los Alamos scientists and those made by the National Academy of Sciences (mentioned above), in which the uranium mining districts were called "national sacrifice areas" and zones in which human habitation should be forbidden, cannot be ignored. Since the Jackpile–Paguate mine was the largest in the area (and one of the largest in the world), it would be safe to assume that it was included in these assessments. In addition, scientists agree universally that uranium mining at this mine has caused cancer and death in miners (if not in nearby residents). Uranium ore and tailings, as well as the water used in the mining process, are known to be radioactive.

The role of the scientist providing "expert knowledge" and scientific validation for both corporations and the government in determining environmental and health standards for the production, processing, and disposal of radioactive materials and for mine reclamation demonstrates a persistent collaboration between some scientific knowledge producers and what can only be described as highly biased interests (in our example, the subsidiary of the Atlantic Richfield Corporation, Anaconda).[30] Of course, such collaborative relations do not include all scientists. Scientific "expert" knowledge is also marshaled *against* government and industry interests by antinuclear activists so that "objective" testimony ends up comprising multiple voices, demonstrating the malleability of scientific data and its interpretation. Even among partners, such as certain scientific communities and energy industries, disagreement exists. "Science" does not come as a hegemonic package of truth when its subject matter concerns politically charged and contested areas such as land and the environment. Though the report from the Anaconda-hired scientists (claiming the uranium mine harmless) seems to contradict the LANL report (claiming the uranium district uninhabitable), the underlying message and the political ends appear to be the same: that the Indians, if not expendable, can be displaced. From the Indian perspective, displacement may mean the same as expendability.[31]

Because scientific analysis is costly and requires specialized skills, open hearings more often than not consist of contestations between "expert" scientific knowledge and local "commonsense" anecdotal knowledge. Confronting the "experts" in formal public hearings, such as those held for the reclamation of the Jackpile–Paguate mine, often feels like an exercise in futility—especially when technoscientific discourse is marshaled in opposition to "simple" fears and commonsense knowledge—to those most affected, the local populace.

The discourses of science (and of the law) are formidable tools for legitimating dubious claims and delegitimating counterclaims. As became apparent in the hearings on reclamation mandates, Anaconda attempted to shield itself with scientific discourse that claims one of the world's largest uranium mines did not need to be reclaimed, that it could be left open with its tailings blowing in the wind, that it posed no risk to human or animal health. In response to the "experts," the Pueblo Indians of Laguna cited case after case of deaths caused by cancer. As Herman Garcia of the village of Paguate commented:

> [A]nd now I think the reason why the people in the Pueblo of Laguna are kind of concerned about this cancer illness is because like—and please don't compare it with the City of Albuquerque or New York. I come from a very small village, and I don't know how you'd figure that out; but, last year, in the Village of Paguate alone, we lost five people from cancer . . . these people that I'm talking about were nondrinkers and nonsmokers. . . .
>
> That's why we're having such a hard time, and I think we've been as reasonable as we possibly could be, but how much longer do we have to wait to cover the land, the one we consider dangerous? I have to work because I can't really go by these studies, I'm no expert, and I think it would really make me feel good—like the ponds we consider hazardous, I'd like for some of these experts to go out there and swim in those ponds. Then when I see them swim, then maybe I feel more secure, and we might be able to swallow some of these studies that have been introduced here today.[32]

Besides presenting the oral accounts in open hearings, Anaconda substantiated its claims with voluminous scientific texts in the form of technical documentation produced by expert witnesses. In addition to the obscurity of the language, the sheer volume of documentation functions as a barrier to the uninitiated.

The dominance of text-based scientific and legal arguments and validation of the "facts" concerning Indian cultures by Euroamerican scientific experts is particularly problematic, because Indian peoples' heritage of knowledge is often based on oral traditions and organized around a very different set of legitimating strategies. Of course, increasing numbers of Indians wield the sword of legal and scientific discourse today with great skill and some notable success, but many Indians still do not use (and disdain to use) the master's tools to bring down the master's house.

Confronting scientific "truth" for many Indians, as well as non-Indians, in the nuclear landscape can be an extremely disempowering experience. Those not trained in the specialized discourse of radiation science confront an apparent discrepancy between what they experience in their bodies, such as cancer and its connection to the open uranium mine down the road, and what they are told is the "truth" about the risks from radiation exposure.

THE GLOBAL PICTURE

By 1982 uranium production had been greatly curtailed in the Grants Uranium Belt, since even cheaper sources had been found outside the continental United States. The same transnational energy corporations that played so significant a role in the creation of the U.S. nuclear landscape are, of course, players in a larger global military economy in which uranium mining remains a requirement for the continuation of nuclear energy and weapons development. The extractive resources that fuel nuclear power are mined in many "Fourth World" lands, demonstrating further that nuclear colonialism follows a global pattern of exploitation. For example, as of 1980 "seventy percent of France's uranium [came] from Niger and Gabon in west Africa."[33] Transnational energy corporations have reaped maximum profits at the expense of many indigenous populations around the world. The uranium sacrifice zone has not been limited to the Grants Uranium Belt in the U.S.:

> Significantly, large proportions of the uranium production and reserves controlled within the five developed nations are located either within internal colonies of those nations, such as Indian reservations in the United States and aborigine reserves in Australia, or in colonies or neocolonies whose resources and labor are being exploited considerably by energy resource corporations. In Australia, it is estimated that eighty percent of all uranium reserves lie on aboriginal lands. Aboriginal people in Australia, like American Indians, were pushed on to the least desirable lands within nations and have been virtually forced

into accepting miserable agreements with energy corporations. The 1978 agreement between the aborigines and the companies (Ranger Uranium Agreement) gave the aborigines only 4.25 percent of the revenues of the uranium mine royalties.[34]

For many indigenous communities historically, as well as in many cases today, uranium mining is only a form of resource extraction for export. Because of this, native communities become "raw materials colonies" for the uranium companies and their home nation-states. The following list shows the aboriginal communities with the most significant uranium reserves:

1. *Australia*: particularly the Arnhem Land Area of the Northern Territory, home to a large existing aboriginal community;
2. *Canada*: particularly in a northern Saskatchewan area inhabited by Cree-Dene Native Americans;
3. *Southwest Africa (Namibia):* under South African mining concessions in the "last colony in Africa";
4. *United States*: on Navajo, Laguna Pueblo, Havasupai, and Colville Confederated Tribal lands, along with pre-1848 Hispanic land grants at Cebolleta and San Mateo Springs.[35] Also included are the Sioux lands in the Black Hills of Dakota, and the Spokane Reservation (thirty miles upstream from the Yakima Reservation) in the state of Washington.

The United States uranium region forms the first layer of the map showing the transformation of land under nuclear colonialism. Its story spans forty-plus years of uranium booms and busts, concerns millions of acres, massive environmental pollution still left unreclaimed, and generations of Indians dying of cancer. Behind this landscape stand wealthy corporations, powerful federal agencies such as the Department of Energy (formerly the Atomic Energy Commission) and the Department of Defense, and scientific centers such as Los Alamos National Laboratory, Lawrence Livermore Laboratories, and Sandia National Laboratories in Albuquerque. But this particular part of the nuclear landscape does not exist in isolation. It is part of a larger terrain—part of a number of interconnected transformative processes that emerged in the postwar West and Southwest. As the United States marked its entry into the nuclear age, the uranium zones of sacrifice were a fundamental part of the emergence of a new technological era that began in the 1940s. They are also the first sites in a constellation of toxic sites that are the product of a technological society unwilling to look closely at the human and environmental costs of its maintenance.

Without uranium there is no nuclear landscape, no nuclear weapons development, no nuclear energy industry. It underlies the creation of nuclear power centers hidden in the desert—centers of first-rate scientific research and development. After all, it all began in order to provide the scientists at Los Alamos with the material for making bombs.

NOTES

1. Dorothy A. Purley, interview by author, tape recording, Paguate Village, Laguna Pueblo reservation, New Mexico, 16 September 1995. Dorothy Purley's statement should be read as a personal discussion with the author only, not as an official statement from the Laguna Pueblo. Dorothy's outspoken stand and her criticism of the uranium mines are not necessarily shared by all Pueblo or Navajo people.

2. Ibid.

3. Charles C. Reith and Bruce M. Thomson, *Deserts as Dumps?* (Albuquerque: University of New Mexico Press, 1992), 38–39.

4. Ward Churchill, *Struggle for the Land* (Monroe, Maine.: Common Courage Press, 1993),264. For an excellent account (with footnote resources) of the uranium industry in Indian country, see the chapter titled "Radioactive Colonization: Hidden Holocaust in Native North America." Other sources cited by Churchill to substantiate this claim are Richard Hoppe, "A Stretch of Desert along Route 66—the Grants Belt—Is Chief Locale for U.S. Uranium," *Engineering and Mining Journal* 79, no. 11 (1978): 79–93. Also see Winona LaDuke, "A History of Uranium Mining," *Black Hills/Paha Sapa Report* 1, no. 1 (1979).

5. [Hosteen Kinlichee], "An Overview of Uranium and Nuclear Development on Indian Lands in the Southwest," *Southwest Indigenous Uranium Forum Newsletter* (Gallup, N.M.), September 1993, 5.

6. This was the famous Project Trinity. The Alamogordo Range site was, and still is, near the Mescalero Apache reservation in southern New Mexico. Because of their proximity to the explosion site some Mescalero Apache claim to be among the first victims (along with the Atomic Veterans present at this site during the explosion) of atmospheric nuclear weapons testing because of downwind contamination.

7. [Kinlichee], "Overview of Uranium," 6.

8. Ibid.

9. Marjane Ambler, *Breaking the Iron Bonds* (Lawrence: University Press of Kansas, 1990), 150.

10. U.S. Department of the Interior, *Final Report Environmental Impact Statement for the Jackpile–Paguate Uranium Mine Reclamation Project II* (Albuquerque: Dept. of the Interior, October 1986), A-35. Statement by Chester T. Fernando, governor of Pueblo Laguna.

11. Ibid., A-36.

12. "Colorado and Utah led the country in uranium production in the 1950s and early 1960s, with New Mexico and Wyoming gaining first place in the 1970s." Arjun Makhijani, Howard Hu, and Katherine Yih, *Nuclear Wastelands* (Cambridge, Mass.: MIT Press, 1995), 113.

13. Churchill, *Struggle for the Land,* 264.

14. Ibid., 262, citing Joseph G. Jorgenson, "The Political Economy of the Native American Energy Business" in *Native Americans and Energy Development,* II, ed. Joseph G. Jorgenson (Boston: Anthropology Resource Center/ Seventh Generation Fund, 1984), 9–20.

15. For more information on the health risks associated with uranium mining and milling, see Linda Taylor, "Uranium Legacy," *The Workbook* 8, no. 6 (Albuquerque: Southwest Research and Information Center, November/December 1983); Jonathan M. Samet et al., "Uranium Mining and Lung Cancer in Navajo Men," *New England Journal of Medicine* 310, no. 23 (7 June 1984); Donald Calloway, "Neoplasms Among Navajo Children," grant proposal (Window Rock, Ariz.: Navajo Health Authority, 24 February 1981); Paul Robinson, "Uranium Production and Its Effects on Navajo Communities Along the Rio Puerco in Western New Mexico," in *Proceedings of the Michigan Conference on Race and the Incidence of Environmental Hazards,* ed. Bunyan Bryant and Paul Nohai (Ann Arbor: University of Michigan School of Natural Resources, 1990). See also Makhijani, Hu, and Yih, *Nuclear Wastelands,* chapter 5. *Wastelands* identifies the major health studies conducted on uranium miners. It also documents the historical disregard of the studies' results (that certain aspects of uranium mining were dangerous to miners and should be altered) by the uranium companies and the Atomic Energy Commission.

16. U.S. Environmental Protection Agency, *Radiological Quality of the Environment in the United States* (Washington, D.C.: U.S. Government Printing Office, 1977), 62–66 (cited in Churchill, *Struggle for the Land,* 266). See also L. M. Shields et al., "Navajo Birth Outcomes in the Shiprock Uranium Mining Area," *Health Physics* 63, 542–551; and Calloway, "Neoplasms Among Navajo Children."

17. Calloway, "Neoplasms Among Navajo Children," cited in *The Workbook* 8, no. 6 (November/December 1983).

18. *The Workbook* 8, no. 6 (November/December 1983).

19. Ambler, *Breaking the Iron Bonds*, 174.

20. Rita Begay, quoted in Melissa Schlanger, "Right Off We Could Tell It Was Unusual," *Gallup* (N.M.) *Independent*, 18 July 1989.

21. Chris Shuey, "The Rio Puerco River: Where Did the Water Go?" *The Workbook* 9, no. 1 (January/March, 1986).

22. Makhijani, Hu, and Yih, *Nuclear Wastelands*, 121.

23. Churchill, *Struggle for the Land*, 271, citing Environmental Protection Agency, *Potential Health and Environmental Hazards of Uranium Mine Wastes* (Washington, D.C.: U.S. Government Printing Office, 1983), 1–23.

24. D. R. Dreeson, "Uranium Mill Tailings: Environmental Implications," *Los Alamos Scientific Laboratory Mini-Report* (February 1978), 1–4. Cited in Churchill, *Struggle for the Land*, 275.

25. Churchill, *Struggle for the Land*, 275, citing Thadias Box et al., *Rehabilitation Potential for Western Coal Lands* (Cambridge, Mass.: Ballinger, 1974).

26. Shields et al., "Navajo Birth Outcomes."

27. Taylor, "Uranium Legacy," 199.

28. Shields et al., "Navajo Birth Outcomes," 550.

29. U.S. Department of the Interior, *Final Report Environmental Impact Statement*, A-10.

30. This kind of collaboration between scientists and private or government interests also occurred in lawsuits between the Department of Energy and downwind victims of nuclear testing at the Nevada Test Site.

31. Even though the final settlement with the Anaconda Company gave the Laguna Pueblo Indians enough money to unsatisfactorily reclaim the mine, they are still left working with uranium tailings as one of their primary means of making a living. Again, they appear to be at risk, excluded, and expendable.

32. U.S. Department of the Interior, *Final Report Environmental Impact Statement*, A-62, A-63, statement by Mr. Herman Garcia of Paguate village.

33. Richard Nafziger, "Transnational Energy Corporations and American Indian Development," in *American Indian Energy Resources and Development*, Development Series no. 2 (Albuquerque: Native American Studies Dept., University of New Mexico, 1980), 14.

34. Ibid.

35. Robinson, "Uranium Production and Its Effects," 176.

Coyote Learns to Glow

RICHARD RAWLES

I

A sign near the entrance to the Nevada Test Site reads:

> Desert Tortoise Habitat
> Threatened Species
> It is unlawful to possess, harass, transport,
> injure, kill, receive or remove
> a threatened or endangered species
> 16 USC Sec. 1538

By those standards of criminality, the entire Department of Energy (DOE) operation at Mercury, Nevada, should be subject to arrest. The amount of radiation the tortoises have been exposed to should qualify as injury. As part of the department's "bugs and bunnies" environmental research program, the reptiles are routinely rounded up and tagged for monitoring.

But instead of DOE officials, a score or more of demonstrators are arrested one Easter noontide in the mid-1990s as they cross the barbed-wire fence and cattle guard separating the crowd from camouflage-clad Wackenhut security guards and a contingent from the Nye County Sheriff's Department. The sheriff himself squints at the ragtag assembly of Indians, Atomic Veterans, cassocked monks, and latter-day hippies, turning now and again to one of his men to whisper an order. He's a smaller, blond version of Clint Eastwood, an image he evidently cultivates. "We've got traffic," he says, looking up the road. Then, to the soldier nearest him: "Pay attention," as if the protesters were about to mass behind the incoming car and storm the corrugated metal shack off to the side that serves as the base entrance's sentry post.

It's a ritual that has been repeated twice yearly for over twelve years—on Indigenous People's Day (October 12) and Easter. Protesters wave Western Shoshone visas as they are led off to a holding pen—built specially for the purpose in the heyday of mass demonstrations—on the other side of the entrance. Although nowhere near in numbers to the crowds that converged here in the late 1980s, when full-scale nuclear tests were still conducted across Mercury Valley, beyond the first range of mountains, demonstrators still show up. They are led by Corbin Harney, the Western Shoshone spiritual leader, who warns of a new danger, just visible through a gap in the Skull Mountains: a low-lying, gently sloping ridge—Yucca Mountain—that would be unremarkable but for the fact that it is slated to store seventy thousand tons of high-level nuclear waste from America's aging, ailing nuclear power industry.

It's typical of the American government's professed concern for the "environment" that it should regard the desert tortoise as endangered—but not the region's longtime Shoshone inhabitants, whose leaders have brought the protesters to the fence. Americans prefer to think of their wilderness as uninhabited; it makes it easier to reconcile setting aside certain areas for military activities, such as bomb tests. If their sacrifice is necessary for national security, well, tortoises don't protest their extinction, and if they must go, they go quietly. Put up signs around the perimeter to make it look as though civilians are responsible for their disappearance, not the military. Never mind the fact that the tortoise (*Gopherus agassizii*) is totem to some people who have lived in the region as long as the tortoise has—some ten to twelve thousand years.

The Nevada Test Site and the overlapping Yucca Mountain Project to the north rest on traditional native lands. In fact, despite efforts by the federal government to buy them out, the Western Shoshone hold title to the land based on the 1863 Treaty of Ruby Valley. They have resisted assimilation to varying degrees, often supplementing a subsistence living from diminishing reserves of game animals and pine nuts with ranching and mining jobs. Their grievances against government intrusion into their affairs go deeper and farther back in time than those of the Nye County ranchers, spearheaded by Dick Carver, who made headlines and the cover of *Time* magazine over the issue of access to public lands.[1]

Far from being an uninhabited wilderness, the desert regions in and around the Nevada Test Site show archaeological evidence of human habitation for thousands of years until the land was withdrawn from public use by the military. These "invisible people" fight the very thing that the tortoise sign warns of: extinction. They have allied themselves with white environmental and antinuclear activists not only to protest the desecration of their homeland by nuclear activities but also to bolster their own cultural survival, which they have managed to a remarkable degree.

Not all the Americans of European descent who come to the Nevada Test Site do so out of political idealism or a sense of environmental justice, although they certainly voice support for these causes during the three-day gatherings, which include workshops on nonviolence and Western Shoshone land rights as well as nuclear politics. Most come seeking spiritual solace and not, incidentally, a good time. They arrive by the bus- and vanload and set up camp, sometimes drumming and dancing far into the night. At sweat lodge ceremonies before the protests, the white people crowd into tarpaulin-covered huts for a ritual that has become commonplace among Native Americans. They listen to Firefly, a sixty-year-old, self-described ex-con and ex-addict, chant in his native tongue, tell his life story, and explain native ways. Despite his relatively hoary age, he is not, he says, an elder, or a medicine man, or teacher, or anything so exotic; he is a "helper," like the man tending the fire and pitchforking stones into the makeshift wickiup. The rocks used to heat the sweat lodges, he explains, are "stone people." They represent the heart that warms the body. One enters and leaves the lodge saying "all my relations"—meaning animals, birds, plants, rocks, as well as people.

In the lodge we are enjoined to keep them all in mind. But when the time comes to "pray together," the white Americans are consumed with their own concerns—praying for themselves, their families, their finances—and the result is a kind of cacophony. Others take part in the ceremonies to express New Age religious sentiments, believing the Indians possess insight into what white people have come to term "Earth-based spirituality"—sentiments the Indians tend to disdain as misappropriation of their customs. As a consequence, many Indians avoid the Peace Camp ceremonies. But whatever their shortcomings, the white protesters bring numbers to the gatherings and public attention to Sho-shone land rights struggles. What's more, they are ready and willing to put their bodies on the cattle guard, in effect making visible the invisible radiation that blows in from the Nevada Test Site.

These foreign Americans, of whom I am one, are, in contrast to Native Americans, a displaced lot. We drive along the surface of the desert landscapes in our cars, looking at the pristine scenery, turning a blind eye to the weapons complexes that checker the desert landscape. If we feel particularly adventuresome, we head off on a wilderness trek, careful to avoid others, and count it a blessing if we see no one else on the trail. Nature is elsewhere, apart from our human settlements. The human and the nonhuman are divided by our technology of cars, media—and weapons. Despite Shoshone reliance on some of the same technology, much of their activity takes place out-of-doors—eating, talking, dancing, singing, praying. Some seem to live as itinerant an existence as their seminomadic forebears; their connection is not to buildings. Land, not a house, is home. Many other native peoples who espouse an ethic of living within the natural world seem to do so in the belief that human and nonhuman are dependent on each other for continued survival. Water resources, for instance, are cared for as much as any plant or animal, particularly in the desert. Instead of an eco-systems ethic of "managing natural resources" (read: controlled plun-dering), their ecology stems from an ethic of reciprocity between what we classify as dead "nature"—water, rocks, the air—and the living.

The distinction may seem academic until viewed in context. For instance, Harney's emphasis on "one water, one air, one Mother Earth" may sound like the Gaia hypothesis simplified for New Age consump-tion, but in practice it speaks to a radically different ethos—one that is not a further abstraction from ecosystemic cycles of nitrogen and car-bon, as it is for Western ecologists. It speaks to how we might live on the Earth differently, not as selfish, self-sufficient individuals, but as people with responsibilities to the resources we use—allowing time for cultiva-tion and renewal of those resources. It is a message that resonates clearly in the desert, where water, although largely invisible, is a resource easily damaged or drained through overuse.

Ours is a culture of displacement, and it is as displaced people that we comb the American West for signs of meaning, whether in geologic formations or in traces of a hidden Indian presence. Such is the American heritage of immigration—that we must, perhaps forever, regard ourselves as newcomers in a land peopled by others, by aboriginals, or even by other "settlers" whom we displace by degrees. While our own origins as a people, as Euro-Americans, may be lost in the Aryan mists, it is possible to examine this pervasive sense of displacement and trace its current to a cultural stratum that finds its expression in a mythology that reveals a split within ourselves—between what we idealistically espouse and how we act. It is a tale of conquest, of plunder, and of moving on. Except that now there is nowhere left to go and no turning back. Having reached the physical limits of our frontier, we turn back in on ourselves, as we must, and come face to face with the legacy of our pursuit of unlimited energy and world dominance—seventy thousand tons of deadly radioactive waste.

II

I have a recurrent fantasy. Drilling into Yucca Mountain, scientists discover a large vault. Teams of archaeologists are called in. An underground city, perhaps? Maybe a rumored golden city of Cibola, a scene reminiscent of recent tomb discoveries in Egypt, unimagined treasures, or of the discovery of the lunar monolith in Kubrick's *2001: A Space Odyssey*? Speculation abounds. Finally workers clear away enough debris for scientists to enter the cavern. What they discover is a vast chamber, vaguely familiar, where large casks of steel, some corroded beyond all recognition, lie in disarray. An eerie glow, like some primeval mist, pervades the cavern, the floor of which is flooded up to the scientists' knees. And then the realization. This is an atomic vault, a radiation waste dump of a civilization long since vanished from the face of the Earth.

Science fiction? Yes, but we easily forget how much science is fiction—how predisposed we are to conceive of problems in certain ways. The scene I envision could easily be enacted ten thousand years hence, during a future waste crisis. The scale of time by which scientists calculate the outcomes of intervention at Yucca Mountain is geologic, longer than recorded history. No man-made container can be guaranteed to stand up for more than a few hundred years. Russian engineers will count their blessings if the specially designed materials they've used to seal the damaged Chernobyl reactor last two hundred years. Any estimates of a material's durability beyond that remain as speculative as any science fiction. Instead scientists are relying on supposedly water-impermeable welded tuff, of which the Yucca Mountain formation is composed, to hold the most toxic waste in check.

No, the crisis is now. Not in some unimaginable past or future.

We are fond of the stories scientists tell us. They are somehow reassuring, comforting in the face of what we don't fully comprehend. (Myth, it is sometimes argued, serves a similar function in less "advanced" cultures.) Chaos theory, for instance, reduces the forces of entropy and disintegration to human scale: something almost imaginable, even manageable, something that we can visualize in computer simulation, rendered harmless by innocuous terms like "the Butterfly Effect." The implication—that small, even infinitesimal anomalies in the initial conditions of a system can magnify over time, with massive repercussions—is ignored when science wants the outcome of its experiments predetermined. The massive "experiment" at Yucca Mountain—testing the feasibility of siting a radioactive dump there—has a foregone conclusion. Theories to the contrary, such as the "critical mass" theory, in which physicists speculate that storing all that plutonium in one place could lead to an explosion, are summarily dismissed.

I read a Louis L'Amour western, I forget its name, written before chaos theory was popularized by James Gleick and *Jurassic Park*. It begins its saga with a coyote scratching at a piece of dirt, which loosens some rocks. After years of erosion, a vein of gold is exposed that would otherwise have remained hidden, perhaps forever, had the coyote not loosened the rock. Discovery of the gold ushers in a gold rush, of course, forever altering the natural history of the West. What chaoticists call the Butterfly Effect, here I would rename the Coyote Principle.

Extrapolating the Coyote Principle to the Yucca Mountain story, the use of a tunnel-boring machine to drill a hundred miles of twenty-five-foot-diameter tunnels into the mountain will have consequences far beyond what we can currently imagine. The site, selected for its relative remoteness and particular geology, is nestled among dozens of known earthquake faults and recently active (within the last fifteen thousand years) volcanoes. Ironically, Yucca Mountain was chosen as the site to house high-level radioactive waste for its inertness, and yet the surrounding area is quite active geologically. A 5.5 temblor shook the area a few years back, damaging facilities at the neighboring Nevada Test Site. Within the mountain itself, water is perched on ledges, ready to seep downward through fissures should conditions change. We can well imagine the current drilling into the mountainside serving as the agent of such a change. And the area is not active just geologically. Until weapons testing ceased in 1992, hundreds of underground nuclear tests rocked the region.

No one can watch a film of an aerial view of an underground nuclear test and go away believing that it has no effect on the land. Spreading outward from the epicenter, the land buckles up like a souffle before subsiding into a kind of sink. Rocks in the interior of the Earth are subjected to temperatures found only on the surface of the sun. Corbin Harney asks, "What does that do to the groundwater?" The aquifer under the Nevada desert, the third largest in the United States, is already receding due to the demands of a booming Las Vegas. Add possible radiation, and you don't need to worry about the desert tortoise, except for a few possible mutants. Nor do you have to worry about the few troublesome Shoshone who cling to the land. In time, however, the water will drain past Ash Meadows, the oasis twenty miles to the southeast, ultimately affecting the Colorado River that supplies Los Angeles and that, if irradiated, will make the news too late to do anything about it.

The quarter-of-a-million-year legacy (equal to the *half*-lifes of plutonium) of our fifty-year experiment with nuclear energy is further evidence of the Coyote Principle. Little could Americans have imagined in 1945 the scope of the problem that attempting to harness the nuclear fire would engender. Little can we imagine it now. But imagine it we must. In thinking about such time scales, which are well beyond the scope of the historical imagination, we must revert to the language of myth. Science offers little help.

Coyote, of course, is the culture bringer, mischief maker par excellence in western Native American Indian traditions, and, like Prometheus in our Western mythology, the bringer of fire, stolen not from gods but from other humans during the time when animals were human—or, as Westerners prefer to think of it, when *humans* were animal.

Atomic energy represents another cycle in the myth of the stolen fire. Like Coyote, who lights his tail in order to transport the fire and whose fur consequently catches fire during his getaway, we are experiencing a difficult time putting out the fire. Every attempt to douse the flames only seems to spread them. It is out of control. In one version of the story, the people who are the keepers of the fire eventually catch up with and kill Coyote. Like his cartoon counterpart, Coyote is of course immortal, and goes on to other misadventures. Our species may not be so lucky.

But compare the Greek myth of Prometheus, the immortal Titan who has a soft spot for humanity. Remember the quarrel that started it all. Asked by Zeus for an offering in return for the gift of fire, humans offer up the bones and offal of slaughtered animals, keeping the best part, the flesh, for themselves. Incensed at the mortals' efforts to trick him with mere incense, Zeus rescinds his gift of fire. Prometheus steals it back, for which he is punished by being chained to a rock as food for an eagle (sacred to Zeus), who comes daily to feast on his liver. To punish the humans, Zeus sends the beautiful but airheaded Pandora, who unleashes all the ills of the world, not least of which is cruel and delusive hope.

The emphasis on gifts in this story is not incidental. The human sin is that Zeus's gift of fire is not reciprocated in kind. Deferring for the moment the answer to the question of how gods could consume flesh even if it was offered them, it's evident that humans hoard the food for themselves; it's not shared with other species. In rescinding the gift, Zeus punishes humans for upsetting the balance of what Lewis Hyde in *The Gift* calls the economy of gift exchange, and what Edgar Wind in *Pagan Mysteries of the Renaissance* identifies as the principle of reciprocity— what moderns might call the balance of nature. Such a principle seems more closely aligned with "natural" laws of conservation, laws whose implications we ignore when the purpose suits us. In stealing back the fire, Prometheus demonstrates what the German philosopher and cultural historian Hans Blumenberg in *Work on Myth*, his monumental exegesis of the Prometheus myth, characterizes as an evolutionary step forward in (at least Western) consciousness—deceit, cleverness, cunning, guile (i.e., the calculating intelligence) in its relation to the natural world—humans' ability to trick nature into providing more than they return to their surroundings—in more modern terms, to extract more from the "system" than one puts into it.

That's civilization—the negentropic ability to gather together resources from the surrounding chaos to construct order without, in effect, having to suffer the consequences. Everything depends on what you include in the description of your environment, your "ecosystem," or, in mythological terms, your cosmos. It's comforting to believe that the resources being consumed lie outside your system, that the gods are somewhere else and not paying attention, and that you can get away with theft. If the resource being consumed happens to lie in a desert outside your productive economic system, in land occupied by unproductive "savages," so much the better. You don't need to calculate the effect consuming those resources has on the surroundings or the marginalized inhabitants. Not until the waste comes back to haunt you, and the no-man's-land becomes a dumping ground for deadly detritus.

Humans, having gathered uranium from the New Mexican desert not all that far from Yucca Mountain, have harnessed the energy within the atom, for commercial and security purposes, in effect by "tricking" nature out of its secret power. We are aided in our industry by this supposedly "free" energy source. As Martin Heidegger observed, we regard the natural world as a "standing reserve," there for the plundering—the military metaphor is more than apt in this case. Having stolen from nature its hidden fire, we delude ourselves into believing that there's no reckoning, no balancing of accounts, despite even the scientific evidence, which tells us there are no free meals in nature's unforgiving cycles. We are burdened by the waste from this virtual cornucopia, much as the Greeks of the early classical period projected into Pandora's box of woes the burdens of civilizing fire—its destructive aspects, along with the rituals needed to maintain the fire.

Our modern economic system encourages us in the belief that we can obtain something for nothing, or at least more for less. The industries fueled by the electrical power generated from nuclear energy (or any source) operate on the principle of replacing human energy with power obtained from machine-transformed natural resources. We want to believe that we can produce, consume, and amass unlimited quantities of products with no obvious side effects. For instance, when it comes to modern food production, we are haunted by the chemicals used to increase yield.

We of the West are the children of Prometheus. The heart of the Promethean story is a contention over how food is obtained and processed. Food is one of the products transformed by energy. Eating meat that is not cooked makes one no different from the animal "red in tooth and claw." According to Claude Lévi-Strauss in *The Raw and the Cooked,* the ability to cook food is the great socializer, the great civilizer. Besides setting humans apart from animals, the cooking of food brings people together around the fire, the energy source. In Lewis Hyde's book *The Gift,* food operates as a medium for gift exchange: hoarding it results in disaster; it is *meant* to be consumed. Of course, keeping food for lean periods is a civilizing practice: it allows cities, those islands of negentropy, to flourish; people can remain where they are rather than follow food sources. An entire economic network of food exchange grows up around the city, where food from outlying areas is brought to market to exchange for the products of industry.

But what is the price paid for the privilege of transforming food into a caloric commodity? In a reversal from the original sin of humans eating the flesh of sacrificial animals, Prometheus is condemned to having his liver (flesh) consumed by Zeus, the eagle spirit, showing how it is that gods can consume flesh—through an animal higher, closer to the gods, than humans. In effect the human being becomes carrion, the food of the gods, consumed, reabsorbed into nature in a rather painful way: not to die but to suffer, because the food can no longer be processed as it should be. The cooked flesh of animals is tainted: the violence of the sacrifice remains within the body. Ritual cleanses it. A parallel with our modern nuclear dilemma can be drawn. The radionuclides that invade the body represent an invisible nature spirit—Zeus's revenge, or his brother Pluto's revenge against humans for having plundered the chthonic realms of riches. But in our era of conspicuous consumption, there is no ritual, no mythic eagle, to cleanse the Promethean landscape of radiation.

According to a study sponsored by the Massachusetts-based Childhood Cancer Research Institute, Indians living around the Nevada Test Site, both Shoshone and Paiute, have long supplemented their diets with game and pine nuts from the region, much as their ancestors subsisted on these foods for centuries before the West was "won." In fact their subsistence economies contributed to the view, promulgated by "pioneers," of the Shoshone and Paiute as savages and something less than human. Because of the fallout entering the food chain from nearly one hundred on-continent atmospheric nuclear tests conducted in the late 1950s and early 1960s, Indians who relied on these food sources proved far more susceptible to radiation than city-dwelling downwinders. It is a tale seldom told in the controversies over radiation experiments and those downwind populations, who obtained food from the wider-ranging commercial network. Medical records are sealed. In partially documenting Indian exposure, my wife, Valerie Kuletz, a sociologist, and I interviewed members of the Moapa Paiute tribe to the southeast of the Nevada Test Site for her book, *The Tainted Desert*. Sitting around the table at their community center, Moapa Indian women told us of case after case of cancer in their small tribal community. They added that we were the first outsiders to inquire after their public health. They said animal and plant species that they used to harvest in the wild are rarer now. Dismissed by government agencies as anecdotal, the evidence nonetheless suggests that downwind Indian communities were at higher risk from fallout—were, in effect, experimental subjects.

III

It is not the need to transform flesh into food that fuels our drive to harness nuclear power. Ordinary fire has given us the means to cook for millennia. What is it, then, that nuclear energy brings us that we cannot otherwise have? The power that feeds the lights of Las Vegas, although symbolic of our consumption habits, an economic black hole that reabsorbs the wealth produced by the average American citizen, is not generated in nuclear facilities.

Complex social and political factors contribute to our reliance on such power, and the reader is referred to *The Tainted Desert* for those. But there are cultural reasons as well: a need to dominate, a need to feel like masters of a nature that is so often portrayed in our literature as fickle or cruel. It's true that nature has not been kind to the white race. Sensitive to the sun, we are drawn to more northerly, colder climates where exposure (to, ironically, a form of radiation) is limited. Our revenge has been to conquer nature, first by setting ourselves apart and then by devising technologies to dominate. We are not born to the out-of-doors. But nature, as even our myths tell us, cannot be trifled with, and in unlocking its secrets, we pay a price.

Such bald-faced assertions are of course speculation. But science, in all its rationalism, has failed to provide a solution to a problem it was instrumental in creating. From speculation may emerge productive and unexpected avenues of thought. Our myths, endlessly reinterpreted and subject to countless retellings, provide a basis for such speculation. You don't have to be a nuclear physicist to realize that something of mythic proportions has been happening, is happening, in the Nevada desert. From films like *Hair* and *Desert Bloom* to *Blue Sky* and *Independence Day*, the desert around the Nevada Test Site figures in the popular imagination as the signifier of what we have become and what we fear most. It is a chaotic attractor, a vortex that transforms culture, where we are face to face against an other we don't comprehend. Area 51 on the Nevada Test Site has become the locus of our myth of the alien. Yet to longtime inhabitants of the region, aliens are us. Humans mythologize their technologies, ascribing to them supernumerary powers. At the same time that we create self-destructive technologies such as nuclear power, we project onto the cosmos, in the form of aliens, a superior technology with a power to destroy us. The aliens are gods whose powers we have stolen. And, like Zeus, they seek revenge in our myths.

In the Native American mythic tradition, there is also a recognition that fire brings cultural transformation, and with it problems that need tending. Life becomes more complex—humans must ensure that the fire doesn't go out or get out of hand. Fire itself brings culture; its use separates humans from animals. Animals become food that is cooked. But eating animals in a time when humans are animals is like eating yourself—it's cannibalistic, thus problematic. In the Shoshone tale "Coyote Learns to Fly," a dilemma arises over the killing of animals. When Coyote ends up eating his own brains, remarking, "That's good gravy," he becomes aware that killing any animal is akin to killing yourself, a dilemma difficult to reconcile. There's a right way and a wrong way to go about it, however. To kill for food is permissible. To kill for sport is a punishable transgression.

Nor does Coyote's theft of fire go unpunished. Coyote's hair bursts into flame after his escape from the women's camp from which he has stolen the fire. The guardians of the fire, the women, catch up with and kill him. Fire escapes only because Pack Rat, a negentropic character if there ever was one—hoarding, gathering, accumulating stuff from his surroundings—runs off with it. The fact that it is a woman who must be duped in order to obtain the fire (not some Olympian sky god) speaks to a difference in the two myths, and thus in the two cultures.

Women are made powerful in their roles as keepers of the fire, whether in Greek or Native American myth. They tend the hearth; they embody a life force alien to "Man." In the Promethean tale, Pandora, the first woman in Hesiod's cosmology, is the thunder god Zeus's poisoned gift to humanity. Before her, there are only men. She is beautiful, alluring, but she signifies trouble to the Greek male mind. As Jane Caputi has argued convincingly in *Gossips, Gorgons and Crones,* nuclear energy has often been regarded as possessing an alluring yet dangerous femininity. She cites one advertisement depicting a woman in a diaphanous negligee with copy that poses the riddle: Why is a beautiful woman like a nuclear power plant? Answer: She must take good care of herself, schedule regular rests and visits to her doctor, and never let herself get out of shape. "She's as trim now as she was ten years ago." She exemplifies the principle of preventive maintenance. She is the "good wife" who never goes off or gets out of line. We must remember, however, who the modern Pandora is that pried open the box of nature, releasing the ills of nuclear waste into the environment. Is it not the nuclear scientist who justifies every excess with humanity's supposedly insatiable need to know the secrets of "Nature"?

In the Native American myth, troublemaker and culture bringer combine into one figure, Coyote, who, while gendered male, is often depicted attempting to perform female functions like childbirth and menstruation. He seems jealous of woman's ability to create new life. In the Greek myth, man is clearly the culture bringer and woman the troublemaker. Such cultural differences can be illuminating. Promethean man sacrifices himself for the betterment of Man; Pandoran woman is relegated to the status of one who is deceptive, insubordinate, and plain stupid. Pandora (from *pan* = all, *dora* = gift) is the all-giving mother of life. Coyote, in the Shoshone tale "Coyote Learns to Fly," understands the power women hold and attempts to emulate it, using the hot-rock birthing bed to simulate giving birth and, later, to bring down the Sky Boys, who wantonly killed his cousin Mountain Sheep Boy for sport, creating unnecessary waste in the process.

The rocks from which uranium ore is milled protect us from the harmful effects of this radiant transformative energy—but disturb the delicate balance, unlock the safeguards, and we put ourselves at risk. According to Corbin Harney, Indians of the region have long been aware of the radioactivity of the earth and its effects; it is simply a product of the earth being alive. Indians, he said to me on a visit to my home in the Santa Cruz Mountains, would cover themselves in a white chalk dust to protect themselves from the more deleterious effects in areas where there were concentrations of such power. Later, on reflection, I could not help but think of the "white clay men" who dance around the infant Zeus to protect him from the wrath of his father, Chronos (time), who wishes him dead.

Unlike the hot rocks from which we obtain uranium, the hot rocks found in the sweat lodge bring people together to minister to their spiritual health, to cleanse themselves of impurities—a ritual that must be performed regularly. The importance placed on "stone people" in sweat lodge ceremonies demonstrates the belief in a power inherent in rock. Radiant energy brought out by the fire is—under the proper conditions, with respect for the rocks—a transformative healing power. Our nuclear culture and industry, needless to say, show none of that respect. While scientists insist on the inertness of the Earth, they name the power that emanates from it "radiation," and it is deadly. Concentrations of this power, left intact, are recognized by some Indians as *puha*— a power immanent within the Earth that makes it alive.

Nuclear power abrogates the healing property of rocks—of the earth. It finds an echo of the original hot rocks in the use to which radiation is put in modern cancer therapy, an attempt to purify the body of toxins that have sent the body into revolt, perhaps by the very vector that caused the disease. Nuclear apologists often point to radiation's medicinal effects as justification for continued research into and testing of nuclear power. But by far the dominant role played by nuclear energy is to further our self-aggrandizement. We have power to burn. We can barely imagine what modern conveniences we would have to give up without nuclear power. Our microwaves? Our computers? A recent ad from Pacific Gas and Electric, which runs California's nuclear power plants, touts the role it plays in brewing the sixty-five million cups of coffee consumed in the state each day. More important, ending the reliance on nuclear power, in whatever form, would mean loss of power in the world—economic, military, scientific. We are dependent on exporting nuclear technology to developing nations to make them dependent on us. With our nuclear arsenal, we can still bully our way around the hemisphere or simply negotiate softly, carrying our big stick as a silent but constant threat.

IV

Native Americans of the Yucca Mountain region proclaim Yucca Mountain a sacred mountain, a claim that the Western mind derides as disingenuous because to us it seems such an uninteresting piece of igneous rock. It is low, flat, and elongated, and stands out only in contrast to the higher peaks around it. But on closer inspection, archaeologists have found many ceremonial sites on the mountain—in particular, the Prow, at the eastern end of the mountain—to be of unusual significance. Nearby Forty-Mile Wash appears to have been a major trade route, judging from the artifacts left behind. An Indian spokesperson for the Yucca Mountain Project with whom Valerie spoke said that Paiutes believe Yucca Mountain serves as a passageway from this world to the next for the newly dead.

While it has become fashionable for some environmentalists and academics bent on demythologizing the romantic view of nature-loving natives to dismiss appeals to sacredness as political posturing, pointing to past Indian practices of clearing land by burning as evidence of Indian callousness to the environment, such protestations must be seen in the context of those whose interest is in preserving "wilderness" as empty space for the white man's recreation—"pure" parks outside civilization's putrefying cities, where one can escape and be renewed. More accurately, as Dennis Martinez, founder of the Indigenous Peoples Restoration Network, pointed out in *Sierra,* Indian efforts to control fire are evidence of the sophistication of their environmental awareness *and* culture. University of Nevada, Reno, anthropologist Kay Fowler has shown how, historically, Shoshone cultivated mesquite and pine. Cultivation equals culture. Julian Stewart, the founder of cultural ecology, showed how the Owens Valley Paiute irrigated the land. Claims by some that such practices evince a disregard for "the environment" miss the point entirely. Historically, Shoshone in particular have been derided as virtually without culture, as living on insects and grass, as being in some primitive state of nature, making it easier to eradicate the uncultured, the less than human. Efforts to redress such stereotypes do not mean that, conversely, they possess no ecological awareness.

As inheritors of a Greek culture that Euro-Americans have claimed as the ancestor of their own, we see ourselves always spreading locustlike over the Earth. In contrast, many Native American cultures share a belief in autochthonic origins, that the land they live on gave birth to their people. We have abandoned any belief in an autochthonous origin in favor of continual expansion. In those cultures we see as the wellspring of our own—the Greek and the Hebrew—displacement is in fact part of the origin myth, and in fact it could be argued that the expulsion from Eden into a wilderness fraught with danger is the displacement myth par excellence. Like Peter Rugg in the story by the early-nineteenth-century American writer William Austin, we travel farther and farther from our destination in an effort to return to some semblance of an origin, only to find that we "can't go home again." We lack an origin myth, and postmodern celebrations of that lack reflect, in fact, the loss of a sense of origins.

The Western fixation on the "underground" as a source of energy often reflects a colonialism spearheaded by mining interests—our efforts to extract resources from "unsettled" regions in fact constituted the first industry. Some modern scholars of ancient Greece have noted that the journey to the underworld in Greek myth often masks a tale of expansion: Orpheus must descend to the underworld to rescue Eurydice (a name that means "wide ruling"). In the nineteenth century, Edward Bulwer-Lytton, who became colonial secretary, wrote a book called *Vril*, subtitled *The Coming Race*, about an underground civilization powered by a strange magnetic force. It became a favorite of Hitler's as he developed his fantasies of a master race.

Some Western Shoshone say that a serpent lives within Yucca Mountain, and that recent earthquake activity in the region points to the serpent's restlessness and eventual awakening. Both these assertions reflect evidence of the mountain's special status, its sacredness. In Western mythos, the sacred is inevitably distinguished from the profane. Both Émile Durkheim and Mircea Eliade have made this absolute distinction, relegating to the sacred that which cannot be touched or approached because of its purity and inviolability. To touch or approach brings almost certain death. When Oedipus enters the sacred grove at Colonus, for instance, he is destroyed. In a study conducted to design an appropriate signifier for the Waste Isolation Pilot Project radiation waste dump near Carlsbad, New Mexico, scientists, linguists, and artists proposed monuments designed to ward off future-world trespassers who might not read a present-day language (or any language). Proposals included the landscape of thorns (giant spikes in the ground), the black hole (a heat-absorbing field that would be too hot to approach), and the menacing earthworks. (There seem no more menacing earthworks than those around Paguate Pueblo.) Here again, the nuclear enters the realm of the mythological. Ironically, all the proposals would generate the curiosity of a Pandora. But the greater irony is that in a belief system which draws distinctions between sacred and profane, such monuments would make our nuclear waste dumps indistinguishable from the "sacred"—a zone that cannot be entered without fatal consequences.

In the Judaic account of the ark of the covenant, the power of God rests in a box that must be enshrined in a holy of holies, approachable only by those anointed as its keepers. Its supernatural power is ultimately destructive to Israel's enemies. In the case of our nuclear waste dumps, however, it is not its purity that makes the site off-limits but its potential for destructiveness, its lethality, its polluting effect. The material world—symbolized by the atom—in all its godlike power becomes the source of pollution. In this sense nuclear waste is more akin to the Greek notion of miasma, that which must be shunned because of its polluting effects, and which requires a sacrifice to expunge. Miasma emerges from the contamination believed to come from the committing of a crime. In that sense our crime against the Indians—genocide—results in a miasma of radiation. Somewhat analogously, the Jewish hell—Gehenna, the communal dump—is situated next to Tophet, the site of human sacrifice.

Perhaps it would have been better never to have discovered the atomic fire; its potential destructiveness so far outweighs its imagined benefits. But like the technology of fire, it's not going away. If it goes out, we fear we will lose the power associated with it. Does the use of nuclear power represent a situation analogous to that of fire? Can we simply control our use of nuclear power for benign purposes? I believe there is an analogy, but we must remember the price paid by Prometheus: having his liver gouged out on a daily basis. We have to ask ourselves, What is the benefit derived from the nuclear fire? Are our all-night cities blazing up out of the desert worth a potentially terrible price? What is the price already paid? For the Indians who have suffered from nuclear exposure and harvested little of the benefits, the answer might seem obvious. Are we willing to sacrifice their bodies on the altar of industry? Of course we are; they're not our bodies. Or are they? Can there be any real separation in a nuclear age? Is there any real safety in entombing waste in a mountain ninety miles from Las Vegas, that city of eternal light?

When the Western Shoshone say "Ours is the most bombed nation on Earth," it is not an exaggeration. Nor are they simply referring to Newe Segobia, their homeland. To the extent they are Americans—and they are *native* Americans; we are the *foreign* Americans—America is the most bombed nation on Earth. It has bombed itself. The fact that it is desert believed by scientists to be uninhabitable should not obscure the fact. That which is sacred is made so through sacrifice, the spilling of blood, the taking of life. We have sacrificed Indian lives to sanctify the Nevada Test Site as our holy of holy lands—where our power is tested—where we meet the ultimate threat of the alien we imagine coming to conquer *us*. And we will sacrifice ourselves in the long run to consecrate Yucca Mountain. But for the Shoshone and Paiute, the land is the body, the water is the blood flowing through that body. It is already sacred for the simple reason that it is alive.

However much I have drawn on the Promethean and Coyote myths to illuminate aspects of the cultures confronting nuclear waste, I believe that the situation with nuclear energy and power is categorically different from that of fire. Everyone recalls Disney's *Our Friend the Atom,* and the boy's encounter with the atomic genie. But perhaps the Sorcerer's Apprentice scene from *Fantasia* is the more apt cartoon. Whatever we do to try and stop it, more and more radioactivity is produced. It is uncontrollable. And we do not possess the magic formula by which to stop it.

Are we to assume that over hundreds of years, thousands of years, some catastrophe will not disrupt the Yucca Mountain site and contaminate the groundwater? We cannot. We cannot put the nuclear genie back into its Pandoran box. We *can* stop producing more waste. We can reduce our energy consumption by the amount we rely on nuclear power, and end our dependence on nuclear weapons to "deter" aggression abroad. We can devote our scientific resources to solving what is arguably the greatest technical challenge humanity has faced—not the "sexiest" or the "sweetest," but the greatest—instead of finding ever new uses for nuclear energy. We do not have to continue swallowing the condescending reassurances of science. We must now use those "hot rocks" to bring the sky boys—those scientists, generals, and politicians who believe nuclear supremacy justifies every act of injury—down to Earth. Perhaps the answer lies in returning the waste to the earth, to be reabsorbed. But two things must happen. No more of it must be produced, which means abandoning nuclear weapons and the government's plans for "stockpile stewardship"—maintaining a nuclear arsenal into the twenty-first century. And the land taken from the Shoshone and Paiute must be returned to them for real stewardship. It is amazing that they still want it, but they do. They take the long view we seem incapable of taking.

Sometimes I can't help but think that those Greek myths of monstrous hybrids were articulations of some distant future in which mutations run rampant over the world, victims of our experiments in radiation. Like 1950s science fiction movies such as *Them!*, depicting mutated giant insects, I imagine giant desert tortoises coming out from behind the hills at the Nevada Test Site.

Undoubtedly the Greek myths depict an undifferentiated chaos full of hybrids at a time when humans *were* animals from which, in the evolutionary view, the modern Euro-American emerged, and for every beneficial mutation, many harmful ones must be overcome in the course of human evolution. But who is to say which mutation is ultimately harmful and which beneficial—the strain that has produced a world of inert matter that, when unlocked, radiates deadly, gene-altering particles, or a worldview that sees the earth as alive, with concentrations of energy that ought to be respected, not tapped and exploited in the hope of obtaining unlimited energy or power over others? Strange how shortsighted science, which prides itself on its long views of evolution and geology, can be when its interests—or those of the state that supports it—are at stake. What scientists see as inert matter capable of both containing and producing radiation, others view as a living entity with water running, connecting its tissues. But even some scientists recognize that the major threat posed by insertion of radioactive waste at Yucca Mountain comes from the water, the characteristics of which may vary radically from kilometer to kilometer, and of which almost nothing is known other than that the aquifer is some forty-five hundred square miles, most of which drains into Ash Meadows, near the town of Pahrump, the root of which (*pa*) means water in Paiute (a name whose root also is *pa*).

As cautionary tales, those of Prometheus and Coyote offer different outcomes: on the one hand, endless death-in-life, chained to the Caucasus Mountains, mythical home of the Caucasian race; and on the other, rebirth, renewal, through cultural transformation and a recognition of our limitations and responsibilities—to the Indians we have overrun and to the land we have despoiled. Yet we possess the potential for renewal. The promise of Ash Meadows, twenty miles from the Nevada Test Site, where the aquifer bubbles up into crystal blue ponds, should provide us an image of a place where species found nowhere else are beginning to thrive again after the ravages of modern agriculture and mining. We must allow time for renewal. We must recognize that the water that feeds these springs must not be contaminated. Eventually the water will quench thirsts in Pahrump and Las Vegas. Seventy thousand tons of radioactive waste entombed inside Yucca Mountain, perched precariously atop this water table, is not going to remain sealed forever.

On October 10, 1994, the usual crowd gathered at the cattle guard in front of the Nevada Test Site. The ceremony has long been ritualized. It's polite political confrontation. But on this day the familiar was broken by the arrival of two busloads of Japanese tourists. They unfurled the banner of their peace group, and among them were *hibakusha*, survivors of the atomic bombings of Hiroshima and Nagasaki. To them this must have seemed a strange and mysterious place. Here were actual Indians drumming in a wide-open space, hippies in tie-dyed shirts. In the first flush of recognition, there were tears of joy. For us, they represented conciliation, the ability to communicate across borders, races, oceans. Introductions were quickly organized. There was only one translator. A few spoke English. But somehow, it all came off. We were brought together in a circle, just as we had been for the sunrise ceremonies. Leaders of the various groups shook hands with the spokesperson for the *hibakusha,* who had to be pushed to the circle in a wheelchair, but rose for the introductions. Corbin Harney welcomed him, as did the spokesmen for the Atomic Vets, and a Fransciscan monk. It was an incredibly moving scene, spontaneously arranged. A bustling middle-aged Japanese woman, too young to be one of the *hibakusha,* who seemed to be the tour organizer, selected a ten-year-old boy from the children of the activists, and presented him with a paper crane, which she held over his head, invoking the spirit of Sadako and the story of the thousand cranes, saying that what they were doing was for the children. The boy looked as though he wished he could be anywhere else but here.

Valerie leaned over to me and, nodding in the direction of the boy, remarked, "Talk about being destined." The mood was such that I couldn't agree more. When it came Valerie's turn to meet the *hibakusha* elder, I saw him look around Mercury Valley. He was fixated on the building in the center of the valley, one that had always fascinated me because its dome is eerily reminiscent of the cenotaph in the center of Hiroshima. I knew he recognized it as such. Yes, our joy was mitigated by the recognition of what crimes our country had committed in our name. But we believed, this group of a hundred or so, that we could do better. There were no television crews to record the event, but I was filled with Pandora's greatest gift—hope. I do not think it was an illusion.

Not far from here Wovoka received his vision of a renewed Indian culture—the white man dead and the Indian restored to a former glory—that became the Ghost Dance religion. We laugh now and think it tragically quaint, this crisis cult, but I think the menace from the Nevada Test Site and the Yucca Mountain project make Wovoka still relevant. We do not have to believe in the Ghost Dance to learn from it. All prophecy is a warning. If we heed the warning, the prophecy is disproved. Does that mean the prophet was wrong? If we do not heed the warning, I'm afraid Wovoka's prophecy of a decimated white population will come true. As for the Shoshone and Paiute, I believe they will remain long after the white "settlers," having decimated the land to the point where it is of no use to them, abandon the land. That's the long view.

It is a tribute to Harney's leadership that he does not exclude anyone from participating in the ceremonies outside the gates of Mercury. All who respect Indian sensibilities are welcome, and there is probably no more poignant symbol of the harmony possible between Indian and white than that which exists between the Western Shoshone elders at Peace Camp and the Atomic Veterans, soldiers and sailors who were placed in harm's way during atomic tests, and who have banded together to buy land nearby, from which they maintain a constant vigil. Both are the experimental subjects of those tests, united in adversity and commemoration.

The highway that runs from Las Vegas to Beatty along the western edge of the Nevada Test Site and the Yucca Mountain Project is called the Veterans Memorial Highway. Someone wrote the word *Atomic* over the sign. Having suffered the consequences and witnessed the magnitude of the nuclear experiment, the vets, too, take the long view from Yucca Mountain. Like the desert tortoise, noted for its longevity, the people who have come here, have come to stay.

NOTE

1. Western Shoshone ranchers Mary and Carrie Dann have been entangled in disputes over grazing rights in central Nevada for years, but it is the white ranchers like Carver who have made headlines. Ironically, what brought Carver national prominence was his insistence on building an access road on public lands that had not been surveyed for Indian artifacts. But both Indians and ranchers oppose siting nuclear waste at Yucca Mountain.

The Pentagon's Radioactive Bullet

BILL MESLER

*I*t is about two feet long, cylindrical, and far denser than steel. When fired from a U.S. Army M1 Abrams tank, it is capable of drilling a hole through the strongest of tank armors. The makers of this tank-killing ammunition say it is the best in the world. But there is one problem with the Pentagon's super bullet: It is made of radioactive waste.

The first time the Army used this "depleted uranium" (DU) ammunition on a battlefield was during the Gulf War, in 1991. Yet despite Pentagon assurances that only a small number of U.S. troops were exposed to dangerous levels of DU, a two-month investigation by *The Nation* has discovered that hundreds and perhaps thousands of U.S. veterans were unknowingly exposed to potentially hazardous levels of depleted uranium, or uranium 238, in the Persian Gulf. Some soldiers inhaled it when they pulled wounded comrades from tanks hit by DU "friendly fire" (U.S. forces mistakenly fire on other U.S. forces) or when they clambered into destroyed Iraqi vehicles. Others picked up expended rounds as war trophies. Thousands of other Americans were near accidental explosions of DU munitions.

The Army never told combat engineer Dwayne Mowrer or his fellow soldiers in the First Infantry Division much about DU. But the GIs learned how effective the radioactive rounds were as the "Big Red One" made its way up the carnage-ridden four-lane Kuwaiti road known as the "highway of death." Mowrer and his company saw the unique signature of a DU hit on nearly half the disabled Iraqi vehicles encountered. "It leaves a nice round hole, almost like someone has welded it out," Mowrer recalled.

What Mowrer and others didn't know was the DU is highly toxic and, according to the *Encyclopedia of Occupational Health and Safety,* can cause lung cancer, bone cancer, and kidney disease. All they heard were rumors.

"Once in a while you'd hear some guy say, 'Hey, I heard those things were radioactive,'" Mowrer said. "Of course, everybody else says, 'Yeah, right!' We really thought all that Agent Orange stuff and human radiation experiments were a thing of the past."

So Mowrer and his comrades didn't worry when a forty-ton HEMTT transport vehicle packed with DU rounds accidentally exploded near their camp. "We heard this tremendous boom and saw this black cloud blowing our way," he said. "The cloud went right over us, blew right over our camp."

Before they left the Gulf, Mowrer and other soldiers in the 651st Combat Support Attachment began experiencing strange flu-like symptoms. He figured the symptoms would fade once he was back in the United States. They didn't. Mowrer's personal doctor and physicians at the local Veterans Administration could find nothing wrong with him. Meanwhile, his health worsened: fatigue, memory loss, bloody noses, and diarrhea. Then the single parent of two began experiencing problems with motor skills, bloody stools, bleeding gums, rashes, and strange bumps on his eyelids, nose, and tongue. Mowrer thinks his problems can be traced to his exposure to DU.

The Pentagon says problems like Mowrer's could not have been caused by DU, a weapon that many Americans have heard mentioned, if at all, only in the movie *Courage under Fire,* which was based on a real-life DU friendly-fire incident. The Defense Department insists that DU radiation is relatively harmless—only about 60 percent as radioactive as regular uranium. When properly encased, DU gives off so little radiation, the Pentagon says, that a soldier would have to sit surrounded by it for twenty hours to get the equivalent radiation of one chest X-ray. (According to scientists, a DU antitank round outside its metal casing can emit as much radiation in one hour as fifty chest X-rays.) Plus, the military brass argues that DU rounds so effectively destroyed Iraqi tanks that the weapons saved many more U.S. lives than radiation from them could possibly endanger.

But the Pentagon has a credibility gap. For years, it has denied that U.S. soldiers in the Persian Gulf were exposed to chemical weapons. In September 1996, Pentagon officials admitted that troops were exposed when they destroyed Iraqi stores of chemical weapons, as Congress held hearings on "Gulf War Syndrome." The Pentagon also argued, in its own defense, that exposure to chemical weapons could not fully explain the diverse range of illnesses that have plagued thousands of soldiers who served in the Persian Gulf. Exposure to DU—our own weaponry, in other words—could well be among the missing links.

Scientists point out that DU becomes much more dangerous when it burns. When fired, it combusts on impact. As much as 70 percent of the material is released as a radioactive and highly toxic dust that can be inhaled or ingested and then trapped in the lungs or kidneys. "This is when it becomes most dangerous," says Arjun Makhijani, president of the Institute for Energy and Environmental Research. "It becomes a powder in the air that can irradiate you." Some scientists speculate that veterans' health problems stem from exposure to chemical agents combined with DU, burning oil-field vapors, and a new nerve-gas vaccine given to U.S. troops. "We know that depleted uranium is toxic and can cause diseases," said Dr. Howard Urnovitz, a microbiologist who has testified before the Presidential Advisory Committee on Gulf War Veterans' Illnesses. "We also know these soldiers were exposed to large amounts of nerve-gas agents. What we don't know is how the combination of these toxic and radioactive materials affect [sic] the immune system."

Exactly how many U.S. soldiers were exposed to dangerous levels of DU during the Gulf War remains in dispute. Friendly-fire incidents left at least twenty-two veterans with DU shrapnel embedded in their bodies. The Veterans Administration is also monitoring the health of eleven more soldiers who were in tanks hit by DU but who were not hit by shrapnel, and twenty-five soldiers who helped prepare DU-contaminated tanks for shipment back to the United States without being told of the risk. The tanks were later buried in a radioactive waste disposal site run by the Energy Department.

NO PROTECTION

The Nation's investigation has also discovered that the average infantry soldier is still receiving no training on how to protect against exposure to DU, although such training was called for by an Army report on depleted uranium completed in June 1995. On the training lapses, the Pentagon does acknowledge past mistakes. Today the Army is providing new training in DU safety procedures for more soldiers, particularly members of armor, ordnance, or medical teams that handle DU on a routine basis. "I feel confident that if an individual soldier has a need to know, they will be provided that training from the basic level on," Army Colonel H. E. Wolfe told *The Nation*. But Wolfe confirmed that even now, not all infantry will get DU training.

Although the full hazards of these weapons are still not known, the law allows the President to waive restrictions on the sale of DU to foreign armies. Documents obtained under the Freedom of Information Act show that the Pentagon has already sold the radioactive ammunition to Thailand, Taiwan, Bahrain, Israel, Saudi Arabia, Greece, Korea, Turkey, Kuwait, and other countries which the Pentagon will not disclose for national security reasons. The proliferation of DU ammunition around the world boosts the chance that U.S. soldiers will eventually be on the receiving end of the devastating weapon.

A broad coalition of veterans organizations, environmental groups, and scientists hope that won't happen. On September 12, 1996, they met in New York to kick off a campaign calling for an international ban on DU weapons. Even the conservative-minded Veterans of Foreign Wars and the American Legion recently passed resolutions calling on the Defense Department to reconsider its use of the controversial weapon.

"Clearly the Department of Defense hasn't thought through the use of DU on the battlefield and what kind of exposure they are subjecting our troops to," charged Matt Puglisi, the assistant director of veterans affairs and rehabilitation for the American Legion. "It is a very effective weapon, which is why the DOD really doesn't want to see it re-examined. We only spent a couple of days [in winning the Gulf War].

But what if we had a fight that took years and years? We could have tens of thousands of vets with DU shrapnel in them."

THE GULF WAR TEST

The U.S. Army began introducing DU ammo into its stockpiles in 1978, when the United States and the Soviet Union were engaged in intense competition over which side would develop the most effective tank. Washington feared that the Soviets with their T-72 had jumped ahead in the development of armor that was nearly impenetrable by traditional weapons. It was thought that DU rounds could counter the improved Soviet armor. But not until Iraq's Soviet-supplied army invaded oil-rich Kuwait and President Bush sent an expeditionary force of 500,000 to dislodge it was there a chance to battle-test the DU rounds.

American M1 Abrams tanks and Bradley armored personnel carriers fired DU rounds; the A-10 Warthog aircraft, which provided close support for combat troops, fired twin 30-millimeter guns with small-caliber DU bullets. All told, in the one hundred hours of the February ground war, U.S. tanks fired at least 14,000 large-caliber DU rounds, and U.S. planes some 940,000 smaller-caliber rounds. DU rounds left about 1,400 Iraqi tanks smoldering in the desert. Gen. Norman Schwarzkopf recalled one commander saying his unit "went through a whole field of burning Iraqi tanks."

The DU weapons succeeded beyond the Pentagon's wildest dreams. But they received little public attention compared with the fanfare over other high-tech weapons: smart bombs, stealth fighters, and Patriot missiles (which looked good, even if they didn't, as it turned out, work). DU, perhaps the most effective new weapon of them all, was mentioned only in passing. "People have a fear of radioactivity and radioactive materials," explained Dan Fahey, a former Navy officer who served in the Gulf. "The Army seems to think that if they are going to keep using DU, the less they tell people about it, the better."

As the U.S.-led coalition forces swept to victory, many celebrating GIs scrambled onto—or into—disabled Iraqi vehicles. "When you get a lot of soldiers out on a battlefield, they are going to be curious," observed Chris Kornkven, a staff sergeant with the 304th Combat Support Company. "The Gulf War was the first time we saw Soviet tanks. Many of us started climbing around these destroyed vehicles." Indeed, a study by the Operation Desert Shield/Desert Storm Association found that out of 10,051 Gulf War veterans who have reported mysterious illnesses, 82 percent had entered captured enemy vehicles.

Other soldiers might have been exposed to harmful levels of DU as they rescued comrades from vehicles hit by friendly fire. A Gulf War book, *Triumph in the Desert*, contains one dramatic picture of soldiers pulling wounded Americans from the burning hull of an Abrams tank that had been hit by a DU round. Black smoke from the depleted-uranium explosion billows around the rescuers. Still other GIs picked up fragments of large-caliber DU rounds or unexploded small rounds and wore them as jewelry, hung around the soldiers' necks. "We didn't know any better," said Kornkven. "We didn't find out until after we were home that there even was such a thing as DU."

But the Americans facing perhaps the great risk from DU were those who had been hit by DU shrapnel, especially those still carrying radioactive fragments in their bodies. Robert Sanders, who drove a tank, was one apparent casualty. On the third day of the ground war, his tank was hit by a DU round fired from another U.S. tank. "I had stinging pain in my shoulder and a stinging pain in my face from the shrapnel," Sanders said.

Military doctors removed the shrapnel. Several years later, however, Sanders heard that DU was radioactive and toxic, so he obtained his medical records. He found an interdepartmental fax saying doctors had removed bits of an "unknown metal" from his shoulder and that it was "probably DU." Four years later, after he was wounded, Sanders took a urine test for depleted uranium which revealed high levels of it in his system. The Pentagon had never made an effort to tell him of his likely exposure.

Even the end of the ground war on February 28, 1991, did not end the threat of exposure to U.S. soldiers. Government documents reveal that in one accident alone, at a camp at Doha, about twelve miles from Kuwait City, as many as 660 rounds weighing 7,062 pounds burned, releasing dark clouds of DU particles. Many of the 3,000 U.S. troops stationed at the base participated in cleanup operations without protective gear and without knowledge of the potential dangers.

At war's end, U.S. forces left behind about 300 tons of expended DU ammunition in Kuwait and Iraq, a veritable radioactive waste dump that could haunt inhabitants of the region for years. In August 1995, Iraq presented a study to the United Nations demonstrating sharp increases in leukemia and other cancers as well as other unexplained diseases around the Basra region of the country's south. Iraqi scientists attributed some of the cancers to the depleted uranium.

Some U.S. officials and scientists have questioned the Iraqi claims. But former Attorney General Ramsey Clark, who has made two recent trips to Iraq, observes that "the health ministry and doctors particularly in Basra and the south are terribly concerned about a range of problems that were not experienced before: fetuses with tumors, high rates of leukemia." And a secret British Atomic Energy Authority report leaked to the London *Independent* in November 1991 warned that there was enough depleted uranium left behind in the Persian Gulf to account for "500,000 potential deaths" through increased cancer rates, although it noted that such a figure was an unlikely, worst-case scenario. That figure was based on an estimate that only forty tons of DU was left behind.

Another study, by Siegwart Gunther, president of the Austrian chapter of Yellow Cross International, reported that DU projectiles "were gathered by children and used as toys." The study noted that a little girl who collected twelve of the projectiles died of leukemia. Gunther collected some DU rounds in southern Iraq and took them to Germany for analysis. However, when Gunther entered Germany, the DU rounds were seized. The authorities claimed that just one projectile emitted more radiation in five hours than is allowed per year under German regulations.

Cleaning up the radioactive mess in the Persian Gulf would cost "billions," even if it were feasible, said Leonard Dietz, an atomic scientist who wrote a report on depleted uranium for the Energy Department. But the Pentagon maintained in a report that "no international law, treaty, regulation, or custom requires the U.S. to remediate Operation Desert Shield/Desert Storm battlefields."

Those who suggest otherwise have found that they must fight the military industry as well as the Pentagon. In January 1993, Eric Hoskins, a public health specialist who surveyed Iraq as a member of a Harvard team, wrote an op-ed piece in the *New York Times* warning that DU may be causing health problems in Iraqi children. A few weeks later a harsh letter to the editor accused Hoskins of "making readers of limited scientific literacy the lawful prey of his hyperbole," which reaches the "bizarre conclusion that the environmental aftermath of the Persian Gulf war is not Iraq's fault but ours!" The author, Russell Seitz, was identified as an associate with the "Olin Institute for Strategic Studies, Harvard University."

Though the letter appeared to be the work of a neutral scientist, the Olin Institute at Harvard was established by the John M. Olin Foundation, which grew out of the manufacturing fortune created by the Olin Corporation, currently the nation's only maker of DU antitank rounds. Seitz did not answer a request from *The Nation* seeking comment.

Despite the Pentagon's love affair with DU, there is an alternative—tank ammunition made from tungsten. Matt Kagan, a former munitions analyst for *Jane's Defense Weekly,* said the latest developments in tungsten technology have made it "almost as effective as D.U." That assessment is shared by Bill Arkin, a columnist for the *Bulletin of the Atomic Scientists* who has consulted on DU for Greenpeace and Human Rights Watch. "It comes down to this," Arkin said. "Is there a logical alternative that provides the same military capability and doesn't leave us with the legacy? The answer is yes, tungsten."

But tungsten is more expensive and must be imported, while the United States has more than 500,000 tons of depleted uranium, waste left behind by the production of nuclear weapons and by nuclear generators. Scientists have long looked for a way to re-use what otherwise must be stored at great expense in remote sites.

"It's just a cost issue," argued Arkin. "But nobody ever thought through what would happen when we shoot a lot of this stuff around the battlefield. It's not a question of whether a thousand soldiers were exposed or fifty soldiers were exposed. We were probably lucky in the Gulf War. What happens when we're fighting a war that makes the Gulf War look like small potatoes?"

Brighter than the Brightest Star

KARL GROSSMAN

*I*t was brighter than the brightest star, said John Van der Brink, and had a tail about twelve times the width of the full moon with "sparkling bits sort of coming off the back of it. This was an extraordinary spectacular event."[1] From his vantage point in the mountains of northern Chile where he and his wife had gone to watch meteors, he had "no illusions that it was anything other than a piece of space debris" falling to Earth through the ink-black night sky. Van der Brink recently retired as an electronics specialist from the European Southern Observatory in Chile.

Leo Alvarado, a postgraduate student of geology from Chile's Universidad Católica del Norte, who had been driving with four colleagues across the Atacama Desert in northern Chile, saw it too, changing brilliant colors as it came down. "We watched it break up into many pieces and burn," he recounted.[2]

What they and other eyewitnesses saw November 16, 1996, was Russia's Mars 96 space probe descending along a swath of Chile and Bolivia and scattering its remains across a 10,000-square-mile area. The probe carried about a half-pound of deadly plutonium divided into four battery canisters that were to serve as electricity sources for Mars rovers. Like their U.S. counterparts, the containers were touted as sufficiently strong and heat resistant to remain intact, no matter what. The U.S. is now admitting that may not have been the case.

"There are two possibilities," said Gordon Bendick, director of legislative affairs of the National Security Council, about the fate of the canisters. "One, they were destroyed coming through the atmosphere [and the plutonium dispersed]. Two, they survived and impacted the earth and drove through, penetrating the surface . . . or could have hit rock and bounced off like an agate marble. . . . I don't give credence for any one [possibility] because I don't know."[3]

"Named after Pluto, god of the underworld, [plutonium] is so toxic that less than one-millionth of a gram, an invisible particle, is a carcinogenic dose," emphasized Dr. Helen Caldicott, president emeritus of Physicians for Social Responsibility. "One pound, if uniformly distributed, could hypothetically induce lung cancer in every person on Earth."[4]

If the probe "burned up and formed fine plutonium oxide particles . . . [t]here would be an increased hazard of lung cancer," commented Dr. John Gofman, professor emeritus of radiological physics at the University of California at Berkeley, who investigated the 1964 crash back to Earth of a U.S. SNAP-9A (Systems for Nuclear Auxiliary Power). When its plutonium-fueled space power system burned up in the atmosphere, 2.1 pounds of plutonium vaporized and dispersed worldwide. Dr. Gofman has long linked that accident with an increased level of lung cancer.[5]

If the battery canisters somehow landed intact, there is also the question of nuclear proliferation. The U.S. displays concern over the spread of nuclear material that could be used by "rogue" states, terrorist groups, and the like. Although the probe's plutonium-238 could not be used to make bombs—it does not fission (split) like the plutonium-239 used in nuclear weapons—it could still be extremely dangerous in the wrong hands. Plutonium-238's relatively shorter half-life of 87.8 years, compared to a half-life of 24,500 years for plutonium-239, is why it is used in space probes—its comparatively rapid disintegration produces heat which is translated into electricity. The quick decay also makes plutonium-238 some 280 times more radioactive than plutonium-239, and thus a more extraordinarily toxic nuclear poison if inhaled as vapor or small particles that become lodged in the lung.

HOT PANTS AND COOL RESPONSES

Bendick discounts the dangers. "If [the canisters] burned up in the atmosphere, bottom line here, if they weren't heat resistant enough to stand what I would call a nonstandard reentry pattern, the release was maybe up to two hundred grams of plutonium, which is like a drop of blood in the Pacific Ocean. There is no environmental problem with a couple of hundred grams. . . . If in fact this thing survived reentry into the atmosphere and these things came down and crash-impacted on the earth—they were meant to penetrate the earth, much as the containers with the plutonium-238 were meant to penetrate Mars, their original target—they'll never be found. And even if they did and were found, people could walk around with them in their pants pockets for the rest of their lives and never be bothered. . . . If it became particulate matter after diffusing in the atmosphere, burned plutonium would be much similar to open air testing that the French did in the Pacific as recently as a few years ago." Nor was that possibility dangerous, since "we can find no positive causal link" between radioactivity released in atomic bomb testing done by the U.S. in Utah, for example, and cancer, the N.S.C. director of legislative affairs claimed.[6]

Such serenity did not always reign. When the U.S. Space Command announced on November 17, 1996, that the wayward Russian probe "will reenter the Earth's atmosphere . . . with a predicted impact point . . . in east-central Australia" in a matter of hours, President Bill Clinton telephoned Australian Prime Minister John Howard. He offered the "assets we have in the Department of Energy" to deal with any radioactive contamination.[7] (Clinton was planning to fly to Australia the following day for a state visit, the first stop before an Asia tour.)

Howard placed the Australian military and government on full alert. He held a press conference to inform the Australian people of the potential danger and called on them to remain calm. "I can't tell you where it is going to land. I can't tell you when," the prime minister declared.[8] He thanked Clinton for his call and warned Australians to use "extreme caution" if they came in contact with remnants of the Russian space probe.[9] The U.S. television networks all featured stories on their Sunday evening news programs. "Mars probe expected to fall within hours," reported CNN.[10]

Russian Space Agency spokesman Vladimir Ananyev admitted: "We've got a problem."[11] Russian NTV television reported: "Unburned bits of the station could hit the Earth. To make matters worse the station has four thermoelectric generators fueled by radioactive plutonium."[12]

The global media attention made "the danger of a disaster involving a plutonium space project real . . . to people of the world," commented Bruce Gagnon, co-coordinator of the Global Network Against Weapons and Nuclear Power in Space.[13]

Back in Australia, some people "hit the panic button when President Clinton rang the Prime Minister," reported the *Irish Times* from Adelaide: A "national crisis" had been "sparked by this interplanetary ballistic bungle."[14] Others hit the bottle: "A barkeeper in the tiny outback town of Tibooburra offered his customers free beer after officials announced the probe might land in a nearby swamp. A bookmaker in central Australia's Alice Springs said dozens of gamblers tried to place bets on where the Russian probe would crash."[15]

In fact, belying its motto "Masters of Space," the U.S. Space Command (USSPACECOM)—the arm of the U.S. Air Force charged with space warfare and tracking man-made objects in space—had made the first of a series of blunders. Through November 17, the day *after* the Mars 96 space probe had already fallen on South America, the Space Command remained focused down under.

The succession of errors caused "a government source" to tell *Space News:* "I think it's a real black eye for the U.S. Space Command and their space tracking capabilities."[16]

In fact, on November 17, the Space Command made another not-so-masterly prediction: The probe would fall not on Australia, but to the east, in the Pacific.[17] It then updated this report with news that Mars 96 had fallen in the Pacific just west of South America—between Easter Island and the coast of Chile.[18] Meanwhile, Russia's *Rossiiskiye Vesti* announced the probe had "crashed to its doom in the Pacific Ocean west of Australia" [sic],[19] and then put the site in another patch of Pacific, east of Australia and west of South America.[20]

"The thing both agree on is that the Mars 96 probe landed in the water," heralded *USA Today.* "That means the radioactive batteries in its lander vehicles with their . . . ounces of potentially lethal plutonium, lie at the bottom of the ocean."[21]

Prime Minister Howard went before Australia's House of Representatives: "It does appear that what we all have is a happy ending to the saga of the Russian spacecraft."[22] The *Washington Post* ran the headline: "Errant Russian Spacecraft Crashes Harmlessly After Scaring Australia."[23]

They were all wrong. On November 29, eleven days later, the U.S. Space Command completely revised its account yet again: It changed not only *where* but also *when* the probe fell—not *off* South America but *on* Chile and Bolivia, and not on November 17 but the night before. "We now believe that the object that reentered on November 17, which we first thought to be the Mars 96 probe, was in fact the fourth stage of the booster rocket [rather than the probe itself and the batteries]. Confusion has surrounded key events and times in this mission, including the last stages of the rocket burn, the separation of the Mars 96 probe from the rocket, and the final reentry into the Earth's atmosphere of the booster and the probe. USSPACECOM has now completed an extensive post-event analysis that has led to this new conclusion which supports Russian statements about when their Mars 96 probe reentered the atmosphere. The area where any debris surviving this reentry could have fallen is located along an approximately fifty-mile-wide and two hundred-mile-long path, oriented southwest to northeast. This path is centered approximately twenty miles east of the Chilean city of Iquique and includes Chilean territory, the border area of Bolivia, and the Pacific Ocean."[24]

"The fact that the U.S. government initially missed the reentry of the Mars 96 space probe is embarrassing and worse," commented Steve Aftergood, a senior research analyst for the Federation of American Scientists. "It calls into question the quality of our space tracking abilities. When you consider that this issue reached all the way up to the White House and had the president contacting the prime minister of Australia over a re-entry that already occurred, it's borderline scandalous."[25]

RACISM AND SPACISM

But the problem went beyond simple technical incompetence. "You can clearly see the double standard," charged Houston aerospace engineer James Oberg, who specializes in following Russian space missions. "Australia got a phone call from the President, and [Chile] got a two-week-old fax from somebody." Manuel Baquedano, director of the Institute for Ecological Policy in Chile, asked, "Are the lives of Australians worth more than the lives [of Chileans]?"[26]

Months later, the fate of the probe and the plutonium it carried remains unclear. The U.S., which gave a presidential-level pledge of "assets" to Australia to deal with any radioactive contamination when it looked like the probe was falling on Australia, was not providing any major assistance to Chile or Bolivia.[27] Dr. Luis Barrera, an astrophysicist and director of the Astronomy Institute at the Universidad Católica del Norte, said that NASA officials had e-mailed him for gathering eyewitness accounts of the probe's disintegration. Then the agency's interest subsided. He suspects NASA doesn't want too much attention paid because bad publicity might impact on NASA's already controversial plan to launch a record 72.3 pounds of plutonium on its Cassini probe.[28] The Russian government has been "uncooperative," said Barrera, still not giving Chile a description of the canisters so that searchers would know what to look for—if the batteries remained intact.

The U.S. news media were similarly blasé about the implications for Latin America. The *New York Times* relegated the story to a five-paragraph Reuters dispatch under "World News Briefs" buried inside its December 14 edition.[29]

As to why the U.S. was not providing the "assets we have in the Department of Energy" that Clinton promised Australia, *Space News* reported in January 1997 that it was told by a "U.S. government source" that "specially-equipped Department of Energy aircraft capable of spotting from the air the nuclear material carried in the Russian spacecraft . . . were not deployed as the aircraft cannot operate at the altitudes and terrain where Mars 96 may have hit Earth."[30] According to Bendick at the NSC, "It's not the United States' responsibility to protect the world from this. . . . We told Bolivia and Chile that we would provide technical assistance, but they haven't requested any. They asked for technical data and we provided [information on] the radioactive combination of the air, the ground, and the water, and we said it is negligible."[31]

There did not, however, seem to be any hard evidence for that optimistic assessment. In January, the Chilean government asked its ministries of Defense and Interior and the Chilean Nuclear Energy Commission to conduct a study "to determine with absolute certainty [if there was] radioactive contamination."[32] "The impacts on health are not clear," said Barrera, but there is concern because the water source for several cities is in the impacted region. Scientists from his university,

Barrera explained, have gone to the approximate scene to test water for plutonium.

Also, Bolivian officials reported that a police unit had found debris of the Mars 96 probe in Bolivia near the Chilean border, but that report was later called "unofficial" and is not supported by other reports.[33]

ACCIDENTS HAPPEN

While the Mars 96 accident was an embarrassment to the Russian space program and the U.S. Space Command, as well as a potential nightmare for the region affected, it "is a gift to those who would challenge the Cassini mission and other nuclear-powered space missions," commented Aftergood. "It reminds us all that not only can accidents happen, but they do happen with disturbing regularity."[34]

Bringing that message home in a spectacular way was the January 17 explosion of a Delta II rocket lofting a forty-million-dollar Air Force navigational satellite. The twelve-story, fifty-five-million-dollar rocket blew up thirteen seconds after launch, turning the winter sky over the Cape Canaveral Air Station into a distinctly unpatriotic Fourth of July–style fireworks display. "Take cover immediately from falling debris," announced an Air Force officer over the public address system at the launch site. "I say again, take cover immediately from falling debris." As the burning fragments descended over a wide area, a cloud of toxic chemicals formed above the site and began drifting out to sea, then back to land and then south along Florida's Atlantic coast.[35] It contained nitrogen tetroxide and monomethylhydrazine, components of the rocket's fuel—both described by NASA documents as "deadly if a person comes into contact" with them. Residents as far south as Vero Beach, one hundred miles away, were told by the Cape Canaveral officials to stay inside, close all windows and doors, and turn off the air conditioning and heating units. At the Cape Canaveral Elementary School, Brad Smith, a fourth- and fifth-grade teacher, described the cloud as having "weird purples and blues and reds." He said he pushed wet paper towels under the door to his classroom to keep the rocket fumes away from his students."[36]

The Delta II blowup further demonstrates that "space technology can fail and accidents can happen," said Bruce Gagnon of the Global

Network Against Weapons and Nuclear Power in Space.[37] Said Global Network co-coordinator Bill Sulzman, also director of the Colorado-based Citizens for Peace in Space: "They show that launch and flight failures are routine and that any claims that there is no real danger from Cassini is false. In fact, adding nuclear cargo to the situation is a setup for catastrophe."[38]

DISPERSING DANGER

Cassini's use of radioactive material has already done damage. In July 1996, Los Alamos National Laboratory reported increased contamination of workers and equipment and cited work on Cassini's plutonium-fueled systems as the primary cause.[39] Plutonium, stresses Greg Mello of the Los Alamos Study Group, is inherently dangerous to work with and "increased work with plutonium will cause increases in worker exposure."[40]

As the Cassini mission goes forward, many more people could be impacted. The initial danger was that a blowup on launch could break open or melt the plutonium-carrying canisters and spread radioactivity. The second potential flash point is the "slingshot maneuver" planned for 1999. In this "flyby" scheme, twenty-two months after launch, NASA will swing Cassini back toward Earth in order to use the planet's gravitational force to gain enough velocity to propel the probe on to Saturn, its final destination. During that pass, Cassini is to fly just 312 miles above the Earth's surface. But if there is a miscalculation or malfunction and it comes in too close and undergoes what NASA calls an "inadvertent reentry," it could burn up on hitting the seventy-five-mile-high atmosphere, spreading plutonium over a wide area.

NASA public-relations material gives the impression that even then, the plutonium would not be dispersed as cancer-causing vapor and respirable particles. But, in fact, the space agency's *Final Environmental Impact Statement for the Cassini Mission* totally contradicts that, saying, if the Cassini probe slips into the Earth's atmosphere during the "flyby," a sizable portion of the plutonium fuel *would* be released, including much of it as "vapor or respirable particles."[41]

The NASA *Final Environmental Impact Statement for the Cassini Mission* also says that if there is such an "inadvertent reentry" during the planned Earth "flyby" of Cassini on August 16, 1999, and the probe breaks up, dispersing plutonium, "approximately five billion of the estimated seven to eight billion world population . . . could receive ninety-nine percent or more of the radiation exposure."[42]

Despite the danger signs with which Mars 96 and Delta II lit the sky, the Clinton administration is pushing ahead with other nukes in space. In September, the administration announced a national space policy that included the development of nuclear-propelled rockets for military and civilian uses. The Defense Special Weapons Agency will work on "multiple nuclear propulsion concepts" for military missions, while NASA's Marshall Space Flight Center's Advanced Concepts Division, along with Los Alamos National Laboratory, will develop propulsion for civilian uses.[43]

Meanwhile, at the 14th Symposium on Space Nuclear Power and Propulsion in Albuquerque in January, scientists from Brookhaven National Laboratory recycled a plan to rocket high-level nuclear waste into space.[44] The U.S. government had proposed this same scheme decades ago, but rejected it out of fear that an accident on launch or a fall back to Earth would douse the planet with atomic waste.

Recent events, says Gagnon, "show that despite all the claims by NASA and others, technology can fail, that spacecraft can fall out of the sky and burn up on reentry."[45] U.S. acknowledgment that radiation may well have been released over Chile and Bolivia when the Mars probe nose-dived back to Earth is tacit admission that safety systems are not foolproof.

NOTES

1. David L. Chandler, "Eyewitnesses in Chile Shed Light on Russian Probe's Spectacular Fall," *Boston Globe*, 5 December 1996, A2.

2. Chris Bryson, "How Safe Are Nuclear-Powered Space Missions?" *Christian Science Monitor*, 17 December 1996, 12.

3. Interview, February 1997.

4. Helen Caldicott, *Nuclear Madness* (New York: Norton, 1994), 81.

5. Interview, January 1997.

6. Interview, February 1997.

7. "Reentry of Russian Space Probe," statement by the Press Secretary, White House, 17 November 1996.

8. Associated Press, "Crippled Mars Probe Crashes Harmlessly to Earth in South Pacific Waters," 18 November 1996.

9. Cable News Network (CNN), 18 November 1996.

10. CNN, 17 November 1996.

11. Reuters, "Russians Try to Put Space Probe Back on Course," 17 November 1996.

12. Reuters, "Parts of Space Probe Could Hit Earth—TV," 17 November 1996.

13. Interview, November 1996. The Global Network (P.O. Box 90035, Gainesville, FL 32607, 352-468-3295) is leading the challenge to the Cassini launch and other planned space projects using nuclear power.

14. Brian Donaghy, "Mars Probe Crash Puts Australia on Red Alert," *Irish Times*, 18 November 1996, 1.

15. Associated Press, "Crippled Mars Probe," 18 November 1996.

16. Leonard David, "Mars 96 Mishap Highlights Weak Coordination," *Space News*, 20–26 January 1997, 18.

17. CNN, 17 November 1996.

18. Associated Press, "Russian Mars Probe Falls, Australians Were Ready to Duck, but It Hit Pacific," 18 November 1996.

19. "Russian Space Probe Crashes Near Australia," *Rossiiskiye Vesti*, 19 November 1996.

20. Veronika Romanenkova, "Russia Says Probe's Debris Poses No Threat to Any State," *ITAR-TASS*, 19 November 1996.

21. Paul Hoverstein, "U.S., Russia Differ by a Day on Crash of Mars 96 Probe," *USA Today*, 19 November 1996.

22. Xinhua News Agency, "Australia Calls Russian Rocket Crash 'Happy Ending,' " 18 November 1996.

23. David Hoffman and Peter Barker, "Errant Russian Spacecraft Crashes Harmlessly After Scaring Australia," *Washington Post*, 18 November 1996, A18.

24. "Update on Russian Space Probe," Directorate of Public Affairs, United States Space Command, Release no. 41–96, 29 November 1996.

25. Interview, January 1997.

26. David L. Chandler, "U.S. Said to Fumble Space Debris Alert," *Boston Globe*, 4 December 1996, 1.

27. Interviews with Barrera, January 1997; and Gordon Bendick, February 1997.

28. Interview, January 1997.

29. Reuters, "Russian Mars Craft Said to Have Fallen in Bolivia," *New York Times*, 14 December 1996, 7.

30. David, "Mars 96 Mishap."

31. Interview, February 1997.

32. Sergio Velásquez, "Por Eventual Caida de Sonda Rusa: Piden Investigar Posible Radiactividad en Norte," *El Mercurio* (Santiago, Chile), 3 January 1997, CO5; and Kristi Coale, "Chile Investigates Plutonium Threat," Wired News Stories, 3 January 1997.

33. Sergio Monivero Brunz, "Se Informo en Iquique: Sonda Rusa Cayo en Suelo Boliviano," *El Mercurio,* 13 December 1996, CO8; and interviews with Franklin Bustillos, press attaché, Bolivian Embassy, Washington, D.C., February 1997.

34. Interview, January 1997.

35. Todd Halvorson, "Delta 2 Rocket Explodes," *Florida Today,* 18 January 1997.

36. Frank Oliveri, "Residents Take Shelter from Toxic Cloud," *Florida Today,* 18 January 1997, 1; and interview with Bruce Gagnon, January 1997.

37. Interview, January 1997.

38. Interview, February 1997.

39. Keith Easthouse, "Radioactive Mishaps Rising at LANL," *New Mexican,* 29 July 1996, 1.

40. Ibid.

41. *Final Environmental Impact Statement for the Cassini Mission,* Solar System Exploration Division, Office of Space Science, NASA, June 1995, 4–51.

42. Ibid., 4–76.

43. Anne Eisele, "Nuclear Research Initiated, NASA's Marshall, Pentagon Advance Propulsion Concepts," *Space News,* 14–20 October 1996, 1.

44. Hiroshi Takahashi and An Yu, "Use of Ion Thrusters for Disposal of Type II Long Lived Fission Products into Outer Space," presentation at 14th Symposium on Space Nuclear Power and Propulsion, co-sponsored by Defense Special Weapons Agency, NASA, and the Department of Energy, 28 January 1997.

45. Interview, January 1997.

For Us All

KAY MACK

JULY 1997. NEAR MY ROCKY MOUNTAIN HOME

*I*t's hot, blazing hot. The dogs don't bark anymore; they pant, their sides heaving. Deer and elk shear every flower bud—even the poisonous ones—the very day we smile and call them *Bud*. Snow-melt rivers are thinner than usual, so are the forests, so are we, so are the Earth and its atmosphere.

It all began for me, this bonding with Earth Home, near the Himalayan headwaters of the holy Ganges, in India, when I was a boarding school fourth grader. From Woodstock School, I gazed at vast ranges of snow, razor-edged against unearthly blues—colors only angels could fathom. Thick ferns, nourished by monsoon rains, waved their welcome from host trees and shady nooks. Millennial lichen and tiny moss carpets dappled the rocks with a tapestry of greens. Meandering brooks burbled their canticles, joining the winds' cadences through oaks and evergreens. At night, the jackals tuned their ancient songs carefully, and long.

When the time came to leave my mountain homeland and return to my birthland America for college, I knelt in a corner of my favorite hideaway—Fairy Glen near Tehri road—and sang my farewell. Clutched in my hand was a marble of pine pitch whose scent for years reminded me of my Himalayan home.

FEBRUARY 1992. AUSTIN, TEXAS

My youngest daughter invited me to join her at a national conference on nuclear production, waste, and health-related issues.

Sponsored by a national organization, she and her barrel-chested dog, Gus, lived for a year in a tipi in the searing/freezing desert as caretakers of a fifteen-foot-by-fifteen-foot, straw bales and stucco, open-air peace place across the highway from the most nuked place on earth—the Nevada Nuclear Weapons Test Site. Visitors came from fifteen nations and most states to pray and to gaze in great sadness out over the land—birthright lands taken away from the Western Shoshone for purposes of testing weapons of death.

"Sure," I agreed, eager to share a five-day experience with her, the youngest of my grown daughters—all of whom are good friends.

Flying in on an "economy run," we arrived in Austin, hot, damp, hungry. We, people and organizations from six countries and half the states, gathered at our university conference site, where everything smelled faintly of paper, projectors, air conditioners, and old gum. After a cafeteria chicken salad sandwich, I found Room 30C. There, I waited with fifty other people behind two rows of rumpled faculty, maybe scientists. We murmured, rustled. It was really siesta time.

My eyes were closed when there was a sudden hush in the room. On the raised platform stood two men, both in black. Introductions were made. The younger man was "the university's best Russian Department student." The older man, around fifty, of sturdy six-foot build, ruggedly handsome and spectacled, was Dr. Vladimir Chernousenko, Russian physicist, who had assisted in the "cleanup" of Chornobyl (Russian spelling). The nuclear plant had experienced a horrific meltdown in 1986. He had just flown in from Europe. His face was drained white above his dark shirt.

Dr. Chernousenko spoke in a deep, resonant voice, rolled his words for emphasis, made earnest, sweeping gestures through the air. The interpreter's concentration was remarkable. He sat on the edge of his chair and gazed into the doctor's face as if to inhale his meanings.

We heard facts: The meltdown did not release 7 percent of highly radioactive materials, as our governments had reported. No! It was 70 percent or more. Treated as a hero at first, he was later run out of his homeland when he told the truth to physicists and doctors worldwide. Soils, waters, plants, animals, food chains were profoundly contaminated—especially in Belarus, Ukraine, Russia. Fallout had been detected as far away as Poland, Norway, Sweden. Much more radioactivity now was circling the Earth. Half of the cleanup workers were dead. Millions more were at risk in the next five to twenty years or more. Neurological, endocrine, and cardiovascular problems were considerably higher than usual, especially in children. Cases of leukemia, thyroid cancer, intestinal tract cancerous polyps were being found; weakened immune systems and genetic mutations were already showing up.

Yes! The protective wall built around the reactor was crumbling.

Yes! Many physicists around the world agreed that nuclear power plants should never be converted to alternate uses.

Yes! There was another source of energy, the sun, whose use should be mandatory.

Yes! It was too late in many respects. But there *was* hope! *Stop now!*

Was his life in danger? Silence. Then his suddenly hoarse voice answered.

"The doctors say I have three years . . . maybe." Our interpreter, voice barely above a whisper, choked out the words.

"Well, our time is up. Thank you, Dr. Chernousenko, for your informative presentation. You have given us a better grasp of the enormity of our nuclear problems," the white-haired moderator said matter-of-factly as she gathered up her briefcase.

Anger flashed across his face. He rose, trembling, hands raised, palms toward us, and spoke his first English words.

"You must *understand*! You must be *strong*! You must *work!*"

His words flung me out over an abyss of grief, of dread, where I could hear Earth, life, keening over itself. I was one of the voices. I walked through broken cloud cover for the rest of our conference days. Information flowed out in torrents from research, medical, and eyewitness accounts, and personal experiences. We heard:

—from Dr. Jay Gould about steeply increased numbers of breast cancer in women living downwind from nuclear power plants, and from Dr. Rosalie Bertell about no amount of radioactive exposure being "safe";

—a daughter's account of the involuntary plutonium injections given to her black father, who was one of twenty-three thousand victims of plutonium research during our government's secret 1950s research projects;

—radioactive, hazardous, toxic wastes consistently dumped in ethnic areas and American Indian lands, where the people were perceived, by some, to be less educated, less organized, less possessed of political and economic power—ethnic colonialism, they called it;

—toxic work sites where worker-mothers gave birth to malformed babies, some with no brains;

—antinuclear activists' properties and businesses purposely destroyed by fire, their pets poisoned or shot dead from helicopters, their families threatened;

—the United States routinely buying, or receiving by prior agreement, worldwide nuclear and toxic wastes;

—radioactive wastes leaking everywhere;

—fish so radioactive/toxic, they could not be caught or eaten—and so, gone, a whole people's way of life, source of food.

And so it dirged on.

At the final assembly, I yearned for some relief, some drop of joy, some meager note of celebration. But it was not to be. Mother of the Earth, Madre del Mundo, a four-foot white sculpture by Marcia Gomez, sat on the stage cradling the Earth. Members of the Clan of One-Breasted Women, a national organization of breast cancer survivors, read their poetry, danced their agony and survival.

As we left the auditorium, I stumbled into people, careened into walls, bumped into door frames. I could scarcely breathe.

FEBRUARY 1992. KYLE, TEXAS

The next morning, in the nearby country town where we had slept each night, Earth sang exuberantly in tones of jonquil yellow, pansy blue, in scents of fresh-cut grass and hay. Dandelions looked beatific in the early dew. Tall grasses graced a sagging footbridge under which flowed ribbons of ebullient water. Bees hummed million-year-old tunes. I could almost taste the beguiling wine our Montana friends had made from honey. In a little restaurant whose floors tilted into history, red-and-white-checked tablecloths and fresh-cut sweet peas made our breakfast memorable.

MARCH 1992. BACK TO WORK

Back home, apathy hung heavily upon me. My medical clinic and institute's administration work somehow continued. Bits and pieces of it occasionally tugged more insistently at my sleeves, and I tried to respond.

Finally, as I had done four years before, when I struggled for balance following an earlier grim ordeal—the burning, slashing, raping, stabbing of my second daughter by a prison parolee—I found my way to a huge bookstore. It was my favorite in-the-big-city thing to do when I couldn't get away to the mountains. There, with a borrowed headset and some meditative music, I hunkered down in worn, stuffed chairs in the Psychology, Geography & Travel, Gardening, Art, and Literature departments. I must have spent an hour in each, looking at book titles, chapters, pictures—letting the authors reach out to me, infuse me with their humor and wisdom. Finally, I held a book whose title carried the word *Yes*.

"Yes!" I said, looking at a breathtaking photograph of the Himalayas, and later, a lovely little child picking violets in an English cottage garden. "I'll not run away from what I now know. I'll gather more information, work for children, for the Earth, for all life. Yes!"

JUNE 1997. MIDMORNING COFFEE

Dear Dr. Chernousenko,
Your '92 presentation in Austin, Texas, affected me greatly. I accepted your challenge and have become a more dedicated nonviolent, antinuclear activist over the last five years. Sometimes, I do it well. At other times I withdraw, overwhelmed by what I now know of our immense and horrifying worldwide nuclearized life.

There are many who have worked for decades, lifetimes, and I marvel at how they keep going.

I've read magazines and research articles, books, newspapers; tracked worldwide computer Net information; attended conferences, seminars, gatherings; viewed videos and documentaries; made donations; sent letters/faxes/E-mail to federal, state, local officials; given testimony at regional Department of Energy meetings; written and published poetry and prose; given speeches; photographed and distributed color-print postcards of a self-designed glass sculpture—the actual size of the hold-in-the-palm-of-your-hand plutonium triggers used in nuclear bombs. A butterfly—symbol of love and hope—rests lightly on the trigger top.

My profound thanks for your courage and your appeal to us all—to understand, to be strong, and to work.

Sincerely . . .

JUNE 1997. THROUGH THE WINDOW ON A RAINY DAY

I remember one young classmate of mine at the Colorado Institute of Art telling me that he assembled plutonium bomb triggers—" 'pits' in 'glove boxes' at Rocky Flats, near Denver."

"Pits are the fission triggers of a nuclear bomb," he explained, looking blankly into space. It was 1985, and I understood very little of what he was saying. Now, I wonder if he is well or even alive.

Some bright and caring people, upon hearing even a shred of nuclear information, deny the problems, shrug, laugh nervously, walk away. Their eyes glass over. Sometimes, they rage at me.

"Surely our government would not so dupe or endanger us," they shout, throwing their hands into the air.

To stay solvent and sane, I work a regular job that pays my bills; and I journal, cry, pray, sing, laugh, dance, and soar in spirit with my Himalayan eagles. And I act.

AUGUST 1997. NEAR THE RUSHES AT THE EDGE OF THE LAKE

Midafternoon mountain rain patters on my poncho. A slow smile pushes at the edge of my cinched hood as I remember all those monsoons in India. Capillaries of water rush to join rivulets, streams. Crowds of drops pelt the still surface of the lake, marking the spots under which fish might be lazing.

Back from their forays, the geese are gathering for the night. Their fluffed feathers curve into the rising wind like Egyptian papyrus boats of old. I remember Thor Heyerdahl's brave ocean voyage in his fragile *Kon-Tiki*.

Now I sail, fragile but determined, upon murky waters into unknown places where nuclear problems, both present and future, lurk like hideous sea monsters. It's a difficult voyage, this information-gathering, this understanding of the big picture, this work.

NOVEMBER 1998

O, dear heart
must
we now know these things?
must we?

A GLIMPSE AT THE BIG PICTURE—1999

Sixteen-year-old Hillary Kautter wrote to her President: "I belong to a group called The Nuclear Age Peace Foundation . . . I am scared . . . I am afraid of the dark, because I wonder what it's like to never see light. . . . I am afraid of choking. I need fresh air to breathe and live in. . . . I want to live my life to its full extent, and I want everyone around me—and everyone that comes after me—to do the same. A world with nuclear war is a horrible, terrifying place to be. I know—I have seen it in my nightmares many times.[1]

Valerie L. Kuletz, professor and author, writes: " . . . [the] commercial industry legitimates its [nuclear] involvement by claiming a desire to use nuclear power to fuel 'national competitiveness' . . . the military legitimates its involvement through claiming a desire to maintain 'national security.' . . . The scientific community legitimates its involvement by donning the cloak of neutrality . . . and arguing that not to research and develop nuclear technology somehow violates a basic human imperative to pursue knowledge."[2]

OUR RADIOACTIVE "WARS"—HOT, COLD, WASTES, COSTS

Our fifty years of "Hot War," since the creation of the atomic/nuclear bombs, roll on. In the last fifty years, we, the brains and brawn of the world, have continued to pound unrelentingly upon ourselves, upon all that lives. We have poisoned our oceans, rivers, lakes, aquifers, ground-waters, soils,[3] atmosphere, and stratosphere through accidents, purposeful dumping, and leakage. We have destroyed our organs, bones, tissues, immune systems, and, most agonizingly, compromised our genetic pools.

As though in a Dr. Jekyll trance—a kind of psychic numbing[4]—we have managed to dig, like prairie dogs, thousands of uranium mines,[5] to develop hundreds of long-lived radioactive materials[6]—including plutonium-239, uranium-235 and -238, iodine-131, strontium-90, cesium-134 and -137—whose lethal radioactivity will exist for 12,500 to 450,000,000 human generations (one generation=20 years).[7] (By comparison, the 250-generation pyramids and 175-generation Stonehenge are mere infants.)

NUCLEAR WEAPONS AND TESTING

We have built 70,000 nuclear weapons[8] and produced 104 metric tons of plutonium and 994 metric tons of highly enriched uranium.[9] Every four to five years we're making about as much plutonium in the civil sector—mostly nuclear power plants—as we did during the whole Cold War.[10] We have exploded 429.9 tons into the atmosphere; of that amount, 244 tons in 1961–1962 alone. This one-year amount is the equivalent of 16,250 Hiroshima-size bombs.[11]

"The [first] five acknowledged nuclear states possess about 36,000 nuclear warheads . . . of which 22,000 are still active and operational."[12] And 2,051 nuclear tests were conducted by seven nuclear states (1945–1998). The United States and Soviet Union accounted for 85 percent.[13]

Ironically, the United States is the most nuclear-bombed nation in the world.[14] The list includes 935 in Nevada, three in Alaska,[15] three in New Mexico, two in Mississippi, two in Colorado. Of those tests, 528 were conducted in the atmosphere.[16] Radioactive fallout has been found in virtually every state of the United States.[17]

Among the many dire nuclear threats to life must be added, for instance, the catastrophic risks associated with waste tank explosions. The 1957 explosion at Chelyabinsk-65, in Russia, is considered to be the Chernobyl of nuclear weapons production. The tank exploded with a force estimated at seventy-one hundred metric tons of TNT. "In the

United States, tanks at the Savannah River Site contain much more long-lived radioactivity than the Chelyabinsk-65 tank, since cesium-137 is not removed. . . . Therefore, it poses dangers of both external and internal radiation [of the body]."[18]

COMMERCIAL POWER PLANTS

Commercial nuclear fission began, and was pursued, only because government leaders wanted to justify continuing military expenditures in nuclear-related areas and to obtain weapons-grade plutonium.[19] In the private sector, the United States has built 110 commercial nuclear power plants—all of which produce plutonium as a normal part of the fissioning process. Plutonium and/or highly enriched uranium are essential ingredients of nuclear bombs. One hundred five plants are currently active,[20] but aging. All reactor types, developed or designed, pose some level of risk for catastrophic accidents similar to Chernobyl. In its rush to build these reactors, the nuclear industry put development and propaganda before public safety, health, environmental protection, and even economics.[21]

Major sources of nuclear waste[22] are commercial nuclear reactors' electricity production and military plants' weapons development, production, and testing.[23]

RADIOACTIVE WASTE CLASSIFICATIONS

Our current radioactive waste classifications are inappropriately defined, fundamentally flawed, irrational, and incoherent, according to the Institute for Energy and Environmental Research.[24] Classifications are based on the origin of the waste, instead of on the physical or chemical properties that determine the hazards of the waste, and hence its safe and proper management. "Low-level waste" sometimes contains materials more radioactive than "high-level waste."[25]

The most intensely radioactive material on Earth lies in the fuel rods of commercial nuclear power plants. It accounts for 95 percent of the radioactivity generated in the last fifty years from all sources. When removed from the reactor core, the spent fuel rods are about one million times more radioactive than when they were originally loaded.[26]

The Department of Energy (DOE) is responsible for managing some thirty-six million cubic meters of radioactive and hazardous wastes at 137 U.S. sites. Weapons production and related activities have contaminated seventy-nine million cubic meters of soil and almost two billion cubic meters of groundwater.[27]

COSTS

Nuclear-related U.S. costs are astronomical—$6 trillion—to develop, deploy, test, and retire nuclear weapons and their associated delivery systems.[28] Cleanup estimates run from $100 billion to $1 trillion.[29]

THE BACK END OF THE NUCLEAR FUEL CYCLE

"Early on, chemists and chemical engineers were not interested in dealing with waste. It was not glamorous; there were no careers in that field; it was messy; there was no real profit in dealing with the back-end of the fuel cycle."[30]

Killer radioactive wastes—rad wastes—lie in/under/upon/above virtually all life on Earth.[31] They lurk in cracks, crevices, "sealed" rooms, air ducts, pipes, leaking storage containers, soils, and groundwaters[32] near and downwind from[33] our nuclear weapons plants,[34] research labs, power plants. They leak from aboveground and underground holding tanks.[35] They leach into our waterways, travel through our soils, ride the "hides" of radioactive insects.[36] They are mixed into fertilizers[37] and are reprocessed for nuclear weapons or nuclear reactor fuel.[38]

Hundreds of sites, nationwide, are thought to be so radioactively damaged that cleanup, even if such technologies existed, would be impossible. The list of these "national sacrifice zones" is growing.

HOW CLEAN IS "CLEAN"?

Let's talk about Soil Action Levels (SALs) and Standards, since they are the closest thing we have to an official definition of "clean." SALs specify the amount of plutonium and other radioactive materials, in picocuries (a measure of radiation), that may legally remain in each gram of soil after the cleanup of a site is supposedly finished. Once "approved" SALs are met, lands can be used by unsuspecting citizens for recreation, business, and residential needs.

Here's a 1999 example. SALs for our 1955 Pacific bomb test site=40; Hanford Nuclear Reservation (Washington)=34; Nevada Test Site=200; and Rocky Flats Plant (Colorado), a now-closed plutonium trigger production plant=1429. This would be thirty-six thousand times higher than the already arrived fallout from the atmosphere (0.04 picocurie/ gram of soil).[39] Local citizen concern and action continue regarding this enormous threat that could be repeated elsewhere.

OUR HEALTH

In spite of many disclosures that have been made in the last decade, not much is known about radioactive assaults on our health[40] because of "mismanagement, safety violations, environmental contamination, nuclear accidents, unsafe working conditions, equipment failures at weapons plants, faulty radiation dose record-keeping, secrecy, a focus on deaths rather than illness, and the lack of long-term follow up."[41] Increasingly disturbing information has been/is being collected about the health of uranium miners,[42] nuclear plant workers,[43] and "regular" citizens in the surrounding, or downwind, communities.[44]

Dr. Dudley Goodhead, Director of Britain's Medical Research Council, reports that "[I]f one cell gets [a radioactive] alpha particle, there is a finite . . . chance of that cell becoming cancerous. . . . A single alpha particle may be carcinogenic."[45] The U.S. Department of Energy estimates that as little as one ten-millionth of a curie of plutonium, if inhaled, can cause cancer.

According to recent studies, small doses of radiation over long periods of time are no less severe than massive one-time doses. Long-term effects of chronic exposure to radiation are cancer, reproductive failure, birth defects, genetic defects, and death.[46]

It is now said that no level of exposure is safe.[47]

On August 1, 1997, the National Cancer Institute revealed that as a result of U.S. nuclear tests (mostly 1951–1958) conducted in the atmosphere at the Nevada Test Site, radioactive iodine-131 fallout had rained down on virtually everyone living in the United States. Hot spots occurred over large portions of the Midwest, parts of New England, and areas east and northeast of the Test Site—Idaho, Montana, and the Dakotas. Ten thousand to seventy-five thousand excess thyroid cancers are predicted.[48]

AUGUST 1998. LYING ON A MOUNTAINSIDE

Stars fling galaxies of laughter across dark meadows.
Come play with us
Leap lithe and strong upon the plains of infinity.

WHY DIDN'T WE KNOW?

"The public has tolerated nuclearism . . . because it has been kept in abysmal ignorance and deliberately deceived. Archival material was classified as secret, environmental and dosimetric data were kept poorly, journalists were fed slanted intelligence, and public relations pros spewed propaganda to soothe an anxious citizenry."[49]

"George Orwell wrote about the role of language in shaping understanding . . . our world view . . . our system of beliefs. . . . Language and mindset continually reinforce each other."[50] So we have been tranquilized through the "engineering" of emotionally sterile, value-palatable words that some have labeled "nukespeak."[51] Here are some examples:

—atomic bombs are "projectile units";
—millions of dead people are "megadeaths";
—bomb-destroyed areas are "units taken out";
—target bombings are "surgical strikes";
—missing plutonium or uranium is a "random measurement error";
—nuclear weapons accidents are "broken arrows" or "bent spears";[52]
—Three Mile Island's partial nuclear reactor meltdown was "a normal aberration";
—the Chornobyl meltdown was a "unique event, on a scale by itself";
—current activities in design and testing programs, leading to a new class of thermonuclear weapons, are "Stockpile Stewardship Programs."[53]

WHAT SOME LEADING VOICES HAVE SAID

Our technical civilization has just reached its greatest level of savagery.—Albert Camus, 1945[54]

Early on, physicist Niels Bohr said that the Super Bomb could never be made without turning the U.S. into one huge factory. Years later, he said that we had done just that.—Laura Frank[55]

Nuclear weapons are inherently dangerous, hugely expensive, militarily inefficient, and morally indefensible.—General Lee Butler, former Commander, Strategic Air Command, 1996[56]

The proposition that nuclear weapons can be retained in perpetuity and never used—accidentally or by decision—defies credibility. The only complete defence is the elimination of nuclear weapons and assurance that they will never be produced again.—Canberra Commission on the Elimination of Nuclear Weapons[57]

It is up to . . . us to determine whether we have the courage to ensure that Chornobyl is the last gasp of a dying nuclear age, or whether Chornobyl is the future of a damaged, dying Earth.—Michael Mariotte, Director of the Nuclear Information Service[58]

THE PLEA FROM MILLIONS

I am persuaded that in every corner of the planet, the tide of public sentiment is now running strongly in favor of diminishing the role of nuclear weapons. . . . I am convinced that most [of the] public are well out in front of governments.—General Lee Butler[59]

International peace and disarmament organizations' and individuals' efforts have resulted in

—the 1968 Nuclear Non-Proliferation Treaty's 1995 Review and Extension Conference;
—the Comprehensive Test Ban Treaty;
—the International Court of Justice's opinion;[60]
—the International Court of Justice's 1996 decision regarding the illegality of testing, use, or threat of use of nuclear weapons;

—the twelve hundred nongovernmental organizations' Abolition 2000 Initiative;

—the seventeen-state Canberra Commission for the Elimination of Nuclear Weapons;

—the eight-state New Agenda Coalition and its Joint Ministerial Declaration.[61]

AND YET . . . AND YET . . . IT CONTINUES

In 1946, Albert Einstein said, "The unleashed power of the atom has changed everything save our modes of thinking, and thus we drift toward unparalleled catastrophe."[62]

The United States has been a signatory of many historic international treaties and promises, yet numbers of new weapons—warheads, missiles, and more—are in the pipeline.[63] Advances in precision-strike weapon capabilities have been made. U.S. forces [now] "may be able to engage 1,500 targets in the first hour, if not the first minutes, of a conflict."[64]

Since 1997, U.S. research labs have detonated six subcritical underground nuclear plutonium tests at the Nevada Test Site.[65]

The military and civilian sectors are soon to be overtly linked. Commercial nuclear power plants are now to be used for military purposes—to produce mixed-oxide (MOX)[66] fuel and tritium,[67] an essential "enhancer" for nuclear bomb triggers.

Work proceeds on a thirteen-year, $60 billion "Stockpile Stewardship Program" designed to underwrite a number of nuclear weapons research, development, testing, and production programs leading to the next generation of thermonuclear weapons.[68] One of the many programs that clearly violate the Comprehensive Test Ban Treaty—signed by 150 countries, including the United States—is the California-based National Ignition Facility (NIF), a $2.2 billion complex (about the size of the Rose Bowl) due to be completed by 2002. Laser beams are to create thermonuclear explosions by beaming a titanic bolt of energy onto a tiny pellet of hydrogen fuel. The heat generated would be hotter than the surface of the sun and would cause the hydrogen atoms to fuse into helium in a burst of pure fusion energy.[69]

Suddenly from the rim of the moon, in long, slow-motion moments of immense majesty, there emerges a sparkling blue and white jewel, a light delicate sky-blue sphere laced with slowly swirling veils of white, rising gradually like a small pearl in the thick sea of black mystery. It takes more than a moment to fully realize this is Earth . . . Home.[70]

WE MUST BE THE CHANGE WE WISH TO SEE IN THE WORLD[71]

We must

- —stop routine venting of radioactive materials directly into the atmosphere;[72]
- —stop unsafe burning of wastes;[73]
- —stop unsafe containerization and recontainerization of wastes in thus far poorly tested, dangerous casks that supposedly are to last an impossible one hundred to ten thousand years . . . and longer;[74]
- —stop the transportation (and inevitable accidents) of wastes in trucks, trains, boats, and barges over millions of U.S. highway, track, and waterway miles, through almost all the U.S. states;[75]
- —stop "shallow" dumping of wastes on unlined trenches—sure to leak—at the Nevada Test Site;[76] Ward Valley, California;[77] Sierra Blanca, Texas;[78] and many other sites, both known and unknown to U.S. citizens;
- —stop deep vault and tunnel, out-of-sight-out-of-mind, geologically/seismically unsound, irretrievable waste burial in sites— challenged by hundreds of environmental, scientific, and anti-nuclear groups—such as the Waste Isolation Pilot Project (WIPP) near Carlsbad, New Mexico,[79] and at Yucca Mountain, Nevada, where ten miles of waste burial tunnels are to be gouged out of this Western Shoshone sacred site;[80]
- —stop private dump sites;
- —stop the reprocessing of radioactive wastes into MOX;[81]
- —stop the reprocessing of radioactive materials to make more tritium, a nuclear bomb trigger "enhancer";[82]
- —stop the Stockpile Stewardship Program[s], including the National Ignition Facility;[83]

—connect with nuclear-concerned organizations near you. Their newsletters, bulletins, magazines, and well-researched books are very helpful;

—promote the twelve Cleanup and Waste Management Recommendations suggested by the Institute for Energy and Environmental Research.[84]

Here are some of the Cleanup and Waste Management Recommendations:

1. Create a new . . . environmentally-protective system of radioactive waste classification. . . .

4. Suspend the politically expedient Yucca Mountain and WIPP repository programs. . . .

5. Provide funds and technical support to communities that have residual contamination so that they can monitor the environment and keep themselves informed. . . .

9. If sound remediation technologies are not available . . . make investments in research and development. . . .

10. Make public all information that was created at taxpayer expense relating to health and the environment . . . [with] explicit public right to this information. . . .

11. Impose stringent financial accountability on the contractors and institute engineering-based methods to review. . . .

12. Create national clean-up standards that allow state and local governments and Indian tribes to apply stricter clean-up standards. . . .

ALL THIS WORK, DOES IT DO ANY GOOD? YES!

Citizens' actions have led to closed nuclear sites, blocked radioactive dump sites, stopped nuclear production and transportation, litigation, agencies fined, revoked licenses, raised safety standards, medical training, health testing, antinuclear media programs, and more.

JULY 1998. SITTING NEAR A MAGNIFICENT PONDEROSA PINE

The news is that Dr. Chernousenko died some while ago from Chornobyl-induced brain cancer. He has joined the Earth's millions felled by radioactivity. Hopefully, he was spared infernal pain, and his spirit has found eternal peace.

If his address had been available, I would have sent him my letter and the last verse of a poem I wrote.

> Peace is a just and jarring journey of small steps
> and great leaps toward sacred places, times,
> when Earth and all Life become
> Beloved.

JANUARY 1999

The night sky, ablaze above and below, upon the quiet lake waters.

O, our exquisite Earth Carl Sagan called *Pale Blue Dot* in the heavens. From this tranquil mountain lake I see *Blue Dot*'s sky draped in majestic trains of vermilion and magenta all shafting through layers of wisteria, indigo, and goldenrod.

O, the sunrise light from thousands/thousands, growing in awareness and moral determination.

> I pray daily for clarity and courage,
> for all those who choose to understand, to be strong, to act,
> and
> For Us All.

NOTES

1. Hillary Kautter, "Dear Mr. President," *Waging Peace Worldwide: Journal of the Nuclear Age Peace Foundation* (Summer 1998): 15.

2. Valerie L. Kuletz, *The Tainted Desert: Environmental and Social Ruin in the American West* (New York: Routledge, 1998), 16–17.

3. For instance, 750,000 gallons of high-level waste have leaked into the soil from Hanford, Washington, tanks. A typical U.S. tank holds about one million gallons. Arjun Makhijani, Howard Hu, and Katherine Yih, eds., *Nuclear Wastelands: A Global Guide to Nuclear Weapons Production and Its Health and Environmental Effects* (Cambridge, Mass.: MIT Press, 1995), 53–55.

4. Psychologist Robert Jay Lifton believes that " . . . nuclear weapons have generated a worldwide psychological health crisis of massive proportions, an epidemic of psychic numbing." Ira Chernus, *Nuclear Madness: Religion and the*

Psychology of the Nuclear Age (New York: State University of New York Press, 1991), 9.

5. "Peak Number of Operating Domestic Uranium Mines (1955)," in "50 Facts About U.S. Nuclear Weapons," *The U.S. Nuclear Weapons Cost Study Project,* Brookings Institution, Internet posting, 24 November 1998.

6. Fissile materials are composed of atoms that can be split by neutrons in a self-sustaining chain reaction to release enormous amounts of energy. In nuclear reactors, the fission process is controlled and the energy is harnessed to produce electricity. In nuclear weapons, the fission energy is released at once to produce a violent explosion. The most important fissile materials for nuclear energy and nuclear weapons are plutonium-239 and uranium-235. See "Fissile Material Basics," Institute for Energy and Environmental Research (IEER), 21 March 1996; Internet posting, 20 November 1998.

7. Ibid.

8. Arjun Makhijani and Marc Fioravanti, "Cleaning Up the Cold War Mess," *Science for Democratic Action* (Institute for Energy and Environmental Research) (January 1999): 1.

9. "Fissile Material Basics."

10. Kuletz, *Tainted Desert,* 82.

11. Robert S. Norris and William M. Arkin, "Known Nuclear Tests Worldwide, 1945–98," *Bulletin of the Atomic Scientists* (November/December 1998): 67.

12. Robert S. Norris and William M. Arkin, "Global Nuclear Stockpiles, 1945–1997," *Bulletin of the Atomic Scientists* (November/December 1997): 67.

13. Norris and Arkin, "Known Nuclear Tests Worldwide," 65.

14. Kuletz, *Tainted Desert,* 70.

15. "A comprehensive critical assessment of pathways and exposure routes of radiological and toxic contamination of Amchitka is urgently needed. . . . EPA should place Amchitka Island on the Superfund National Priorities List to ensure maximum public oversight of cleanup." Pam Miller, "Expedition to Amchitka Island, Alaska—Site of the Largest Underground Nuclear Test in U.S. History," *A Greenpeace Report,* 30 October 1996; Internet posting, 24 November 1998.

16. Norris and Arkin, "Known Nuclear Tests," 67.

17. Pat Ortmeyer and Arjun Makhijani, "Worse Than We Knew," *Bulletin of the Atomic Scientists* (November/December 1997): 47.

18. "The Savannah River Site . . . tanks contain much more long-lived radioactivity than . . . the Chelyabinsk-65 tank, since cesium-137 is not removed. Cesium-137 is not only a beta emitter; it also emits gamma radiation . . . it poses

dangers of both external and internal radiation." Makhijani et al., *Nuclear Wastelands,* 55, 56.

19. Kuletz, *Tainted Desert,* 17.

20. "U.S. Nuclear Power Plant Performance," *Nuclear Energy Institute,* Internet posting, 11 December 1998.

21. Arjun Makhijani, "Nuclear Power: No Solution to Global Climate Change," *Science for Democratic Action* (Institute for Energy and Environmental Research) (March 1998): 1.

22. Kuletz, *Tainted Desert,* 16.

23. Some of the nuclear weapons plants and research facilities are Lawrence Livermore National Laboratory, Livermore, California; Rocky Flats Plant, Colorado; Idaho National Engineering Laboratory; Paducah Gaseous Diffusion Plant, Kentucky; Fernald Feed Materials Production Center, Ohio; Mound Plant, Ohio; Portsmouth Gaseous Diffusion Plant, Ohio; Los Alamos National Laboratory, New Mexico; Sandia, New Mexico; Brookhaven National Laboratory, New York; Oak Ridge Reservation, Tennessee; Pantex Plant, Texas; Hanford Nuclear Reservation, Washington. Other listings can be found in Kuletz, *Tainted Desert,* 41–47.

24. Pat Ortmeyer, "Radioactive Waste: The Regulatory Mess," *Science for Democratic Action* (Institute for Energy and Environmental Research) (May 1997): 8–17.

25. Ibid., 8.

26. Mary Olson, "High-Level Radioactive Waste," Nuclear Information and Resource Service fact sheet, January 1995; Internet posting, 11 May 1998.

27. Makhijani and Fioravanti, "Cleaning Up the Cold War Mess," 1.

28. Chuck Hansen, "Not Available in Stores, U.S. Nuclear History: Nuclear Arms and Policy in the Missile Age, 1955–1968," *Bulletin of the Atomic Scientists* (November/December 1998): 60.

29. Makhijani and Fioravanti, "Cleaning Up the Cold War Mess," 1.

30. Carroll Wilson, "Wanted: Sound Radioactive Waste Management Policy," *Science for Democratic Action* (Institute for Energy and Environmental Research) (May 1997): 1.

31. Makhijani et al., *Nuclear Wastelands,* xx.

32. "Groundwater Movement of Radioactive Material Faster Than Thought," *American Chemical Society,* 13 November 1998; Internet posting, 16 November 1998.

33. Kuletz, *Tainted Desert,* 44–45.

34. Ibid., 51. "The Hanford Site . . . along the Columbia River is perhaps the most polluted place in the Western world. Russia's plant near Chelyabinsk may

be the most radioactively contaminated area on Earth." Makhijani et al., *Nuclear Wastelands,* xiv.

35. "High-Level Waste Tanks at Hanford," *Science for Democratic Action* (Institute for Energy and Environmental Research) (January 1999): 5.

36. Kuletz, *Tainted Desert,* 51. See also Nancy Visser, "Research, Medicine and Environment," *Rocky Mountain News,* 19 October 1998.

37. Stephen Hiltgartner, Richard C. Bell, and Rory O'Connor, *Nukespeak: The Selling of Nuclear Technology in America* (New York: Penguin Books, 1983), 44.

38. Gururaj Mutalik and Timothy Takaro, "Physicians Call on President Clinton to Abandon Plans to Re-Use Military Plutonium," Internet posting, 27 November 1990. See also Daryl Kimbal, "Ending Nuclear Materials 'Reprocessing,'" *Nuclear Security Program,* January 1997; Internet posting, 19 November 1997.

39. LeRoy Moore, "Cleanup of Rocky Flats," *Boulder Daily Camera,* 27 September 1998.

40. Terje Langeland, "How Clean Is Clean?" *Colorado Daily,* 26 October 1998.

41. Pat Ortmeyer, "Fissile Materials, Health and Environmental Dangers," *Institute for Energy and Environmental Research,* 21 March 1996; Internet posting, 20 November 1998.

42. Arjun Makhijani and Bernd Franke, "Worker Radiation Dose Records Deeply Flawed," *Science for Democratic Action* (Institute for Energy and Environmental Research) (November 1997): 1–7.

43. Makhijani et al., *Nuclear Wastelands,* 72.

44. Makhijani and Franke, "Worker Radiation Dose Records Deeply Flawed," 1–7.

45. International Physicians for the Prevention of Nuclear War (IPPNW) emerged in the early 1980s to educate the public on the consequences of nuclear war and nuclearism. Recipient of the Nobel Peace Prize in 1985, it now has a constituency of 200,000 health workers in 83 countries. IPPNW and IEER have issued two books, *Radioactive Heaven and Earth* (Takoma Park, Md.: IERR, 1991) and *Plutonium: Deadly Gold of the Nuclear Age* (Takoma Park, Md.: IERR, 1992). See also "Health Effects of Ionizing Radiation (HEIR) Reports," *Committee for Nuclear Responsibility,* Internet posting, 11 September 1998. The first two HEIR reports were *Radiation-Induced Cancer from Low-Dose Exposure: An Independent Analysis* (1990; updated 1998), and *Preventing Breast Cancer: The Story of a Major, Proven, Preventable Cause of This Disease* (1996, 1998). See also "Bio-Medical 'Un-Knowledge' and Nuclear Pollution: A Common-Sense Pro-

posal," Gofman's speech on the acceptance of the 1992 Right Livelihood Award in Stockholm, for his pioneering work in exposing the health effects of low-level radiation; Sam Miller, "Why Should I Be Involved in Monitoring the Local Nuke?" *Downwinders' Page*, Critical Information Project, CNR/HEIR Reports; Internet posting, 9 November 1998; and Tricia Pritikin: "Preserving the Health Histories," *Waging Peace Worldwide. Journal of the Nuclear Age Peace Foundation* (Fall/Winter) 1997): 10–11. "A new study suggests higher levels of radiation were released during the 1979 Three Mile Island-2 accident than so far revealed. . . . leukemia and lung cancer rates downwind of TMI were five to ten times higher than upwind." Dr. Steven Wing conducted a reevaluation of the Columbia University Three Mile Island study and discovered that people living closer to the path of the escaping radiation cloud developed all cancer types more frequently. Lung cancer and leukemia rates were two or three times higher than they were near the plant but upwind from the plumes. Among those in the most direct path of the plumes, lung cancer incidence was elevated by 300 to 400 percent, and leukemia rates were up by 600 to 700 percent. "The Wing Study Re-examines TMI Accident Cancer," *NIRS Nuclear Monitor,* Inernet posting, 29 May 1999.

46. "No Radiation Dose Safe, Study Says," *Boston Globe,* 20 November 1997. Posted on Internet by Robert Schaeffer, Public Policy Communications, Belmont, Mass., July. 1998.

47. Kuletz, *Tainted Desert,* 85.

48. Rosalie Bertell, Ph.D, "Limitations of the ICRP Recommendations for Worker and Public Protection from Ionizing Radiation: Survey and Evaluation of Criticism of Basic Safety Standards for the Protection of Workers and the Public Against Ionizing Radiation," presented at STOA Workshop, European Parliament, Brussels, 5 February 1998. See also Ian Fairlie and Marvin Reshikoff, "No Dose Too Low," *Bulletin of the Atomic Scientists* (November/December 1997): 52–56.

49. Ortmeyer, "Worse Than We Knew," 47.

50. Makhijani et al., *Nuclear Wastelands,* xv.

51. Hiltgartner et al, *Nukespeak,* xiii–xiv.

52. Ibid., xiii–xiv, 36, 50, 65, 125, 159, 169, 172, 174, 209.

53. There were 44 nuclear weapons "accidents," according to the Air Force and Department of Energy (1950–1980); 12, according to the Navy (1959–1984). A total of 563 nuclear "incidents" were reported by the Navy (1965–1983). No public information is available about nuclear weapons accidents involving the Army. Jaya Tiwara and Cleve J. Gray, "U.S. Nuclear Weapons Accidents," *Center for Defense Information,* Internet posting, 24 November 1998.

54. Andrew Koch, "Selected Nuclear Quotations," *Center for Defense Information*, Internet posting, 24 November 1998.

55. Laura Frank, "Cleanup as Challenging as Building Bomb," in *The Tennesseean: Special Report—An Investigation into Illnesses Around the Nation's Nuclear Weapons Sites*, 10 February 1997; Internet posting dated 19 November 1998.

56. Koch, "Selected Nuclear Quotations."

57. Linda Pentz, "Not One Cent, Red or Otherwise," *Bulletin of the Atomic Scientists* (November/December 1997): 64.

58. Michael Mariotte, "Chernobyl Diary 1996. This Is How the World Ends . . . ," *NIRS: The Nuclear Monitor*, Internet posting dated 30 October 1998.

59. General Lee Butler, "The Risks of Nuclear Deterrence: From Superpowers to Rogue Leaders," speech at National Press Club, 2 February 1998.

60. "Nuclear Weapons Are Illegal! World Court Issues Landmark Opinion," *NGO Committee on Disarmament*, 8 July 1996; Internet posting, 24 November 1998.

61. David Krieger, "Open Letter to President Clinton," *Waging Peace Worldwide* (Summer 1998): 3.

62. Hiltgartner et al., *Nukespeak*, 1.

63. William M. Arkin, "What's 'New'?" *Bulletin of the Atomic Scientists* (November/December 1997): 23.

64. Andrew F. Krepinevich and Steven Kosiak, "Smarter Bombs, Fewer Nukes," *Bulletin of the Atomic Scientists* (November/December 1998): 26–31.

65. Plutonium is blown up with chemical explosives 1,000 feet below the Nevada desert without causing a chain reaction—and hence is called subcritical. Stanley K. Sheinbaum and Alice Slater, "It's Time to Abolish Nuclear Arms—It's Too Late Merely to Control Them," *Waging Peace Worldwide: Journal of the Nuclear Age Peace Foundation* (Summer 1998): 11.

66. Nuclear Information and Resource Service, *What Is MOX?* (Washington, D.C., 1996).

67. Hisham Zeffriffi, "Tritium: The Environmental, Health, Budgetary and Strategic Effects of the Department of Energy's Decision to Produce Tritium," *Institute for Energy and Research*, Internet posting, 20 November 1998.

68. Brad Morse, "Stockpile Stewardship Resolution," *Alliance for Nuclear Accountability*, Internet posting, 17 December 1998.

69. William J. Broad, "Fusion Research Effort Draws Fire," *IERR Study on Weapons Development*, Internet Posting, 16 July 1998.

70. Edgar Mitchell, in Kevin W. Kelley, ed., *The Home Planet* (Reading, Mass.: Addison-Wesley, 1988), 42–43.

71. *Waging Peace Worldwide* (Summer 1998): front cover.

72. Kuletz, *Tainted Desert*, 70.

73. "Incineration of Radioactive and Mixed Waste," *Institute for Energy and Environmental Research,* August 1996; Internet posting, 20 November 1998.

74. Mary Olson, "Multi-purpose Canisters," *Radioactive Waste Project,* January 1995; Internet posting, 5 November 1998. See also Diane D'Arrigo, "Low-Level Radioactive Waste," *NIRS Fact Sheet,* March 1992; Internet posting, November 1998; and "NRC Warns Sierra Nuclear on Faulty Casks," *NIRS Monoline,* Internet posting, 30 October 1998.

75. "Radioactive Waste Transportation," *Radioactive Waste Management Associates,* New York, January 1995; Internet posting, 5 November 1998. See also "It Takes a Police State to Move a Waste Cask," *NIRS Report,* 1998; Internet posting, 5 November 1998.

76. Kuletz, *Tainted Desert,* 128.

77. "Save Ward Valley," *NIRS Monoline,* Internet posting, 30 October 1998.

78. Bill Addington, "President Clinton Pulls Trigger on Minority Community: OK's Sending Radioactive Waste to Texas Border," *NIRS Monoline,* 22 September 1998; Internet posting, 13 December 1998. See also Diane D'Arrigo, "Sierra Blanca License Denied!" *NIRS Monoline,* 26 October 1998.

79. LeRoy Moore, "Camera Was Wrong about WIPP," *Boulder Daily Camera,* 13 June, 1998. See also "WIPP: No Solution for Radioactive Waste Danger for Colorado," fact sheet, Rocky Mountain Peace and Justice Center, June 1998.

80. Michael Mariotte, "Dump Yucca Mountain," *Nuclear Information and Resource Service,* 18 November 1998; Internet posting, 25 November 1998.

81. "DOE Prepared to Approve Use of MOX Fuel," *NIRS,* November 1996; Internet posting, 5 November 1998. Reprocessing operations—both civilian and military—can be dangerous to workers, the public, and the environment. Accidental criticalities can occur. Makhijani et al., *Nuclear Wastelands,* 53.

82. "Dear President Clinton," *Physicians for Social Responsibility,* 28 July 1998; Internet posting, 19 November 1998. See also Rachel Zoll, "Tennessee Valley Authority to Make Tritium for Bombs at Power Reactor," *Boulder Daily Camera,* 23 December 1998.

83. Brad Morse, "Stockpile Stewardship Resolution," *Alliance for Nuclear Accountability,* 17 December 1998; Internet posting, 18 December 1998.

84. Makhijani and Fioravanti," Cleaning Up the Cold War Mess."

PART III

Beyond Despair

Baring the Atom's Mother Heart

MARILOU AWIAKTA

"What is the atom, Mother? Will it hurt us?"

I was nine years old. It was December 1945. Four months earlier, in the heat of an August morning—Hiroshima. Destruction. Death. Power beyond belief, released from something invisible. Without knowing its name, I'd already felt the atom's power in another form. Since 1943, my father had commuted eighteen miles from our apartment in Knoxville to the plant in Oak Ridge—the atomic frontier where the atom had been split, where it still was splitting. He left before dawn and came home long after dark.

"What do you do, Daddy?"

"I can't tell you, Marilou. It's part of something for the war. I don't know what they're making out there or how my job fits into it."

"What's inside the maze?"

"Something important . . . and strange. I see long, heavy trucks coming in. What they're bringing just seems to disappear. Somebody must know what happens to it, but nobody ever talks about it. One thing for sure—the government doesn't spend millions of dollars for nothing. It's something big. I can't imagine what."

I couldn't either. But I could feel its energy like a great hum.

Then, suddenly, it had an image: the mushroom cloud. It had a name: the atom. And our family was then living in Oak Ridge. My father had given me the facts. I also needed an interpreter.

"What is the atom, Mother? Will it hurt us?"

"It can be used to hurt everybody, Marilou. It killed thousands of people in Hiroshima and Nagasaki. But the atom itself . . . ? It's invisible, the smallest bit of matter. And it's in everything. Your hand, my dress, the milk you're drinking—all of it is made with millions and millions of atoms and they're all moving. But what the atom means? I don't think anyone knows yet. We have to have reverence for its nature and learn to live in harmony with it. Remember the burning man."

"I remember."

When I was six years old, his screams had brought my mother and me running to our front porch. Mother was eight months pregnant. What we saw made her hold me tight against her side. Across the street, in the small parking lot of the dry cleaner's, a man in flames ran, waving his arms. Another man chased him, carrying a garden hose turned on full force, and shouting, "Stop, stop!" The burning man stumbled and sank to his knees, shrieking, clawing the air, trying to climb out of his pain. When water hit his arms, flesh fell off in fiery chunks. As the flames went out, his cries ceased. He collapsed slowly into a charred and steaming heap.

Silence. Burned flesh. Water trickling into the gutter. . . .

The memory flowed between Mother and me, and she said, as she had said that day, "Never tempt nature, Marilou. It's the nature of fire to burn. And of cleaning fluid to flame near heat. The man had been warned over and over not to work with the fluid, then stoke the furnace. But he kept doing it. Nothing happened. He thought he was in control. Then one day a spark. . . . The atom is like the fire."

"So it *will* hurt us."

"That depends on us, Marilou."

I understood. Mother already had taught me that beyond surface differences, everything is in physical and spiritual connection—God, nature, humanity. All are one, a circle. It seemed natural for the atom to be part of this connection. At school, when I was introduced to Einstein's theory of relativity—that energy and matter are one—I accepted the concept easily.

Peacetime brought relaxation of some restrictions in Oak Ridge. I learned that my father was an accountant. The "long, heavy trucks" brought uranium ore to the graphite reactor, which was still guarded by a maze of fences. The reactor reduced the ore to a small amount of radioactive material. Safety required care and caution. Scientists called the reactor "The Lady" and, in moments of high emotion, referred to her as "our beloved reactor."

"What does she look like, Daddy?"

"They tell me she has a seven-foot shield of concrete around a graphite core, where the atom is split." I asked the color of the graphite. "Black," he said. And I imagined a great, black queen, standing behind her shield, holding the splitting atom in the shelter of her arms.

I also saw the immense nurturing potential of the atom. There was intensive research into fuels, fertilizers, mechanical and interpretative tools. Crops and animals were studied for the effects of radiation. Terminal cancer patients came from everywhere to the research hospital. I especially remember one newspaper picture of a man with incredibly thin hands reaching for the "atomic cocktail" (a container of radioactive isotopes). His face was lighted with hope.

At school we had disaster drills in case of nuclear attack (or in case someone got careless around the reactor). Scientists explained the effects of an explosion—from "death light" to fallout. They also emphasized the peaceful potential of the atom and the importance of personal commitment in using it. Essentially, their message was the same as my mother's: "If we treat the atom with reverence, all will be well."

But all is not well now with the atom. The arms race, the entry of Big Business into the nuclear industry, and accidents like Three Mile Island cause alarm. Along with me, women protest, organize antinuclear groups, speak out. But we must also take time to ponder woman's affinities with the atom and to consider that our responsibilities for its use are more profound than we may have imagined.

We should begin with the atom itself, which is approximately two trillion times smaller than the point of a pin. We will focus on the nature and movement of the atom, not on the intricacies of nuclear physics. To understand the atom, we must flow with its pattern, which is circular.

During the nineteenth and twentieth centuries, scientists theorized about the atom, isolated it, discovered the nucleus, with its neutrons, protons, electrons. The atom appeared to resemble a Chinese nesting ball—a particle within a particle. Scientists believed the descending order would lead to the ultimate particle—the final, tiny bead. Man would penetrate the secret of matter and dominate it. All life could then be controlled, like a machine.

Around the turn of the century, however, a few scientists began to observe the atom asserting its nature, which was more flexible and unpredictable than had been thought. To explain it required a new logic, and, in 1905, Einstein published his theory of relativity. To describe the atom also required new use of language in science because our senses cannot experience the nuclear world except by analogy. The great Danish physicist, Niels Bohr, said, "When it comes to atoms, language can be used only as in poetry. The poet, too, is not nearly so concerned with describing facts as with creating images and mental connections."

As research progressed, the word *mystery* began to appear in scientific writing, along with theories that matter might not end in a particle after all. Perhaps the universe resembled a great thought more than a great machine. The linear path was bending . . . and in the mid-1970s the path ended in an infinitesimal circle: the quark. A particle so small that even with the help of huge machines, humans can see only its trace, as we see the vapor trail of an airplane in the stratosphere. A particle ten to one hundred million times smaller than the atom. Within the quark, scientists now perceive matter refining beyond space-time into a kind of mathematical operation, as nebulous and real as an unspoken thought. It is a mystery that no conceivable research is likely to dispel, the life force in process nurturing, enabling, enduring, fierce.

I call it the atom's mother heart.

Nuclear energy is the nurturing energy of the universe. Except for stellar explosions, this energy works not by fission (splitting) but by fusion—attraction and melding. With the relational process, the atom creates and transforms life. Women are part of this life force. One of our natural and chosen purposes is to create and sustain life—biological, mental, and spiritual.

Women nurture and enable. Our "process" is to perceive relationships among elements, draw their energies to the center, and fuse them into a whole. Thought is our essence; it is intrinsic for us, not an aberration of our nature, as Western tradition often asserts.

Another commonality with the atom's mother heart is ferocity. When the atom is split—when her whole is disturbed—a chain reaction begins that will end in an explosion unless the reaction is contained, usually by a nuclear reactor. To be productive and safe, the atom must be restored to its harmonic, natural pattern. It has to be treated with respect. Similarly, to split woman from her thought, sexuality, and spirit is unnatural. Explosions are inevitable unless wholeness is restored.

In theory, nature has been linked to woman for centuries—from the cosmic principle of the Great Mother-Goddess to the familiar metaphors of Mother Nature and Mother Earth. But to connect the life force with *living* woman is something only some ancient or so-called "primitive" cultures have been wise enough to do. The linear, Western, masculine mode of thought has been too intent on conquering nature to learn from her a basic truth: *To separate the gender that bears life from the power to sustain it is as destructive as to tempt nature itself.*

This obvious truth is ignored because to accept it would acknowledge woman's power, upset the concept of woman as sentimental—passive, all-giving, all-suffering—and disturb public and private patterns. But the atom's mother heart makes it impossible to ignore this truth any longer. She is the interpreter of new images and mental connections not only for humanity, but most particularly for women, who have profound responsibilities in solving the nuclear dilemma. We can do much to restore harmony. But time is running out. . . .

Shortly after Hiroshima, Albert Einstein said, "The unleashed power of the atom has changed everything save our modes of thought, and thus we drift toward unparalleled catastrophe." Now, deployment of nuclear missiles is increasing. A going phrase in Washington is, "When the war starts. . . ." Many nuclear power plants are being built and operated with money, not safety, as the bottom line. In spite of repeated warnings from scientists and protests from the public, the linear-thinking people continue to ignore the nature of the atom. They act irreverently. They think they're in control. One day a spark. . . .

I look beyond the specters of the burning man and the mushroom cloud to a time two hundred years ago, when destruction was bearing down on the Cherokee nation. My foremothers took their places in the circles of power along with the men. Outnumbered and outgunned, the nation could not be saved. But the Cherokee and their culture survived—and women played a strong part in that survival.

Although the American culture is making only slow progress toward empowering women, there is much we can do to restore productive harmony with the atom. Protest and litigation are important in stopping nuclear abuse, but total polarization between pro- and anti-nuclear people is simplistic and dangerous. It is not true that all who believe in nuclear energy are bent on destruction. Neither is it true that all who oppose it are "kooks" or "against progress." Such linear, polar thinking generates so much anger on both sides that there is no consensual climate where reasonable solutions can be found. The center cannot hold. And the beast of catastrophe slouches toward us. We need a network of the committed to ward it off. Women at large can use our traditional intercessory skills to create this network through organizations, through education, and through weaving together conscientious protagonists in industry, science, and government. Women who are professionals in these fields should share equally in policy making.

Our energies may fuse with energies of others in ways we cannot foresee. I think of two groups of protesters who came to Diablo Canyon, California, in the fall of 1981. Women and men protested the activation of a nuclear power plant so near an earthquake fault. The first group numbered nearly three thousand. The protest was effective, but it says much about the dominant, nonholistic mode of American thought that an article about the second group was buried in the middle of a San Francisco newspaper.

After the three thousand had left Diablo Canyon to wind and silence, a band of about eighty Chumash Indians came to the site of the power plant. They raised a wood-sculptured atom and sat in a circle around it for a daylong prayer vigil. Jonathan Swift Turtle, a Mewok medicine man, said that the Indians did not oppose nuclear technology but objected to the plant's being built atop a sacred Chumash burial site as well as near an earthquake fault. He said he hoped the vigil would bring about "a moment of harmony between the pro- and anti-nuclear factions."

The Chumash understand that to split the atom from the sacred is a deadly fission that will ultimately destroy nature and humanity. I join this circle of belief with an emblem I created for my life and work—the sacred white deer of the Cherokee leaping in the heart of the atom. My ancestors believed that if a hunter took the life of a deer without asking its spirit for pardon, the immortal Little Deer would track the hunter to his home and cripple him. The reverent hunter evoked the white deer's blessing and guidance.

For me, Little Deer is a symbol of reverence. Of hope. Of belief that if we humans relent our anger and create a listening space, we may attain harmony with the atom in time. If we do not, our world will become a charred and steaming heap. Burned flesh. Silence. . . .

There will be no sign of hope except deep in the invisible, where the atom's mother heart—slowly and patiently—bears new life.

At the Crossroads

IN HIROSHIMA AT THE FIFTIETH ANNIVERSARY

EDWARD A. DOUGHERTY

The slogan for the first Peace Restoration Festival in 1946 was "World peace begins from Hiroshima." The deliberate bombing of a civilian population with a nuclear weapon—regardless of the wretchedness of the context—showed that war itself had become too brutal, too capricious, and too inhuman to be allowed to continue. All humanity lost something that day; survivor-poet Sankichi Toge recognizes that loss when he cries out, "Give me back myself./Give back the human race."[1] On August 6, 1995, thousands marked the fiftieth anniversary of that city's atomic bombing. And I was one of them.

My spouse, Beth, and I moved to Hiroshima to become volunteer directors of the World Friendship Center in late August 1993 and stayed until December 1995. Over its thirty years as a guest house and community peace witness, World Friendship Center has welcomed many at this crossroads of history, both as volunteers and as guests from all over the world.

For the fiftieth, there were so many details to attend to that we forgot to reserve seats at the Peace Memorial ceremony for ourselves. Actually, we didn't mind. Having experienced the previous year's ceremony—with its parade of politicians all saying predictable and insubstantial things, its Moment of Silence violated by amateur and professional shutterbugs eager for a snapshot, and the conspicuous absence of the survivors themselves—we weren't upset by not having a seat. We'd been working toward the fiftieth for more than a year, and by the time it came, both Beth and I were in a hurry to see it go. So we guided our guests to Peace Park, got them situated in their seats, and began walking around the ceremony.

We were by the Motoyasu River, which divides the A-Bomb Dome from the rest of Peace Park, when suddenly the air became heavy with bells ringing. That particularly solemn hollow sound came from three directions simultaneously. On both banks of the river, everybody halted. The whirring of cicadas intensified the early-morning heat. Eight-fifteen A.M.—the moment "Little Boy" exploded over Hiroshima. In that stillness, tears welled up, bitter and swollen. Fifty years ago, Robert Lewis, the co-pilot of the *Enola Gay,* said, "My God, what have we done?"[2] Inside me that prayer-plea felt just as urgent, just as insistent.

Then, movement resumed, voices rising again from the podium at the ceremony. We drifted over to the Die-In at the Dome, where every year hundreds of people fall and lie dead on the ground at the sound of those bells—children trying to keep still, a row of people in wheelchairs. That moment of stark stillness, that moment of death. It was a visual echo of the silence after the flash and before the waves of air and noise that were strong enough to knock the stone railings off Miyuki Bridge about a mile and a half away (and about two blocks from where we lived).

On our way out of Peace Park, we ran into Mark, a photographer for *Stars & Stripes.* We'd met him in June down in Nagasaki when the military newspaper was preparing its retrospective article. We observed the writer's interview with a survivor, or *hibakusha* (he-bahk-shah); later we all met again in Hiroshima (we took the same train). We were pleasantly surprised by how Mark had taken time in the museum and seemed personally involved in the experience (unlike the writer); however, we expected he'd be gone, like most journalists, once the assignment was over.

"You came back," I said.

"I felt like I had to," he said.

He told us he'd been to Kobe after the terrible earthquake and resulting fires in January, and saw a city in ruins. Then, he said, hearing the survivors' accounts for days and days, their images, mixed with flattened, ruined Kobe, brewed nightmares in his sleep. He *had to* come back, he said again. Once you learn a fuller story of Nagasaki and Hiroshima, there is a certain imperative; each of us comes to ask "My God, what have we done?" One of the fundamental ways to gain this fuller story is to listen to the witnesses themselves.

On August 6, World Friendship Center asked two men to "tell their experience." In Japanese this is called *kataribe* (ka-ta-ree-bay) which is related to "storytelling" or *shogen* (show-gen) which is more like "giving testimony." Both Hiromu Morishita and Hitoshi Takayama, like thousands of survivors, didn't talk about what they experienced of the atomic bomb for years before bearing witness. In 1968, Mr. Takayama attended a meeting where people claimed "the voice of Hiroshima was slowly disappearing." When he finally spoke out, he created a book—in English—with survivors' accounts, photographs, and reflections by people around the world. He is now preparing a third edition of *Hiroshima: In Memoriam and Today*.

In that book Mr. Takayama writes that when he realized the knowledge was fading because of the silence of survivors, he "felt this bitterly in my heart." Here is his reflection:

> I felt that I must continue to pray and work hard for the cause of peace. Though I am only one humble man, I knew that I had to try to make some contribution, however small, to the cause of peace. I know that the path to peace is a rough one, but I also know as a witness of the A-bomb that all humanity must never again experience such misery and suffering. We must keep telling the truth about that experience to people of good conscience. It is our responsibility to our God and to our fellow men [and women]. The horrible truth about war must be known, and Hiroshima is one of its hardest truths.[3]

"The horrible truth about war" and phrases like it are often used in Hiroshima because there is a basic conviction that if people really knew what war is and what the atomic bomb really did (and could do in exponentially larger terms even now), we would shrink away from choosing it as a way of dealing with conflict. This sense of Hiroshima having more meaning for the future than the past is what motivated teachers like Mr. Morishita to develop peace education around the same time that Mr. Takayama undertook his book. Their deep, personal responsibility felt like an urgency that pressed some hibakusha toward action, beginning with telling the facts of what happened to them as individuals.

Teachers learned that 3 percent of students couldn't answer the question "When did the atomic bomb fall on Hiroshima?" While 3 percent seems small, it was far too many young people for the hibakusha. In addition to ignorance, the survey revealed common feelings that persist today. Students wrote such things as "Atomic bomb affairs don't appeal to me, because I've no experience." And who can't relate to this comment: "I'm too busy with daily affairs to know how to bring about peace." In his essay in *Hiroshima: In Memoriam and Today,* Mr. Morishita responds:

> Should that misery be forgotten? Shouldn't we foster a will toward peace among young people, so that they may not repeat the same error again? If we had a nuclear war again, even those inexperienced youth wouldn't escape it. There is no guarantee that these young people would survive it. Therefore they also have a responsibility to prevent war.[4]

As Mark, the photographer from *Stars & Stripes,* shows, the truth of the survivors' experience can be passed on. The responsibility for making peace, including preventing war—for making "some contribution, however small, to the cause of peace"—can be fostered. I saw this from my own life, which took me as a volunteer to Japan, where I witnessed many other examples.

While living in Hiroshima, we became friends with Paul Quayle, a photographer from England. Somehow he, too, felt this "will toward peace," and it took him to India in the footsteps of Gandhi and then to Japan. He took "snaps" in Hiroshima for more than six years, and the fruit of his labors is a remarkable book, *Hiroshima Calling.*[5] Beth and I, Paul, and countless others have heard the hibakusha, and their message has fostered a sense of responsibility. But it takes all kinds of people waking up to the fact that they must try to make whatever small contribution they can. Teachers, writers, photographers, volunteers. One guest we met was a quiet British physicist who felt she had to make a kind of pilgrimage to Hiroshima. Her personal journey as a scientist crossed the path of history in Hiroshima.

If there is one lesson I've come away with from my time in Hiroshima, it's this: politics and history are murky and painful. It was debilitating to deal with every day. And so the personal aspect of peace work is essential—almost regardless of the results. I must do what I can, if only to practice my own humanity. Meeting people and hearing their stories, not their titles or affiliations, helps us all to recognize our common humanity. We are all the same this way. The survivors who tell their experience appeal to that common ground, warning us that their past experience may be our future. So, on August 6, fifty years after the first inhabited city was destroyed by a nuclear weapon, in addition to the Hiroshima survivors, we asked two U.S. veterans to bear witness to their experience at World Friendship Center.

Anthony Guarisco is a small man who looks at you with intensity. He moves with a stiffness, as if there were something wooden about him. He cannot turn his neck, so he shifts his eyes as much as possible; then if that doesn't work, he turns his entire torso. I'd written to his group, the Association of Atomic Veterans, because there had been some shocking revelations in the past two years.

In November 1993, just after our arrival in the City of Peace, the *Albuquerque Tribune* reported that the U.S. government experimented on hundreds of live human subjects, using radiation. The English-language newspapers in Japan followed the story closely. Some subjects were given doses one hundred times the federal limit on internal radiation for nuclear workers at the time.[6] Some were injected with plutonium, the most lethal substance known.[7] Then, in a flurry of disclosures between 1993 and 1995, we learned that the Department of Defense, Department of Energy, and the Atomic Energy Commission (now called the Nuclear Regulatory Commission) all performed such tests—prison inmates had their reproductive organs bombarded with radiation, others were given hundreds of X-rays; retarded boys who thought they were taking part in a science club were fed radioactive milk; and many others. These tests continued, according to Energy Secretary Hazel O'Leary, into the time of these revelations.[8]

This spirit of experimentation completes the link to the atomic bombs. Some in Hiroshima still harbor resentment over the team of doctors sent by the U.S. government. Called the Atomic Bomb Casualty

Commission, or ABCC, these researchers entered a city where more than 90 percent of the medical personnel were killed or injured, where most hospitals and clinics had only Red Cross medicines, and where knowledge of radiation was extremely limited.

In comes a team of experts from the United States that the Occupation asks (demands? orders?) survivors of the atomic bomb to go see. The doctors examine, measure, and document. Do they diagnose? Prescribe medicines? Provide any answers to the mysterious ailments the survivors are facing? No. ABCC never treated the victims; it was merely gathering information.

Now when people claim that atomic bombs were merely experiments, I know that there is more than a grain of truth to it. If the U.S. government was willing to perform experiments on its own citizens in secret, I am absolutely certain it would do it to "the enemy" regardless of the outcome of the war. The revelations about radiation experiments on human beings made me seek out the testimony of the Atomic Veterans, those servicemen who witnessed nuclear weapons tests.

I was able to meet Anthony because he was attending the Conference Against A- and H-bombs here in Hiroshima. On the fiftieth, he and Bill Bires told a gathering at the World Friendship Center about the other atomic explosions and hibakusha. Anthony was in the Pacific after World War II and witnessed the first bombs used in peacetime, a series of tests called Operation Crossroads. Being on a ship just a few miles away, he could clearly see the power of this weapon—an enormous battleship blasted out of the water only to land, cracking in half.

But he could also witness, firsthand, the radiation. Sick for months, then always more sluggish than ever in his life, Anthony Guarisco became an atomic bomb survivor—a hibakusha, which literally means "one who received the bomb." And the U.S. government denies his ailments are caused by his exposure. The same for Bill Bires, who witnessed blasts in the Nevada desert in the early 1950s. Carole Gallagher's book *American Ground Zero*, on which she labored for ten years, is indescribably heartbreaking because it pairs such personal testimony with portraits of people and places.

Meeting the atomic veterans broke down the idea that all veterans were of the same mind. Japan in general, and Hiroshima in particular, followed the wrangling in the United States over the Smithsonian's proposed, then revised, exhibition of the *Enola Gay*, the plane that dropped the bomb. The media coverage of the fury over the display made "veterans" seem like a single mass. Here were two men—representing hundreds, thousands more—whose combat experience and subsequent military service convinced them that truth brought honor, not war. Like the hibakusha, their experience of the atomic bomb leads them to work for peace.

August brought us another forceful witness of this process. Robert Oliver called us up out of the blue and said he was in Hiroshima for the fiftieth, so we invited him to all our events over those hot August days. Robert had been in the Air National Guard, but slowly the truth about his job became real to him. First, he came upon a used copy of *Unforgettable Fire*, the collection of drawings by hibakusha made in 1970—twenty-five years after "that day." The images showed him what was happening on the ground under the belly of the *Enola Gay*. That book and an offhand comment by one of his officers (something to the effect that "Our job is to destroy things and to kill people") convinced Robert that he could not in good conscience serve in the military any further. A bold step. I wouldn't think conscientious objectors *in the military* are welcomed or respected.

In the afternoon of the fiftieth anniversary, the city hosted Robert Jay Lifton and others in a presentation, but most organizations in the city were having some events, so we missed more than we attended. We were hosting a delegation from World Friendship Center's American Committee (who all stayed with Japanese friends associated with the Center) as well as the Atomic Mirror Pilgrimage (who stayed with us at the Center). Once the evening cooled down, we held *toro-nagashi*. In this beautiful ritual of lantern floating, individuals lit brightly colored paper boxes and floated them down the Motoyasu River, under the A-Bomb Dome. With the special Noh drama on a boat midstream and the hordes of media people and equipment, the intensity of personal expression and communion we felt the previous year was lost. It was like a show. It *was* a show.

Then, it seemed, everyone left. Next stop, Nagasaki. We decided against the trip south because Beth had struggled with Lyme disease the whole time we were volunteers, and the medication was just beginning to make some progress—a whole other story! We also had special events to mark World Friendship Center's thirtieth anniversary in these days, but again, another story. It's enough to say that we were guarding her against the heat, stress, and long hours of going down to Nagasaki.

As a result, Beth and I got a break, a chance to think about all these events and ideas. Peace and justice work seems to start with taking personal responsibility for "history," "politics," "the world," or "the future." Each one of us is urged to this in our own way, and we all name our obligation differently.

Most take a necessary step, once they realize the state of things: they issue a resounding refusal to participate in dehumanizing forces—within our selves and our societies. Like Robert Oliver refusing to participate in the military. Over and over again, people's stories show that if you listen to the truth and act on it, making whatever contribution you can even if it means ridicule or worse, your life takes on a wholeness. One action might even invite the next, leading life into a realm of purpose and meaning you never guessed.

However, it's become clear to me that people must do more than protest. Shouting a profound No to the evil and unthinking cruelty of violence is essential, but ideas are not stamped out by denunciation. They must be displaced by something more viable, more full, and more true. The issue of nuclear weapons, for example, is huge, and it's entangled in politics—international politics, at that—and people are more and more disgusted with politics (both in Japan and the United States). People's contributions can seem minuscule in the face of this. Certainly, we felt this. In our first months in Hiroshima, we were wondering why we quit our jobs and moved across half the world. For peace? Washing guests' sheets? Writing up reports no one will read? Yet, the last nuclear tests by the government of France in the spring and early summer of 1995, like a lightning rod, focused the energy of millions around the world. People boycotted products, sailed into the Pacific, wrote letters, marched at embassies, and held prayer services. Everyone could participate, and no contribution was too small.

Still, how can we go beyond protest? We had a guest from India who teaches Gandhian studies, so we asked Mr. Jeyapragasam to speak one night. He called his presentation "Six Possible Futures." In it he said something I'll never forget: to begin making the future we most desire, we must take non-killing seriously. We need to behave in ways that bring comfort to those who suffer, and we need to begin doing what needs to be done to preserve humanity and life in general. It is essential to draw people to the positive, to call out the best in people.

Another chance meeting at World Friendship Center might illustrate what I mean. After the heat, hecticness, and overextension of the August 6 events, and while the attention turned toward Nagasaki, a Frenchman called from Kyoto, asking if we would accept some roses. Despite the protests, France's announcement that it would resume nuclear tests surrounded the August events with a dark shadow. It was another sign, it seemed, that the testimony and plea from Nagasaki and Hiroshima had not been heard.

Yet, here was a French person in Japan to mark the fiftieth anniversary of the atomic bombings. He had come to present one thousand silk roses and copies of a book he'd written, a lovely edition in French, Spanish, and English. *The Princess and the Birds* was about Sadako, the little girl who died of leukemia ten years after the bomb.[9] Pierre Marchand had arranged to meet international groups, as well as a film crew from France, to make a dignified presentation. Because of a mix-up, he was unable to. Now he had his parcels, but it was too late.

He had read about World Friendship Center in Paul Quayle's *Hiroshima Calling*, so he called and asked for some information. We sent him a brochure so he'd know that the Center was celebrating its thirtieth anniversary this year and that its founder, Barbara Reynolds, was the first woman to be named an honorary citizen of Hiroshima. And we told him we'd love to accept his roses.

Pierre was very pleased. As it turns out, he'd met Barbara in Paris, maybe thirty years ago, when she was on a peace pilgrimage with several survivors. There were other connections, other friendships that could be known only by meeting face-to-face. He further realized that a project he thought was ending with his coming to Hiroshima was just beginning: guests and friends of World Friendship Center can take a rose to Peace Park and offer it. So, even now, one can take a symbolic action. Pierre also encourages anyone who is moved by the story of Sadako to find some way of helping the child-victims of war, because kids still suffer from adult violence—look at Cambodia, anywhere in the former Yugoslavia, Iraq, Liberia, Rwanda. Sadako's story is being relived even now, and each of us can contribute something to help if we have a will toward peace.

The anniversaries are now the far less dramatic fifty-fourth, fifty-fifth, . . . but the survivors are still in Hiroshima and Nagasaki, bearing witness to their experience. We can still listen to them, for a few years anyway. It was a profound experience to meet and get to know Mr. Morishita and translate some of his poems, to become friends with other hibakusha. When she started the Center, Barbara Reynolds wrote, "World Friendship Center is based upon the belief that an individual can and must do something to create peace, and a faith that there is an ultimate power of truth and love that can help each of us to develop a center of peace within ourselves which will be highly contagious." It's as if I've "caught" something from these people, and it encourages me to strive for more.

The value of World Friendship Center, which stands at the crossroads in Hiroshima, is in the power of the individuals who visit. Pilgrims of all sorts come, some with their own pain or their own project, some without knowledge or passion for such far-off events, and they stay overnight. By having breakfast together or talking in a small group, by reading books or seeing a video, people experience that deep, common thread that links us. For more than thirty years, World Friendship Center has been a place of hospitality in Hiroshima, a city where they say peace begins. But we know that peace begins in the folds of the human heart and in the imagination, which is a factory of possibilities.

NOTES

1. Miyao Ohara, ed. and trans, *The Songs of Hiroshima: An Anthology* (Hiroshima: Shunyo-sha Shuppan Co., 1964), 9.

2. Robert Jay Lifton and Greg Mitchell, *Hiroshima in America: Fifty Years of Denial* (New York: Grosset/Putnam, 1995), 233.

3. Hitoshi Takayama, "Instant Inferno," in *Hiroshima: In Memoriam and Today* (Hiroshima: Daigaku Letterpress, 1973), 53.

4. Hiromu Morishita, "Peace Education Based on A-Bomb Experience," in *Hiroshima: In Memoriam and Today* (Hiroshima: Daigaku Letterpress, 1973), 171.

5. Paul Quayle, *Hiroshima Calling* (Self-published, 1995).

6. William B. Falk, "Radiation Guinea Pigs; Hundreds of Humans Used in Federally Sponsored Tests," *Newsday,* 29 September 1993.

7. Jim Morris, "Clampdown: The Silencing of Nuclear Industry Workers; Numerous Experiments Done on 'Nuclear Guinea Pigs' for Decades," *Houston Chronicle,* 26 September 1993.

8. Houston Chronicle News Service, "U.S. Still Funding 200 Human Radiation Experiments," *Houston Chronicle,* 26 January 1994.

9. Yoshiteru Kosakai, *Hiroshima Peace Reader* (Hiroshima: Hiroshima Peace Culture Foundation, 1980), 52.

The Cenotaph

KENNETH ROBBINS

I visited Peace Memorial Park many times during my two stays in Hiroshima. The park, created as a living memorial to the victims of the atomic bomb, is an island buffered by two branches of the Ota River. From the Aioi Bridge (the famous T-shaped bridge at the tip of the island's triangle, the official target for the *Enola Gay* on August 6, 1945) south to Peace Boulevard, the park succeeds in reminding its hordes of visitors that here, half a century ago, too many people to count lost their lives within the blinking of an eye—so many, in fact, that more than likely the exact number will never be known.

The Aioi Bridge offers a telling view of the A-Bomb Dome, the only surviving relic of the actual bombing. Now the internationally known shell of a building is the emblem of Hiroshima and, for some, of the nuclear age. It sits amid fifty-year-old trees flanked on one side by a branch of the Ota, on another by busy Aioi Dori Avenue, and on another by a small but impressive fountain with the new and progressive city beyond.

It is rare to pass the Dome without seeing artists trying to capture its uniqueness on canvas or TV camera crews recording the testimony of an A-bomb survivor.

At the entrance to Aioi Bridge is a granite bust of Tamiki Hara, poet and author who survived the bombing of Hiroshima but not the threat of the bomb's use in the Korean War; rather than live through another holocaust, even from as far away as Korea, Tamiki chose to die under the wheels of a speeding train.

Directly across the river from the Dome and at the apex of the park's triangle is the Peace Clock Tower. Those willing to rise early and make the trip to the site will enjoy the clock's chimes, which sound each day at precisely 8:15 A.M., the exact instant the atomic bomb exploded over fifty years ago.

Immediately south of the clock is the Peace Bell, a large, oval gong typical of bells on the grounds of most Buddhist temples throughout Japan. Here, park visitors may ring the bell for peace. Periodically during any visit to Peace Park, one can hear the bell sending soft and mellow tones from one end of the park to the other.

Further south still is the Children's Peace Monument, a tall and slender four-legged construct that assumes the shape of the Peace Bell, or of the A-Bomb Dome, or of a nuclear missile, the shape of preference probably belonging to each individual observer. Clinging to the sides of the shape are exuberant children, and riding the nose of the missile is a female figure, also a child, standing on tiptoe and reaching out for an armload of peace. The child with angelic overtones represents Sadako, the ten-year-old girl who in 1955 died of leukemia, a disease that was a direct result of her exposure in utero to atomic radiation.

Sadako's story is well known. She believed the Japanese myth that if one folds a thousand origami cranes, she will be healed. She died before folding the magic number. Not only did the tragedy of Sadako's life lead to the creation of the Children's Peace Monument, it also established the ongoing symbol for all nuclear bomb victims, living and dead; that symbol is the paper crane, hand-folded and strung in long, colorful strands. Year round these strands can be found decorating A-bomb monuments throughout Japan. Beginning in the early summer, children from all over Japan make pilgrimages to Sadako's monument in the Hiroshima Peace Park. Usually the ceremony they observe at the site includes the singing of children's songs, the placing of strands of origami cranes, and the taking of group pictures with Sadako's image, arms open and hopeful, high above their heads.

Across a thoroughfare from the Children's Peace Monument is the Flame of Peace, burning eternally at one end of the Pond of Peace. At the other end of the pond sits the Cenotaph. It is here, the center of the park, that one feels most connected to the events of August 1945. For it is here that the list of names, those who died either directly or indirectly from contact with the atomic bomb, is kept. Each August 6, as part of the annual commemoration held in Peace Memorial Park, the names of victims who have died during the past year are entered into the ledger that is carefully maintained inside the concrete coffin. If there is hallowed ground on this Earth, the Cenotaph sits on it.

The true significance of what happened in and to Hiroshima in August 1945 was made clear to me one morning as I wandered past the Cenotaph. I noticed a crowd of people gathered on the south side of the memorial, that in the crowd were television crews as well as a mixture of people who included Japanese and foreigners. Several young men and women were inside the Cenotaph, using a portable hoisting system with chains and hooks to lift the concrete lid from the outer container. Sheets of white cloth had been spread on the gravel outside the Cenotaph. The male workers were dressed in black slacks, white long-sleeved shirts, and black ties; the women wore navy blue skirts and white blouses. All wore white gloves.

First out of the crypt was the mahogany lid of the second container. Then came the unfinished wooden lid of the inner chest. These items were removed in a reverent manner and placed on the white sheeting. Each worker, before stepping on the white cloth, removed his or her shoes. Finally, from inside the elaborate casket, came the names. I had heard that they were kept on a scroll, so I expected to see a large spool of paper or cloth emerge from the sarcophagus, inscribed with thousands upon thousands of names. Instead there emerged a large book, leather bound, perhaps two and a half inches thick and the size of regular typing paper, probably eight and a half by eleven inches. The book was lifted from the Cenotaph and handed to one of the young women, who gave it to a woman who stood, shoeless, on the white sheet. She carried the book to the far corner of the sheet, knelt as she respectfully placed the text on the sheet, and left it there.

My first impression of the contents of the Cenotaph was one of disappointment. I had expected there to be more, I suppose. How much more, I had no idea, but the notion that the book was the sole occupant of the crypt and singular container of the list of names left me feeling cheated.

Then came the second book, equal in size to the first. And the third. The fourth. I felt my breath leave me for a moment as the fifth book emerged from deep inside the coffin. I tried to imagine how many names each book could possibly hold, and with generous spacing, I assumed a minimum of twenty thousand, easily.

People in front of me began to move away. Perhaps the knowledge of what these books contained—the names of all those killed by the bomb affectionately referred to by the American scientists as "Little Boy"—was more than they could take. Or perhaps they had seen enough and were drawn off by the museum, or lunch, or whatever.

I moved to the front of the still large mass of people and watched as the sixth book was lifted from inside the tomb. Then the seventh. The eighth. The ninth. . . .

I felt the need to weep as the tenth book was placed on the white sheeting. I looked around me. Only Japanese were left, silently watching the ritual. I couldn't help but imagine that except for the good fortune of time and place, these books did not contain any of their names. Or mine. I looked at their somber faces—all ages, children, mothers and fathers, the aged, the infirm, the healthy, the important, the less so. There was no difference. The people who stood at the Cenotaph with me were the same as those who had been alive in Hiroshima at 8:14 A.M. on August 6, 1945. They breathed the same, loved the same, cried, bled, ate and drank, shouted, hated, played, and thought the same. No difference. Except the difference timing and place make. For that was then and this was now.

I fought away tears as the fourteenth book was placed on the sheet. I felt dumbfounded when the fifteenth book emerged. Would there be no end to it? How could this be? So many names. I remember sensing similar emotions as I moved down the slope of the Vietnam Memorial in Washington, D.C. There the names etched in granite were touchable, except that at the bottom of the slope, the stacking of names above my head placed them out of reach. That is how I felt as the books of names continued to emerge from the Cenotaph: that the awareness of the atomic blast was moving out of reach. The sixteenth book, reverently placed. The seventeenth. . . . My God, the magnitude! Finally, the last book, the eighteenth, was with silence and awe placed on the white cloth.

I was overwhelmed by what I had seen, and I wanted to see no more. I left the Cenotaph, and have avoided going near it since. I glance in its direction occasionally as I make my way to the International

Conference Center and its holdings of English-language newspapers; I invariably see people of all ages praying in front of it. But that is as close as I wish to get. There is a sorrow at the Cenotaph that I find difficult to abide.

If everyone on this planet could witness the emptying of the Cenotaph and grasp what those eighteen books mean, it is possible that the cry of anguish heard and felt as a result might guarantee that all nuclear arms ever manufactured by human hands would be dismantled without need ever to put them back together again.

Postscript: I shared my observation of the eighteen books encased in the cenotaph with Miyoko Matsubara, *hibakusha* (A-bomb survivor) and former head librarian for the Peace Memorial Museum. She corrected my observation. "Not eighteen," she told me. "Oh, no. That was merely the first layer. Forty-six. There are forty-six books in all. Yes."

And counting.

Beyond Despair

AN IMAGINAL ODYSSEY INTO THE SOUL OF HIROSHIMA

RANDY MORRIS

FINDING THE DOORWAY

*M*y relationship to the bomb as image begins with my birth in 1950 in Richland, Washington, home of the Richland High School Bombers, where pretty cheerleaders still wear the logo of a mushroom cloud across their bosoms. There I grew up among my friends and their parents, workers at the Hanford Nuclear Reservation, the birthplace of the plutonium bomb dropped upon the city of Nagasaki, Japan, an incendiary device that killed seventy thousand human beings. It never occurred to any of us that by virtue of living in this stark desert land by the mighty Columbia River, we were becoming "downwinders," passive recipients of massive radiation leaks from the Hanford Reservation. My dance around the bomb continued through the age of air raid drills ("Get back under that desk, young man!") and bomb shelters ("Mom, will we let our neighbors in or not?").

Later, while attending a boarding school outside of Washington, D.C., I had a dream in which a huge B-52 is flying over the Capitol. Bomb bay doors open, and a man who is partly me straddles a bomb as it falls to Earth. It lands near my dorm. There is a huge flash of light, and I can see the veins behind my eyelids. I wake up in a panic, knowing I have but thirty seconds to live. Sure enough, there is the huge boom that rattles the windows and walls. But survival is a powerful instinct. I jump out of bed and dash for the closet to grab some clothes, then head for the basement, expecting at any moment to be annihilated. Frantically I dig into my closet as my mind begins to split and separate the phenomenal world from the dream world. When the process is complete, I am left standing in my underwear, clothes a jumble, listening to the sharp rain of a thunderstorm clatter against the window.

Circumambulating the bomb as image continued when, in 1981, Ph.D. in hand, I prepared to have a cross-cultural experience in Hiroshima, Japan, home of the Hiroshima International School, where I had secured a teaching position. A month before I was to leave, I had a dream in which I am one of four people in white coats working skillfully but feverishly around a table. Lying like an anesthetized patient on the table is a cylindrical bomb, its innards open, wires sticking out, waiting to explode. To defuse this device will require a great deal of controlled passion. The fate of the world rests on our shoulders. Sweat pours down our foreheads as we try to keep our hands steady. Five-four—we almost have it! We're going to make it! Three-two—Wait! Wait! Just another few seconds!—One—KABOOM! In disbelief at my failure, in anger at not having enough time, I am subjected to the full experience of nuclear annihilation—first the flash of light that lifts and peels the skin, then the explosion that expands and shatters the body, the last sensation memory can sustain.

This was the dream I held in my mind as I first orbited ground zero near the *Hondori* of downtown Hiroshima. It was as if that place, six hundred meters above a hospital door, were an aperture from one world into this. But from what kind of world? Would I ever understand what passed through that door? Would I be required to pass through it myself? Later that day my friend took me to Peace Park. "So this is it!" I thought in ego-based wonder.

"What is that pretty green mound over there, the one with incense trays before it?" I asked.

"Oh, that is the Memorial Mound for the Unknown Dead. Inside it there are tens of thousands of boxes of human remains, most of them unidentified, waiting to be claimed by relatives," my friend said.

To my surprise, I felt hot tears well up spontaneously in my eyes. An unseen hand gripped my chest and squeezed without mercy as sobs rumbled clumsily from my center. I bent my head, half in acknowledgment of the dead, half in shame for my lack of control. It was only then, with that first awakening to the well of grief, the first time I ever recall crying in public, that I began my descent into the soul of Hiroshima.

OVER MY HEAD

Having been awakened by the images of death that lie etched in monuments throughout the city, barely discernible beneath the hustle and bustle of a modern Japanese metropolis, I resolved to do my part for peace. But what could I do? I had no desire to join the political posturing, mostly because I felt that the opposing powers would enact their will anyway, that power has no use for peace. Neither did I feel I was mature or talented enough to create any of the unique and beautiful works of art that have been lovingly dedicated to the city. An idea occurred to me, based on my naive belief that I knew something about dreams. After all, I had studied some dream theory in graduate school and had the benefit of a few years of analysis. I had already come to the conclusion that dreams were an epistemological problem worth meditating upon for a lifetime. How *could* we be both the author and the audience of our own dreams? Why *are* dreams so revered in religious traditions? Why do I find myself so *moved* by certain images in dreams? Perhaps I could change the outcome of my nuclear nightmare by moving more *into* the dreams. I decided to collect the dreams of *hibakusha*, or A-bomb survivors. Wouldn't it be interesting, I thought, to see how the unconscious has come to terms with that event? If there were some new mythology to come out of the A-bomb experience, surely it would appear in the dreams of the hibakusha. But who would share their dreams with me? Brief forays into the field quickly turned up a daunting fact for any dream researcher: the folkways of Japan say that it is a sign of ill health for one to recall dreams, certain exceptions being allowed for dreams that appear at the new year. But with the enthusiasm of youth, I did not give up. Then I was introduced to Tomoko (not her real name), a Japanese hibakusha with massive facial scarring who had dedicated her life to the making of peace. In her somewhat breathless and matter-of-fact way, her English accented and delightful, she offered me this dream story:

"Ah, Randy-san. I will tell you this dream. You see, many years ago I went to America to talk of peace, and every night I had this dream, sometimes two or three times a night. I couldn't get any sleep. We traveled all around the country giving talks, and I was very tired. Finally I couldn't stand it anymore, and I came back home. I didn't leave again for twenty years because I feared this dream.

"You see, in this dream I was twelve years old again, and I woke up on a fine morning. I was walking to school when this big bomb exploded all around me. I was screaming, and my dress was on fire, as was the land all around me. People were yelling and running every which way. I tried to make it to this bridge that would lead me back home. As I crawled over the bridge, I heard my name being called: 'Tomoko! Tomoko!' I looked into the water where all these bodies were floating. And there I saw my friend Akiko. She was still alive, slowly turning in the current. 'Save me, Tomoko, Save me!' Ah, but Randy-san, you see, I was too weak to do anything. I couldn't save her. I turned away and walked on, walked on. And then I woke up feeling terrible! This dream kept happening to me, over and over, and I couldn't get any sleep."

Listening to this dream, I felt the familiar chill that alerts me to the presence of forces larger than myself. However, even while I was still full of the grief of the dream, I thought to myself that, aha, I finally had the dream of a hibakusha with which to work! Then Tomoko turned to me, her eyes burning in her lovely, flawed face. She whispered in a low voice, full of memory and pain, "You see, Randy-san, that is what really happened to me. I dream about what actually happened. I cannot escape. I wish I could have saved my friend Akiko, but, you see, I was too weak and was barely able to help myself. I never saw her again."

Of all the reactions that one could have to such a powerful story, I was surprised to feel shame begin to spread like a crimson tide over my torso until it reached my smooth, inexperienced face. A voice demanded to know who I thought I was, asking people to tell me their most personal inner experiences. No wonder no one would speak to me about their dreams. The secrets of the bomb as image cannot be penetrated so easily, and especially by one who was just awakening to the full extent of the suffering soul of Hiroshima. Clearly there was a region in the collective psyche of this city that relived the apocalypse on a nightly basis in all its particularities, thirty-five years later. Did I really understand how posttraumatic stress syndrome creates a purgatory of repetitious psychic events? Could I understand the magnitude of this suffering? And what about all the nuclear nightmares I had heard from non-Japanese, including my own? Doesn't the experience of apocalyptic terror that is revealed to us in a dream make symbolic hibakushas of us all? *Could it be that the terror is the wake-up call, the revelation itself?* Could it be that this is the meaning of apocalypse in its original sense, "to reveal"? And finally, begrudgingly, how many more lessons in pride awaited me before I could claim any wisdom at all?

WE ARE ALL PARENTS OF FUTURE GENERATIONS

My favorite place in Hiroshima City from which to view the bomb as image is the Buddhist reliquary on the top of Mount Futabayama. Sitting at the base of the silver-lined stupa, inside of which resides the Buddha's knucklebone, one looks out upon the stunning natural beauty of the Ota River delta, surrounded by mountains and emptying into the sea. To the left is Mount Hijiyama, the sacred Buddhist burial ground. That is where the U.S. Army, in its post-Bomb inflation, chose to place the Radiation Effects Research Facility. Behind that hill one can see the brown wooden buildings that represent the only prewar structures left standing in the city. A quaint sight indeed, until one realizes that the neutron firestorms released by "Little Boy" (as the Army affectionately called the atomic bomb) swept rapidly outward from ground zero to consume everything in their path, impeded only by this hill of graves. The quaint old buildings stand because they were protected by the graves. It is just one more irony in the soul of Hiroshima, an irony that lies like shrapnel embedded in a human body. Below and to the left and right, one can see the small valleys in the mountains where survivors fled, some of them outwardly unscathed but already dying from "A-bomb disease." And there are the beautiful stone-lined tributaries of the river, once clogged with the bodies of the dead. The silence of this place is deafening.

I was lying against this silver dome on a brilliant sunny day, the hum of the city below, reading a book that had just been published at the height of America's nuclear fear during the early 1980s. It was *The Fate of the Earth*, written by Jonathan Schell. I was disturbed. The vision that Schell paints of postapocalyptic existence is overwhelming in its detail, all of it based on the latest research into nuclear war. Schell is masterful at exposing the ironies and inconsistencies in our thinking about nuclear conflict. While reading in the reflected light of the silver stupa, I realized that I was sitting on a Buddhist reliquary on Mount Futabayama in the year 1982, imagining life after nuclear war. More specifically, I was imagining life after the extinction of the human species. But then it occurred to me in a flash of insight: nuclear war eliminates the very possibility of imagining anything. The Bomb will eliminate the human consciousness that gave it birth, nurtured it to fruition, and pushed the button. I had to agree with Schell that extinction, like death, is felt not when it has arrived, but beforehand, as a deep shadow cast across the whole of life. It is we the living who experience extinction as it slowly saturates the deep recesses of our psyches.

Depressing, indeed, but then a familiar counterreaction set in, reminding me once more of the numinous quality of the shadow cast by nuclear extinction: *The awareness of what changes when consciousness is no longer extant awakened me to the power of consciousness itself.* Like a fish discovering that it is swimming in water, I realized that I was a carrier of consciousness and that consciousness was the means by which creation looked upon itself. The threat of extinction had awakened me to the God-spark within, had awakened me to the "myth of consciousness." But the revelation did not end there. Another idea of Schell's, a logical extension of the threat of extinction, kept knocking at my door. He said that *whether we have children or not, the possibility of human beings choosing to extinguish themselves makes us all parents of future generations of humankind.* After Hiroshima, humans must actively choose *not* to destroy themselves. To make the choice to live is an act that makes future generations possible. The wonder of this idea washed over me and began to sink into my body. I realized that it was investing my actions with dignity and responsibility. I resolved to do something on behalf of future generations. I took this image to the World Friendship Center, a Quaker peace organization in Hiroshima. From there we developed it into an ongoing community event called Peace Picnic for Future Generations, a quiet walk from Peace Park to the graveyard on Hijiyama and a celebration with games and music for the generations of children yet to be born.

That moment on Mount Futabayama was like an egg cracking open on my head: the idea that we are all parents of future generations has slowly worked its way into everything that I think and do. I see the threat to future generations to be at the psychic root of many of our cultural ills—the neglect of children and the aged, the absence of spiritual rites of passage for our adolescents, the culture of narcissism that mocks our democratic institutions, and much more. The psyche, true to its nature, is throwing up healing counterimages to this threat—searching, probing, for humanly attainable solutions. I believe the revival of indigenous spiritual traditions with their strong ties to the Earth and ancestors to be a key psychic response to the threat to future generations. I believe the current political debates on multiculturalism are psychically based in a desire for our own ethnic stories to be told and heard. Doing so resurrects the imagination of our ancestors and links us, through them, to generations yet unborn. Cultivating the image of future generations in its profundity is a conscious act with moral consequences. *To see one's self as a link, as a choice maker in the continuity of generations, is to invest one's choices with mana or spiritual power, a power grounded in the love of life itself.*

"I MUST TAKE RESPONSIBILITY FOR WHAT HAS HAPPENED HERE"

In the spring of my last year in Hiroshima, during the festival of *Hanami*, when the aroma of warm sake and blizzards of cherry blossoms drench the stone-lined pathways along the Ota River, I boarded the Shinkansen bullet train to Kyoto to attend the fourteenth Annual Meeting of the International Transpersonal Association. I was eager to connect with the world of ideas generated by the concept of the transpersonal. Besides, there is no city on Earth like Kyoto in the spring. It is the ancient spiritual heart of Japan. Making my way as an introvert through the crowds of people, I noticed a brightly dressed, portly black man in traditional garb telling an African folk tale. Intrigued by his voice, and then his demeanor, I paused to listen. Soon I was mesmerized by the lilting tone of his British English and the huge, scintillating images that he was conjuring with his words, images that were redolent with the smells, sounds, and textures of South Africa. I quickly discovered that this man's name was Vusamazulu Credo Mutwa and that he was a witch doctor from Soweto, South Africa. But I already knew him as the greatest storyteller I had ever heard, or was ever likely to hear.

After following him around for several days, just to soak up his stories and to be near a large soul, I was both shocked and delighted when I was asked to lead Credo, his wife, and a small entourage through Hiroshima's Peace Park. During our ride south on the Shinkansen, I sat next to Credo, a striking figure in his African dashiki against the backdrop of Japanese faces. He wore a heavy beaten brass yoke around his neck, from the collarbone of which hung two carved wooden masks. Credo explained that one of the masks was Father Sun; the other, Sister Moon. A chain below their mouths linked them both to a large Coptic cross that rested upon Credo's ample belly. Turning his eyes to me, blurry behind thick spectacles, Credo explained that the cross was the child of Father Sun and Sister Moon. "And that . . . ?" I asked, pointing to a stunning emerald-green stone, the exact size and shape of a human heart, that rested over Credo's own. "It is as you see," he replied cryptically. He went on to explain that the African headband he was wearing was given to his grandfather by Mohandas Gandhi when the Mahatma was experimenting with Truth in South Africa. All in all, Vusamazulu Credo Mutwa was the most impressive spiritual presence I had ever encountered. I knew our trip to Peace Park would be extraordinary.

Indeed, my walk among the memorials to the dead with the black South African witch doctor *was* memorable—the Peace Bell with its hidden image of Africa upon it, Sadako's dome resplendent with a hundred thousand folded paper cranes, even the ever-present pigeons— they all shone forth in a new way on that spring day as Credo Mutwa cast his humanity and wisdom upon them. But even as this walk drew to a close, I was not, nor could I ever be, prepared for the single most illuminating moment during my three years in the International City of Peace. The small group I was leading paused near the entrance to the Peace Museum. Stretching before us was a pathway, stepping-stones to the Cenotaph, upon which is written "Rest In Peace, For We Will Not Repeat The Sin." Each year on August 6, more names of those who have died from the effects of A-bomb disease are added to the stone box tucked beneath the canopy, Eternal Flame burning brightly nearby. I explain to my small band of guests that this is the most sacred spot in the entire park. I add a few more words in a quiet voice as we prepare ourselves emotionally for our encounter with the Cenotaph. But then I hear a loud tapping noise and notice that Credo has turned from our group and is walking slowly and deliberately toward the Cenotaph. The tapping comes from the large black walking staff, a huge brass eagle attached to the top, that Credo carries in his right hand. In the pounding of his walking stick against the stones, we can hear the sound of anger and pain, of power and determination, as Credo walks toward this monument of warning, remembrance, and death. From the other side of the doorway that lies suspended six hundred meters above the hospital entrance, a force descends upon our group and envelops the unfolding scene. Like an electrical field, spiritual energy forms constellations about us and the moment slows to a liquid crawl.

I see Credo reach the stone steps before the Cenotaph. I silently groan as he crashes to his knees. Two pigeons on the Cenotaph roof, their still images vibrating from the heat waves of the eternal flame, etch themselves into my memory. The air is thick and undulating. I see Credo bend over in prayer, his back huge and curved, like the wooden statues of the weeping Buddha. After some time—who knows how long?—I see him remove his African headband, that family heirloom linking him to Gandhi's Truth-force. Credo lays it gently, lovingly, into the ashes on the altar. Then I see him struggle laboriously to his feet. Slowly he turns to face us, and even from this distance I can see that his eye sockets are full of white, their pupils turned in to his head, lost on the other side of Hiroshima's door. Involuntary tears well into my eyes; the now familiar hand squeezes my chest yet again. Oh, the suffering! I can feel its immensity coursing through the solitary body of Vusamazulu Credo Mutwa. Louder now, his walking stick crashing against the stones, threatening to split open the earth beneath his feet, Credo walks toward us wrapped in mystical fire. He is speaking now, and I strain to hear his words. Unmistakably he says to me, he says to us all, "I *must* take responsibility for what has happened here! *I must take responsibility for what has happened here!*"

These words, like an arrow cloaked in mystery, pierced deeply into my heart, where they lie festering today. How can a black South African accept responsibility for a bomb dropped by Americans on the Japanese? What kind of man is it who accepts such responsibility? What is responsibility if it is something that can be accepted in this way? Credo's statement challenges my familiar notions of guilt and responsibility, challenges my ideas of God and redemption, and calls me deeper, ever deeper, into the soul of Hiroshima.

BEYOND DESPAIR

Spiritual revelation is more common than we currently imagine. The hard work is bringing consciousness to the revelatory experience and then converting it into ethical obligation. It has been over ten years since that spring day in Hiroshima, and I struggle with Credo's words like a Zen practitioner would with a Zen koan. I am closer, but I am not there yet. I do know that soon after returning to the States, I was overwhelmed by reading Jim Garrison's book, *The Darkness of God: Theology After Hiroshima*. In this text of theodicy, the first to adequately address the profundity of Hiroshima from my own Christian spiritual perspective, Garrison sees the hand of God at work in Hiroshima. The phenomenology of the bomb is the same as the phenomenology of God—annihilation and judgment, white light, incandescent fire, ultimate concern. While God remains a mystery rooted in antinomy, the Bomb is clearly a god image, an *imago dei*, that is calling for new responses from the human spirit. *To dance around the bomb is to dance around God.* Garrison also gives voice to my experience that Hiroshima has "humanized the eschaton," has placed in the sphere of human choice the future of the created order. To bring consciousness to this new responsibility, a responsibility that could not even be conceived by the human mind prior to Hiroshima, will require a deeper, more holistic education than that currently practiced. I have dedicated my professional life to elucidating an adequate educational response to the terrible beauty/suffering of Hiroshima. I proceed, using the principle of Mahatma Gandhi, each new teaching moment an "experiment with truth," searching and re-searching for the transformative teaching moment when insight is converted into ethical agency.

Fortunately, I am not alone in my quest. I speak here not of my numerous friends and colleagues who are responding to the call of their own muse just as I am, but rather of the spiritual resources that surround us. I speak here of what Thomas Berry, in his *The Dream of the*

Earth: Our Way into the Future, refers to as "genetic guidance." Berry points out that under normal historical conditions we turn for guidance to our cultural traditions; but when cultural traditions are insufficiently imaginative, they are themselves obstacles to healing transformation. In such cases we must turn for guidance to our genetic coding, the spontaneously creative and mysterious impulses that originate in the same instincts through which the Earth itself came into being. The closest I have been able to get to my instinctual source, to my "genetic guidance," has been through my dreams. I pay close attention to them, especially those that illuminate the dark and destructive forces in my own psyche, aware that if the end comes through nuclear war, it will be because some *individual* could not sustain the tension of those very same dark and destructive forces. *Every individual psyche is a field of discovery for genetic guidance.* Following the advice of the dream is to exercise my moral obligations.

One night, in a particularly vivid dream, a well-respected United Nations leader, in a poignant moment of remembrance for all those who have given their lives in service to peace, breaks into a spontaneous speech in which he says, *"We are all, myself included, held in bondage by forces we must begin to identify and break free of, give form to, and consume. The time is now for huge international shifts of consciousness."* On another night I am visited by Mother Teresa, who gifts me with my teaching mantra. She tells me, *"Randy, the point is not to save people. The point is* to create the conditions for the possibility of Grace."

Recently I held a dream conversation with social activist Joanna Macy. In waking life I have admired Joanna's work for some time because it begins with the most honest emotional response we can have to the nuclear threat: complete and total despair. She is able, through a great deal of inner work, to sustain the presence of abject despair in both herself and others. *She has learned how to sustain the gaze of Hiroshima's terror.* The point of her work is to break through psychic numbing and denial, to liberate the imagination into its natural state of sympathetic participation with other and world, so that the heart and will can be moved toward their ethical obligations. In short, *despair awakens and liberates the moral imagination.* It is clear that to break out of our current predicament, we must drink deeply from the well of grief.

In my dream, Joanna and I lie on separate mattresses, a small, glowing pile of gold coins between us. We are immersed in a discussion about the problem of evil as illuminated by Hiroshima. Then our attention turns to a question that troubles me still: Why *wasn't* the nuclear threat sufficient to awaken consciousness in the culture? I awoke before the dream revealed its answer, but on a subsequent night Joanna's spirit returned to talk at great length about meditation practice and techniques of compassion. In one of life's delightful synchronicities, I chanced to meet Joanna Macy in waking life only three weeks after my dream, while on a kayak trip to a remote island in British Columbia. We sat together overlooking the saltwater, and time stood still for me as we continued our conversation on *this* side of the doorway. Through such experiences, imaginal and physical, the genetic guidance system of the Earth lures us to our own healing. Experience reveals to me that there is a symmetry between the inner and outer worlds, a balance which suggests that *political agency and spiritual insight are like Brother Sun and Sister Moon: the product of their union is the redemption of humanity,* a humanity that is now, since Hiroshima, cocreator of the Earth.

I end my imaginal odyssey with this scene: I am standing with Vusamazulu Credo Mutwa on the boarding platform of the Shinkansen bullet train. I know it is the last time I will see him on this Earth. I have been wanting to make a request of him since our ride down from Kyoto, but I am uncertain and indecisive. Finally, however, my importunity wins out. I ask Credo if I can hold the emerald-green heart stone that lies on his chest. He looks at me intently and nods his permission. My hand slowly closes over that stone, surprised by its heat, humbled by the extreme intimacy implied by such an act. I shut my eyes and there, among the surging and rumbling tones of this living rock, I perceive a doorway. Darkness lies before it, but it is slightly ajar, and through that space a ray of light penetrates the gloom. How many, I wonder, are willing to face the darkness, to enter that door and return with rays of hope? How many can drink deeply from the well of grief, can sustain the gaze of Hiroshima's terror? How many are willing to penetrate the dark heart of this city, to re-mythologize out of its wound, so that Hiroshima's healing balm may be spread upon the Earth?

With respect to the soul of Hiroshima, I slowly begin to comprehend Credo's words, "It *is* as you *see*."

Atomic Holocaust, Nazi Holocaust

SOME REFLECTIONS

RICHARD H. MINEAR

AN IMPROBABLE VISION

*I*magine that it is early August in the year 2045. Imagine the scene: the Mall in Washington, D.C. Imagine a gala if somber occasion, the opening of a new national museum. Imagine that the president of the United States, many other heads of state, and grandchildren and great-grandchildren of survivors of the catastrophe have gathered. The museum's motto is a line from the writings of one of the foremost writer-survivors: "For the dead and the living, we *must* bear witness."

Imagine the next day's *New York Times*: "*Atomic* Holocaust Museum Hailed as Sacred Debt to Dead." The article begins: "*One hundred* years after the furnaces of *Hiroshima and Nagasaki* devoured their last victims, *descendants of* survivors and world leaders gathered beneath a bleak, disconsolate sky today to dedicate a museum chronicling man's descent into darkness and the indifference to evil that marked the era. The United States *Atomic* Holocaust Museum was hailed not as the triumph of the human spirit over brutality or survival over genocide, but as a debt to the dead, a warning to future generations of the cost of detachment."

But it is the comments of the president of the United States, long noted for her eloquence, that are the center of attention. Here are excerpts:

It is my purpose on behalf of the United States to commemorate this magnificent museum, meeting as we do among memorials, within the sight of the memorial to Thomas Jefferson, near where Abraham Lincoln is seated, who gave his life so that our Nation might extend its mandate of freedom to all who live within its borders. . . . Here on the town square of our national life, on this *one hundredth* anniversary of the *atomic bombing of Hiroshima* . . . we dedicate the United States *Atomic* Holocaust Museum and so bind one of the darkest lessons in history to the hopeful soul of America.

As we have seen already today, this museum is not for the dead alone nor even for the survivors who have been so beautifully represented; it is perhaps most of all for those of us who were not there at all, to learn the lessons, to deepen our memories and our humanity, and to transmit these lessons from generation to generation.

The *Atomic* Holocaust,[1] to be sure, transformed the entire twentieth century, sweeping aside the Enlightenment hope that evil somehow could be permanently banished from the face of the Earth, demonstrating that there is no war to end all war, that the struggle against the basest tendencies of our nature must continue forever and ever.

The *Atomic* Holocaust began when the most civilized country of its day unleashed unprecedented acts of cruelty and hatred, abetted by perversions of science, philosophy, and law.

The president paused to secure the pages of her speech against a gust of wind. She continued:

The *Atomic* Holocaust reminds us forever that knowledge divorced from values can only serve to deepen the human nightmare, that a head without a heart is not humanity. For those of us here today representing the nations of the West, we must live forever with this knowledge. . . .

The evil represented in this museum is uncontestable. But as we are its witness, so must we remain its adversary in the world in which we live; so we must stop the fabricators of history and the bullies as well. Left unchallenged, they would still prey upon the powerless, and we must not permit this to happen again. . . .

I believe that this museum will touch the life of everyone who enters and leave everyone forever changed; a place of deep sadness and a sanctuary of bright hope; an ally of education against ignorance, of humility against arrogance, an investment in a secure future against whatever insanity lurks ahead. If this museum can mobilize morality, then those who have perished will thereby gain a measure of immortality.

Attached to the new museum is a United States *Atomic* Holocaust Research Institute, which will focus on four main fields of inquiry: historiography and documentation of the *atomic* holocaust, ethics and the *atomic* holocaust, comparative genocide studies, and impact of the *atomic* holocaust on contemporary society and culture. The institute's inaugural academic conference, "The *Atomic* Holocaust: An International Scholars' Conference on the Known, the Unknown, the Disputed, and the Reexamined," will draw more than a hundred specialists from three continents. The institute includes a document archive, a photo archive, an oral history department and archive, a film and video department and archive, and a registry of *atomic* holocaust survivors.

Reacting editorially to the museum's opening, the *New York Times* mentions the debates it has occasioned: "The new *Atomic* Holocaust Memorial Museum was dedicated in Washington yesterday, so America, being America, is all tangled up in debate. Should there be an *Atomic* Holocaust museum in the United States? Couldn't it cheapen or distort this horrific chapter in history? . . . Should it even *be*?" But the editorial answers this last question in the affirmative: "If anything, build more *Atomic* Holocaust museums. Build a memorial museum about slavery, about every brutal event and benighted spot on the planet. They serve, as *did* the struggles of Sarajevo, Belfast, Bombay, Soweto, to remind the world again and again, as the president said yesterday, 'how fragile are the safeguards of civilization.'"

End of improbable vision.

In April 1993 the U.S. Holocaust Memorial Museum opened on the Mall. The words in quotation marks above are from an article by Diana Jean Schemo on page 1 of the *New York Times* for 23 April and an editorial of the same date, the remarks of President Bill Clinton at the dedication, and a brochure, "United States Holocaust Research Institute"; I have italicized my alterations to those sources. ("For the dead and the living, we *must* bear witness" is a quotation from Elie Wiesel.) The new museum on the Mall is one of over a hundred Nazi holocaust museums throughout the world; the number of memorials is in the thousands. James Young writes, "Today nearly every major American city is home to at least one, and often several, memorials commemorating aspects of the Holocaust." Young estimates that perhaps as many people visit Nazi Holocaust museums and memorials worldwide each year as died in the holocaust itself[2]—and his estimate predates the opening of the museum on the Mall. A lunatic fringe today argues that the Nazi holocaust did not happen, but even in a more supportive context, the Holocaust Memorial Museum has an important role to play.

THE MUSEUM THAT ISN'T, AND WHY

There is today no American museum—on the Mall or anywhere else—of the American dropping of the atomic bombs on Hiroshima and Nagasaki. There *are* commemorations. A marker notes the site of the Trinity test at Alamogordo, New Mexico; *Bock's Car*, the B-29 that dropped "Fat Man" on Nagasaki, has long been on display in Ohio; the *Enola Gay* is set to go on display near the nation's capital this year, grotesque commemoration of the fiftieth anniversary of 6 August.[3] As recently as 1976 an air show in Texas conducted a reenactment of the dropping of the Hiroshima bomb. But at the Air and Space Museum on the Mall, just a stone's throw from the new Holocaust Memorial Museum, there is no real attention to the dropping of the atomic bomb on Japan or to the nuclear warheads that were one major purpose behind the development of missiles that served also to launch the United States into the space race.

Museums of the Nazi holocaust present events from the perspectives of the victims—as they should. Monuments in this country to Hiroshima and Nagasaki take the viewpoints of the victimizers. (There are museums in Hiroshima and Nagasaki that attempt to represent the victims, or many of them; those museums raise moral and historical issues of their own. But my topic here is America's Hiroshima, America's

Nagasaki.) And it is still completely acceptable—prize-winningly so—for American writers to treat Hiroshima almost exclusively through the eyes of its victimizers: witness David McCullough's *Truman,* winner of the Pulitzer Prize for biography in 1992. From very early—indeed, from the essay published under Henry L. Stimson's name in the February 1947 *Harper's,*[4] a major part of the justification for dropping the bombs has been that they saved great numbers of American lives—five hundred thousand, one million, two million. The figure has immediate relevance to the issue of proportionality, a key factor in the laws of war. The latest scholarship, that of Barton J. Bernstein, has shown that contemporary (that is, wartime) estimates by the American military ranged from twenty to forty-six thousand American lives lost.[5] McCullough misuses a memorandum of General Thomas Handy and concludes that "figures of such magnitude [no less than 500,000 to 1 million American lives] were then in use at the highest levels." But the memorandum that McCullough cites is evidence of precisely the opposite.[6] Challenged on the issue, McCullough responds that "the point is not that the figures are too high" and that "it didn't matter what they were predicting. It didn't matter whether we were going to lose 5,000 or 50,000 or 500,000—we were not going to make that sacrifice of not just ourselves, but the Japanese lives that would be lost—and that was the decision of the President."[7] In other words, the facts do not matter.

The United States chooses to commemorate Nazi holocaust but not atomic holocaust. Why? The reasons should be clear. First, the Nazi holocaust is someone else's doing, not ours.[8] Nations rarely memorialize their own atrocities, rarely fail to glorify their own wars; Maya Lin's Vietnam Memorial across the Mall from the new museum is a stunning exception. But in what sense does the (Nazi) holocaust belong on the (American) Mall? When pressed on this point, the Memorial Council concluded: "This Museum belongs at the center of American life because as a democratic civilization America is the enemy of racism and its ultimate expression, genocide. An event of universal significance, the Holocaust has special importance for Americans: in act and word the Nazis denied the deepest tenets of the American people."

In the words of James Young, "the U.S. Holocaust Memorial defines what it means to be American by graphically illustrating what it means not to be an American."[9] The United States was not notably victim or victimizer, so the museum's project director can speak of "the Americanization of the Holocaust." Second, many Americans feel kinship with the six million Jewish victims of the death camps, perhaps less so with their five million other victims: non-Jewish Poles, non-Jewish Russians, political dissidents, Gypsies, and gays. Third, those who feel kinship have managed to move the Nazi holocaust to the forefront of the nation's moral and cultural agenda.

In an essay of 1994, Thomas Laqueur—himself the son of Jewish refugees from the Nazi holocaust—concludes that the U.S. Holocaust Museum is out of place on the Mall, that it belongs in Berlin or at the site of one of the camps. He writes:

> Of course the holocaust is a human tragedy and not one belonging to any particular nation; of course America provided a home for many survivors. . . . There is thus no question of whether there should be Holocaust memorials in the United States; most major American cities already have one.
>
> But the Holocaust is not a part of the civic religion of the United States. I say this in part because there are so manifestly other atrocities for which we as a nation are more responsible and might atone—black slavery, or the destruction of indigenous peoples, for example—and because those most concerned with remembering these inhumanities do not have the economic or cultural resources to command a place on the Mall. And even if this were not the case, the Holocaust Memorial Museum would still have no organic connection with American sacred space nor with the sacred spaces of the event itself.[10]

Hiroshima and Nagasaki are *our* doing, not someone else's. There is no need to "Americanize" the atomic holocaust—even though there is clearly room for American memories and memorials to differ somewhat in perspective from Japanese memories and memorials. (It may surprise Americans to learn that Hiroshima and Nagasaki are not widely memorialized in Japan. There are major museums and sites in the two cities, and there is the Maruki Gallery for the Hiroshima Panels north of Tokyo. But that is about it. Because of convenience, many more tourists visit Hiroshima than Nagasaki. Hiroshima's Peace Park includes cenotaph and mass grave and monuments and a convention center and a museum that presents 6 August 1945 virtually in a vacuum, with no mention of what went before. [As of 1995, however, there is a new display in a separate museum in Peace Park that makes clear Hiroshima's complicity in the Japanese war effort.] But my point here is that even in Japan, there are only three museums to the atomic holocaust.) Far fewer Americans feel kinship to victims of Hiroshima and Nagasaki. And those who do feel kinship have not succeeded in placing the issue high on the nation's agenda, either cultural or moral. Note the absence of Hiroshima from the *New York Times* editorial on the U.S. Holocaust Memorial and from Laqueur's list of American atrocities.[11]

HOLOCAUST, NAZI HOLOCAUST, ATOMIC HOLOCAUST

What does the term "holocaust" itself mean? According to the *Oxford English Dictionary* (in its two editions and in the intervening Supplement as well), the basic meaning, from the Greek combination of "whole" and "burnt," is "A sacrifice wholly consumed by fire; a whole burnt offering": its earliest English appearance is about 1250. The second meaning is as follows: "*trans[ferred sense]*. and *fig[urative]*. a. A complete sacrifice or offering. b. A sacrifice on a large scale. . . . c. Complete consumption by fire, or that which is so consumed; complete destruction, esp. of a large number of persons; a great slaughter or massacre." The dictionary cites Milton (*Samson*, 1702) as the earliest use of meaning c. Under this meaning the second edition (1989) lists a 1987 newspaper headline: "AIDS: the new holocaust."

The second edition lists, as its predecessors did not, a new meaning: "the *Holocaust*: the mass murder of the Jews by the Nazis in the war of 1939–1945. Also used *trans[ferred sense]*, of the similar fate of other groups; and *attrib[utive, -ly]*. . . . Hence holocaust *v. trans*, to offer as a holocaust. holocaustal, holocaustic *adjs*., belonging to or of the nature of a holocaust." It appends the following gloss: "The specific application was introduced by historians during the 1950s, probably as an equivalent to Heb. *hurban* and *shoah 'catastrophe'* (used in the same sense); but it had been foreshadowed by contemporary references to the Nazi atrocities as a 'holocaust'. . . . The term is in common use among Jews, but seems to be otherwise relatively rare except among specialists." "Holocaust" clearly applies to Hiroshima and Nagasaki in terms of both burning and scale of destruction. (In its pamphlet, the United States Holocaust Research Institute refers to "Holocaust studies" with a capital *H*. But it publishes an important journal, *Holocaust and Genocide Studies,* which broadens its focus to "other genocides" even as it reserves the term Holocaust for *shoah*.)

As a historian, I find it difficult to deal with the phrase "the Holocaust." To take an obvious parallel, it makes little sense to speak of "the Revolution." Depending on their politics, people take the American Revolution or the French Revolution or the Russian Revolution or the Chinese Revolution or the Vietnamese Revolution as ideal types. But we capitalize Revolution, as in the above instances, only when we imply or state a specific instance. The attempted extermination of Europe's Jews was a particularly huge and gruesome catastrophe. But to capitalize it in the absence of an adjective—European or Nazi—is to absolutize it, to give it in some sense priority over other genocides. The issue is not awareness of magnitude or sympathy for the victims; the issue is one of careful use of language.

Objections to the term "holocaust," whether capitalized or not, come as well from within the Jewish community. As the *OED* indicates, Hebrew offered possible labels: *hurban,* a term associated with the destruction of the Temple, and *shoah,* catastrophe. According to a "Philologos" column "On Language," the secularist and politically left-leaning cultural establishment of the Palestinian Yishuv in the 1940s was unhappy with the notion of viewing the Holocaust in the religious perspective of Jewish martyrology and preferred a more 'neutral' and less freighted word than *hurban*. Its preference was *shoah*.[12] The *OED* definition makes clear that sacrifice is central to the term "holocaust"; like *hurban,* it carries freight. And indeed, in 1955, Yad Vashem (the Holocaust Martyrs' and Heroes' Remembrance Authority) decreed that the proper English translation of *shoah* was "Disaster."[13] Writing in 1984, Yehuda Bauer also expressed a distaste for "Holocaust": "for want of a better term, Holocaust, or more accurately *Shoah* (Catastrophe), using the Hebrew term, which is more appropriate."[14] "Philologos" quotes a 1987 statement of George Steiner—"I now try to avoid that ritual, elevated, and therefore radically inappropriate Greek word Holocaust"—and concludes by speaking of "the growing frequency of 'Shoah' among American Jews."[15] But these are minority voices. Franklin H. Littell of the National Institute on the Holocaust provides a doctrinaire statement: "The Holocaust refers, speaking correctly, to the planned murder of six million Jews in Hitler's area of conquest." Hence: "The use of the atom bomb on Hiroshima and Nagasaki was not 'Holocaust.' Neither was it 'genocide.' Whether it presaged 'omnicide' remains to be seen."[16] The debate over terminology-"*hurban*," "*shoah*," "Disaster," "holocaust," "Holocaust"—makes two points clear: first, language is intensely political; second, if usage has settled on "the Holocaust," that is a recent development.[17]

Consider now the statements of some of those who have linked atomic holocaust and Nazi holocaust. Pride of place undoubtedly goes to Dwight McDonald, for his editorial in *Politics*, August 1945: "This atrocious action places 'us,' the defenders of civilization, on a moral level with 'them,' the beasts of Maidanek."[18] In 1948, in his Dissenting Judgment at the Tokyo trial, the Indian judge, Radhabinod Pal, has this to say:

> Kaiser Wilhelm II was credited with a letter to the Austrian Kaiser Franz Joseph in the early days of [World War I], wherein he stated as follows: "My soul is torn, but everything must be put to fire and sword; men, women and children, and old men must be slaughtered and not a tree or house be left standing. . . ." This showed his ruthless policy, and this policy of indiscriminate murder to shorten the war was considered to be a crime. In the Pacific war under our consideration, if there was anything approaching what is indicated in the above letter of the German Emperor, it is the decision coming from the Allied Powers to use the atom bomb. . . . If any indiscriminate destruction of civilian life and property is still illegitimate in warfare, then, in the Pacific war, this decision to use the atom bomb is the only near approach to the directives of the German emperor during the first world war and of the Nazi leaders during the second world war.[19]

Writing twelve years after the end of the Tokyo trial, Pal's fellow judge, Bert V. A. Röling of the Netherlands, expressed views that he had not expressed in his own dissenting judgment: "from the Second World War above all two things are remembered: the German gas chambers and the American atomic bombings."[20] Neither judge applied the term "holocaust" to the atomic incineration (or, for that matter, to the Nazi genocide). In his 1967 study of survivors of Hiroshima, Robert Jay Lifton compared the patterns he found "to those of other 'extreme' historical experiences, particularly the Nazi persecutions"; Lifton developed the parallels in *The Genocidal Mentality: Nazi Holocaust and Nuclear Threat*.[21] In 1968 Ienaga Saburo, leading Japanese historian, wrote of Auschwitz and Hiroshima as "classic examples of rational atrocities."[22]

In talking about her poetry, Sylvia Plath linked the two holocausts: "I think that personal experience shouldn't be a kind of shut box and mirror-looking narcissistic experience. I believe it should be generally relevant, to such things as Hiroshima and Dachau, and so on." And she attempted to link them in one of her last poems—only to encounter the resistance of a critic whose opinion she respected. A. Alvarez has written of "Lady Lazarus" that Plath "becomes an imaginary Jew." Plath wanted also to become an imaginary Hiroshiman: "Gentlemen, ladies/These are my hands/My knees./I may be skin and bone,/I may be Japanese." But Alvarez discouraged her: "Why '*Japanese*?' I niggled away at her. 'Do you just need the rhyme? Or are you trying to hitch an easy lift by dragging in the atomic victims?'" Plath "argued back sharply" but gave in. Our concern here is with the poet's awareness, not with Alvarez's lesser reach.[23]

In a poem dated 20 November 1978, Primo Levi, survivor of Auschwitz and author of some of the most moving survivor-accounts of the Nazi holocaust, wrote a poem linking Nazi holocaust and atomic holocaust. It is "The Girl-Child of Pompei [*sic*]." The first fourteen lines tell of a victim of Pompeii; the next five speak of Anne Frank; then three lines treat "the Hiroshima schoolgirl/A shadow printed on a wall by the light of a thousand suns,/Victim sacrificed on the altar of fear." The order is chronological, of course: volcano to Nazi holocaust to Hiroshima. But is it *only* chronological? The final four lines are a prayer to the "Powerful of the earth, masters of new poisons,/Sad secret guardians of final thunder" *not* to resort to nuclear war.[24] On the ABC-TV panel that followed the initial showing of *The Day After* in November 1983, Elie Wiesel linked total nuclear war and Nazi holocaust: "Once upon a time it happened to my people, and now it happens to all people. And suddenly I said to myself, maybe the whole world, strangely, has turned

Jewish. Everybody lives now facing the unknown. We are all, in a way, helpless."[25] In May 1994, at a ceremony at UN headquarters in New York, Shimon Peres, Israel's foreign minister, spoke of "two holocausts: the Jewish holocaust and the Japanese holocaust. Because nuclear bombs are like flying holocausts."[26]

Leaders of the Manhattan Project did use the term "holocaust"—its *shoah* meaning was still in the future—for atomic war. As early as September or October 1945, James B. Conant, chemist, president of Harvard University, and Manhattan Project bureaucrat, thought that "survivors of a holocaust" might need printed matter "that would preserve the record of our civilization."[27] In 1949, Conant's coworker Vannevar Bush wondered "if the application of science has finally doomed us all to die in a holocaust." (Bush did not think that this was the case.)[28] As this survey has shown, the term "holocaust" came into use for two events virtually simultaneously; it is only as Nazi holocaust has become "the Holocaust" that resistance has arisen to the term "atomic holocaust."[29]

But the parallels continue to strike thoughtful observers. In 1980 Auschwitz survivor Samuel Pisar linked Auschwitz and things nuclear: "It is as if an Auschwitz fever has taken hold of mankind, pushing it irresistibly toward the precipice, an Auschwitz ideology." In 1981 Archbishop Raymond G. Hunthausen stated that the "Trident [base] is the Auschwitz of Puget Sound." In 1983, nuclear physicist I. I. Rabi joined the chorus: "And now we have the nations lined up, like those prisoners of Auschwitz, going into the ovens, and waiting for the ovens to be perfected, made more efficient."[30] Writing in January 1994 about the American downwinders, Carole Gallagher used the phrase "our nuclear Auschwitz": "Our media has always had a touch of 'the good German,' witnessing the smoke and ashes from our nuclear Auschwitz all these years but never saying a word."[31]

How do people today use the term "holocaust"? A Nexis survey of recent newspapers turned up a significant number of references to "nuclear holocaust." There were scattered other uses: Larry Kramer's essay, "Reports from the Holocaust: The Making of an AIDS Activist"; a review of a book of science fiction that speaks of "waiting for the final holocaust"; global warming as "a holocaust" to environmentalists; the Irish famine of the nineteenth century; the former Yugoslavia should the UN forces depart; the 1994 Los Angeles earthquake as harbinger of a coming holocaust; the Waco, Texas, inferno; rape as the victim's private holocaust; a member of a feuding business family speaking of "a family holocaust"; attacks on Dr. Jocelyn Elders as "director of the Arkansas holocaust" for her support of abortion. Most uses, the overwhelming majority, refer to the Nazi holocaust, but these other uses indicate that as metaphor the term "holocaust" has broad appeal.

Perhaps most striking is the title of David E. Stannard's volume, *American Holocaust: Columbus and the Conquest of the New World*. Although Stannard does not dwell on the use of the term "holocaust," he does address the issue of comparability:

> A secondary tragedy of all these genocides . . . is that partisan representatives among the survivors of particular afflicted groups not uncommonly hold up their peoples' experience as so fundamentally different . . . that not only is scholarly comparison rejected out of hand, but mere cross-referencing or discussion of other genocidal events within the context of their own flatly is prohibited. . . . [S]uch insistence on the incomparability of one's own historical suffering . . . invariably pits one terribly injured group against another—in the all too frequent contemporary disputes between Jews and African Americans, or the recent controversy over the U.S. Holocaust Memorial.[32]

VICTIMS AND MORALISTS

We know Charlotte Delbo, Primo Levi, Nelly Sachs, Elie Wiesel for their brilliant and compelling accounts, in prose and poetry, of the Nazi holocaust. Hara Tamiki, Kurihara Sadako, Ota Yoko, Toge Sankichi—these are the primary writers and poets who experienced Hiroshima and lived to write about it. But how many Americans in 1993 have heard of any of them? Three factors perpetuate our ignorance of the Japanese writer-survivors: the accident of language, and two far-from-accidental factors—lack of identification and lack of interest.[33] Less than forty-eight hours after the bomb fell on Hiroshima, Hara Tamiki jotted down the note: "Miraculously unhurt; must be heaven's will that I survive and report what happened." Ota Yoko later recorded this conversation with her half-sister, a conversation that took place as they walked through the city:

"You're really looking at them—how can you? I can't stand to look at corpses." Sister seemed to be criticizing me. I replied: "I'm looking with two sets of eyes—the eyes of a human being and the eyes of a writer." "Can you write—about something like this?" "Someday I'll have to. That's the responsibility of a writer who's seen it."

Toge Sankichi waited five years before setting his memories into poetry; in "Little One," he addresses a child whose father was killed in battle and whose mother died on 6 August. Three stanzas end with questions: "Who will tell you of that day?" / . . . "Who will tell you of that night?" / . . . "Who will tell you? / Who?" The final stanza ends:

> Right!
> *I'll* search you out,
> put my lips to your tender ear, and tell you. . . .
> I'll tell you the real story—
> I swear I will.

Kurihara Sadako would spend the fifty years after 1945 bearing witness, in poetry, prose, and act. Among her poems is "Hiroshima, Auschwitz: We Must Not Forget."

> What Auschwitz left behind:
> mounds of striped inmate uniforms, children's small shoes,
> and girls' red ribbons,
> eating bowls that served also as chamber pots,
> soap made from human fat,
> cloth woven of human hair.
>
> What Auschwitz left behind:
> turn all the world's blue skies and seas into ink
> and there still wouldn't be enough
>   to express the sadness, the anger,
> the moans of those burned in the ovens.
>
> What Hiroshima and Nagasaki left behind:
> a human shape burned onto stone,
> black rain streaking a wall,
> radioactivity inside bodies,

microcephalic babies irradiated in the womb,
voices of the dead sounding from the skies,
voices of the dead sounding from the bowels of the earth.

Hiroshima, Auschwitz: we must not forget.
Nagasaki, Auschwitz: we must not forget.
Even if the first time was a mistake,
the second time will be a calculated malice.
The vow we made to the dead: we must not forget.[34]

Having translated into English important works by these four survivors of Hiroshima, I identify with the victim, not the victimizers. I
salute Maruki Iri and Maruki Toshi, painters of the Hiroshima murals
that constitute one of the central artistic legacies of the twentieth century, a legacy still all but unknown in this country. When they decided to
paint Hiroshima, the Marukis decided to focus on *people*:

> The few reports of the bomb that had begun to circulate fo-
> cused on how many square kilometers had burned, what had
> happened to buildings and houses, how the concrete buildings
> had been destroyed. There was very little information on what
> happened to the people of Hiroshima, which was the only thing
> that truly mattered. So we decided that we would go to the
> other extreme and paint only people and nothing else.[35]

Sympathy with the victim has become all the easier because there
no longer exists a convincing argument in favor of the bomb—that there
was a military necessity for dropping it or that it convinced the Japanese
leaders to surrender. No serious student today accepts the claim of military necessity. J. Samuel Walker writes: "The consensus among scholars
is that the bomb was not needed to avoid an invasion of Japan and to
end the war within a relatively short time. It is clear that alternatives to
the bomb existed and that Truman and his advisers knew it."[36] As here,
the argument from military necessity is not that the bomb stood between the Allies and defeat (compare Michael Walzer's treatment of the
initial area bombings in Europe, below). It is that the bomb hastened
the defeat or saved lives (both Allied and Japanese, but mainly Allied).
The extent to which the bomb hastened the defeat—if it hastened it at
all—is debatable, but the estimates convincing to me range from days to

weeks. No serious student accepts the claim that the bomb changed the minds of Japan's leaders.

That leaves other motives—intimidating the Russians, for example, or demonstrating the need for control of atomic weapons: James Hershberg's recent biography of James B. Conant shows that Conant favored dropping the bomb "on the grounds . . . (2) that unless actually used in battle there would be no chance of convincing the American public and the world that it should be controlled by international agreement." That posture helps explain Conant's statement of 1974: "We thought, I thought, everybody thought that we must get this war over. We were against the warning [to Japan before the bomb, a warning never issued] *because it would prevent the assurance that the bomb would be dropped.*"[37] Or there are the arguments from "technological fanaticism"[38] and institutional or bureaucratic inertia. It is the latter two that are the most convincing to me.

Paul Kennedy's *The Rise and Fall of the Great Powers* concentrates on economic power and the link between economies and military power; he concluded of World War II: "it is difficult to see how [Allied] productive superiority would not have prevailed in the long term." Japan was considerably weaker than its Axis partner Germany, and the United States was considerably stronger than the other Allies. The figures that Kennedy gives show Japanese capacity to have been far less than that of the United States: in 1943, eighty-six thousand planes produced in the United States, seventeen thousand in Japan; in 1943, $37.5 billion spent for U.S. armaments, $4.5 billion for Japanese. It takes nothing away from the bravery of the fighting forces on both sides to argue that the outcome of the war was never in doubt. Commemorations of the battles of the war—Midway, Leyte Gulf, Okinawa—blind us to underlying issues. Viewed from Kennedy's distance, the Pacific war had no turning points.[39]

There have been moralists since 1945 who have justified Hiroshima and Nagasaki (far more justify the former than the latter), but serious arguments seem to be going in the opposite direction. Major Protestant, Jewish, and Catholic moral philosophers have spoken with broad unanimity. Writing in 1968, Paul Ramsey reaffirmed his own judgment of 1961 that "the obliteration—or area—bombing in the European theater in World War II, the fire-bombing of Tokyo, and the atomic destruction of two Japanese cities were inherently immoral acts of war."[40]

Writing in 1977, Michael Walzer agreed with Ramsey about Hiroshima and Nagasaki: "To use the atomic bomb, to kill and terrorize civilians, without even attempting such an experiment [in negotiation], was a double crime."[41] He did find the European area bombing morally defensible, but only so long as Nazi victory seemed likely—that is, into the summer of 1942. (He conceded immediately that most of the area bombing took place thereafter.[42] And of course, *all* the bombing of Japan—excepting only the Doolittle raid in early 1942—took place well after the tide of war had turned against Japan.)

Consider now *The Challenge of Peace: God's Promise and Our Response,* the pastoral letter of the National Conference of Catholic Bishops (3 May 1983). The letter's focus was on nuclear war and nuclear deterrence *in the future,* so it did not treat the bombing of Hiroshima or Nagasaki explicitly. Still, it is hard not to read into the letter a strong condemnation of Hiroshima. Under "Counter Population Warfare," the bishops stated (para. 147): "Under no circumstances may nuclear weapons or other instruments of mass slaughter be used for the purpose of destroying population centers or other predominantly civilian targets." In the following paragraph, the bishops extend this prohibition even to retaliatory strikes, and state: "No Christian can rightfully carry out orders or policies deliberately aimed at killing non-combatants." Under "The Initiation of Nuclear War," the bishops state (para. 150): "We do not perceive any situation in which the deliberate initiation of nuclear warfare, on however restricted a scale, can be morally justified."[43]

The words of the bishops allow us to see Hiroshima in a new light. Hiroshima was *the* first use of atomic weapons in war; that we always knew. But Hiroshima was also *a* first use, on a predominantly civilian target, against an enemy already demonstrably in the throes of defeat; it was "a deliberate initiation of nuclear warfare."

THE MUSEUM THAT SHOULD BE, AND WHY

I have argued that the dropping of the atomic bombs on Hiroshima and Nagasaki has no justification. I have made clear that my sympathy lies with the victims, not the victimizers. But museums exist not simply to condemn, not simply to express sympathy with victims. Museums exist to memorialize, of course, but they also exist—as does the U.S. Holocaust Memorial—to enable us to study. Historiography and documentation, ethics, comparative genocide, impact on contemporary society and culture: these are the categories the prospectus of the United States Holocaust Research Institute lists. Can anyone doubt that the same categories apply to the atomic holocaust? I think not. The decision to drop the atomic bombs took place in August 1945; it *happened*. We cannot remake it; we must live with its consequences. But we need to study the decision and its consequences before we can achieve a firm sense of where we are today. In a letter of 26 March 1954 to Vannevar Bush, James B. Conant expressed skepticism about the utility of writing the history of the bomb, but the terms in which he did so are remarkable. He wrote:

> the more I think of the past the more certain I am that it would be worse than useless to attempt to write the history of many of the dramatic events regarding the atomic bomb. Subsequent generations may damn all of us who had anything to do with the project for having started down the road which has led to the "atomic age" but unless one goes in for such wholesale emotional condemnation, inquiries into the past would seem to me perhaps worse than fruitless.[44]

In the United States in particular—in particular not because the United States is uniquely guilty but because the United States is uniquely powerful—we need to listen to the voices of those who have suffered from our action. We need to study the atomic holocaust not in the holier-than-thou sense of proclaiming what we are not, of defining ourselves by contrast with evildoers elsewhere, but in the straightforward sense of learning what we are, of defining ourselves in terms of our own acts. We need to hear the voices of the victims. We need a museum to atomic holocaust.

In the period since 1990 the newspapers have offered an almost daily catalog of atomic crimes and unresolved issues: cleanup (lack thereof) at Hanford, the American downwinders, the search for permanent waste sites for radioactive materials, radioactive testing carried out on American citizens. With the end of the Cold War, much of the need for the nuclear weapons themselves evaporates, and the old arguments for secrecy lose whatever cogency they had. Like the constituent parts of the old

Soviet Union, the United States finds itself facing the dilemma of what to do with our nuclear weapons. The Pentagon reportedly is considering targeting them at the Bering Sea instead of at Moscow; critics have suggested removing the warhead from the missiles. But won't someone offer *us* the deal—money for warheads—that we're offering Ukraine?[45]

Much must still transpire before significant numbers of Americans think of Nazi holocaust and atomic holocaust in similar ways. First and foremost, we must stop thinking of Hiroshima (and Nagasaki) as the end of the Pacific war, the end of World War II. How the habit got started is understandable enough: Hiroshima *marked* the end of the fighting even if it did not *cause* it. In the calculus of the time, Hiroshima became the second of a matched pair, the second of two bookends: Pearl Harbor and Hiroshima. Indeed, World War II in the Pacific appears in most high school textbooks *only* as Pearl Harbor and Hiroshima. Japan started the war at Pearl Harbor (the Japanese attack occludes the issue of U.S. policy before 7 December); the United States ended it at Hiroshima. However brutal, Hiroshima was fit punishment for Pearl Harbor.[46] The equation was not merely, or even primarily, historical; it was moral.[47]

In late 1991 McGeorge Bundy, whose covert and overt activities have shaped the American debate on Hiroshima for fifty years, made this extraordinary statement:

> I know that our Japanese friends find it hard to address Pearl Harbor across their memory of Hiroshima and Nagasaki. I agree that those atomic attacks are open to question; I have questioned them myself and so have a good many Americans, while Japanese criticism of the Japanese record from Manchuria to Pearl Harbor remains muted. I think Nagasaki was unnecessary and Hiroshima debatable, and I agree that the Americans remembering the 2,500 victims of Pearl Harbor should not forget that 50 died at Hiroshima for every one at Pearl Harbor. Nonetheless, we can say for Hiroshima that it put an end to the necessary war for which Pearl Harbor was the necessary ignition.[48]

And the context in which I have written this essay—our fiftieth-anniversary commemoration of World War II—likely will reinforce that habit of thought, myopic and self-exculpatory though it is.

But the war was never the true context for Hiroshima. Hiroshima marked the beginning of the rest of history. The apocalyptic rhetoric of J. Robert Oppenheimer in quoting the Bhagavad Gita—"Now I am become death, the destroyer of worlds"—was entirely appropriate. Consider Paul Kennedy's comment: "It is now clear that the dropping of the atomic bombs in 1945 marked a watershed in the military history of the world." (Note that Kennedy does not speak of a watershed in the war.) He continues: "The devastation inflicted upon Hiroshima, together with Berlin's fall into the hands of the Red Army, not only symbolized the end of another war, it also marked the beginning of a new order in world affairs."[49] As Robert J. Lifton wrote in 1967: "We are all survivors of Hiroshima and, in our imaginations, of future nuclear holocaust."[50] To be sure, in some sense we are all survivors of World War II; but we are in a special sense the survivors of Nazi holocaust and atomic holocaust. B. V. A. Röling was right to link the two, but the link goes far beyond memory; it goes to the very essence of our lives today.

Still, despite the improbable vision that opened this essay, I doubt that the day will ever arrive when the president of the United States opens an atomic holocaust memorial museum on the Mall. Of the ongoing debate in Germany over memorializing the Nazi holocaust there, James Young writes: "In fact, the best German memorial to the Fascist era and its victims may not be a single memorial at all—but simply the never-to-be-resolved debate over which kind of memory to preserve, how to do it, in whose name, and to what end?"[51] It is mute testimony to American (un)consciousness of Hiroshima and Nagasaki today that there are no plans for memorials, that there is no debate. The only American memorials to Hiroshima and Nagasaki are to the victimizers, not the victims, and there is no debate.

NOTES

The author wishes to acknowledge the assistance, in various forms, of the following persons, none of whom is responsible for his argument: Dina Abramowicz of YIVO Institute for Jewish Research, Michael Berenbaum, Shmuel Bolozky, Paul Boyer, Milton Cantor, William Christian, Jr., David Glassberg, David Goodman, Hans Janitschek of the

Earth Society Foundation, James Lowe of Merriam-Webster, Gladys and Paul Minear, Larry Minear, Barbara Morgan of the University of Massachusetts Library, Stephen Nissenbaum, Philip Nobile, Larry Owens, Charles Strozier, and James E. Young.

1. In capitalizing "Holocaust," the Clinton White House took a step the Carter White House had been unwilling to take. The act of Congress (1980) establishing the U.S. Holocaust Memorial Council carefully used "holocaust," not "Holocaust," as in its charge to the Council to "provide for appropriate ways for the nation to commemorate the Days of Remembrance, as an annual, national, civic commemoration of the holocaust." See James E. Young, *The Texture of Memory: Holocaust Memorials and Meaning* (New Haven: Yale University Press, 1993), 335, and the discussion of the term *holocaust* below.

2. Ibid., 294, ix–x.

3. See "Notes and Comment," *New Yorker,* 30 September 1991. A report by Hugh Sidey in *Time* (23 May 1994, 64) tells of protest against the plans for the Air and Space exhibit because it involves "an inordinate amount of attention to Japanese suffering." The official Smithsonian response: The script "would not make a judgment on the 'morality of the decision' [to drop the bomb]." The display might have a sign advising "Parental Discretion." Pressure from right-wing forces, including congressional Republicans, led first to the revision and then to the cancellation of the exhibit Air and Space curators had planned. The most useful account is Mike Wallace, "The Battle of the *Enola Gay,*" in his *Mickey Mouse History and Other Essays in American Memory* (Philadelphia: Temple University Press, 1996).

4. Henry L. Stimson, "The Decision to Use the Atomic Bomb," *Harper's* 194 (February 1947): 97–107. As Barton J. Bernstein has demonstrated, the real author is McGeorge Bundy, with major assists from James B. Conant, General Leslie Groves, and others: "Seizing the Contested Terrain of Early Nuclear History: Stimson, Conant, and Their Allies Explain the Decision to Use the Atomic Bomb," *Diplomatic History* 17 (Winter 1993): 35–72.

5. Barton J. Bernstein, "A Postwar Myth: 500,000 U.S. Lives Saved," *Bulletin of the Concerned Atomic Scientists* 42 (June/July 1986): 38–40.

6. Philip Nobile, unpublished manuscript, 45ff.

7. Transcript of phone conversation with Nobile, unpublished essay, 52; transcripts of question-and-answer session following McCullough lecture at Sarah Lawrence, 9 November 1993.

8. But see David S. Wyman, *The Abandonment of the Jews: America and the Holocaust, 1941–1945* (New York: New Press, 1984), for a penetrating analysis of American inaction.

9. Young, *Texture of Memory*, 337. Young is particularly acute on the importance of the national contexts for the various Nazi holocaust memorials.

10. Thomas Laqueur, "The Holocaust Museum," *Threepenny Review* (Winter 1994): 32.

11. In "Imagining Holocaust: Mass Death and American Consciousness at the End of the Second World War" (Ph.D. diss., Northwestern University, 1992), Robert Lane Fenrich offers a thoughtful analysis of the different receptions of the two holocausts, differences that remain significant today.

12. "Philologos," "The Case for 'Shoah,' " *Forward* (14 August 1992): 11.

13. Gerd Korman, "The Holocaust in American Historical Writing," *Societas* 2 (Summer 1972): 260.

14. Yehuda Bauer, "The Place of the Holocaust in Contemporary History," in *Studies in Contemporary Jewry*, vol. 1, ed. Jonathan Frankel (Bloomington: Indiana University Press, 1984), 205.

15. "Philologos," "The Case for 'Shoah,' " 11. See also Jakob J. Petuchowski, "Dissenting Thoughts About the 'Holocaust,' " *Journal of Reform Judaism* (Fall 1981): 1–9.

16. Franklin H. Littell, "Defining the Holocaust," *Martyrdom and Resistance* (March–April 1984): 14–15.

17. See James E. Young, *Writing and Rewriting the Holocaust: Narrative and the Consequence of Interpretation* (Bloomington: Indiana University Press, 1988), 85ff., for a thoughtful discussion of "Naming and Uniqueness," and 92ff. on "Consequences of Metaphor."

18. Dwight McDonald, *Politics* (August 1945): 225.

19. Radhabinod Pal, *International Military Tribunal for the Far East: Dissentient Judgment* (Calcutta: Sanya, 1953), 620–621.

20. Bert V. A. Röling, "The Tokyo Trial in Retrospect," in *Buddhism and Culture*, ed. Susumu Yamaguchi (Kyoto: Nakano Press, 1960), 248.

21. Robert Jay Lifton, *Death in Life: Survivors of Hiroshima* (New York: Random House, 1967), 479. See Lifton and Eric Markusen, *The Genocidal Mentality: Nazi Holocaust and Nuclear Threat* (New York: Basic Books, 1990), esp. 8–14, for a thoughtful discussion of parallels and differences between Nazi holocaust and nuclear genocide.

22. Saburo Ienaga, *The Pacific War: World War II and the Japanese*, trans. Frank Baldwin (New York: Pantheon, 1978). A more literal translation of Ienaga's *reisei na keikaku no moto ni tsuiko-sareta zangyaku koi* (*Taiheiyo senso* [Tokyo: Iwanami, 1968], 216) would be: "atrocities carried out under coolly calculated plans."

23. "Lady Lazarus," in Sylvia Plath, *Ariel* (New York: Harper & Row, 1965),

6–9; A. Alvarez, *The Savage God: A Study of Suicide* (New York: Random House, 1972), 16–18. See also Plath's letter to her mother (October 1962): "It's too bad my poems frighten you—but you've always been afraid of reading or seeing the world's hardest things—like Hiroshima, the Inquisition, or Belsen." Quoted in Janet Malcolm, "The Silent Woman—I," *New Yorker* 69 (23 and 30 August 1993): 89. Alvarez considered the allusion to Hiroshima "apparently not quite relevant." See also Young, *Writing and Rewriting the Holocaust*, pp. 120–121; like Alvarez, Young doubts the aptness of the allusion. Alvarez's intervention has shaped Plath scholarship. In a 1968 essay, George Steiner asks, "Do any of us have license to locate our personal disasters, raw though these may be, in Auschwitz?" (Quoted in Malcolm, "The Silent Woman—I," 109.) The issue is the individual's relation not to Auschwitz but to *any* historical trauma in which the individual is not a participant. See also Malcolm's description of her own coming of age in an era in which "no one was prepared—least of all the shaken returning G.I.s—to face the post-Hiroshima and post-Auschwitz world." ("The Silent Woman—I," 89).

24. *Primo Levi, Collected Poems,* trans. Ruth Feldman and Brian Swann (London: Menard Press, 1976), 34.

25. Quoted in Lifton and Markusen, *Genocidal Mentality,* 1.

26. "Peace Bell Ceremony" (23 May 1994), 7 (typescript). The Peace Bell (stone from Israel, wood from Japan, bell made of coins collected by children around the world) was a gift of the United Nations Association of Japan in 1954, before Japan was admitted to membership; the 1994 ceremony commemorated Earth Day and its cofounder, Margaret Mead. Peres's comments attracted very little notice; a Nexis search turned up no American reference. On 25 May an editorial in the *Jerusalem Post,* "Foot in Mouth," had this to say: "Israelis have always maintained that the Holocaust . . . is a unique event in the annals of mankind. Comparing it to the atrocities of war, or even to genocidal outrages, is a betrayal of its victims and the whole Jewish people. Comparing the bombing of Hiroshima to Nazi deeds is an inexcusable insult to the greatest democracy on earth, a nation which saved humanity from slavery. When such comparisons are made by non-Jews, they are deemed either morally bankrupt or vicious and hateful. That Israel's foreign minister is capable of making them is nothing short of mind-boggling." Writing in the *New York Post* on 2 June, Eric Breindel called Peres's comments "decidedly unfortunate," a "bizarre exercise in moral equivalence," and insisted on "the utter uniqueness of the Nazi attempt to wipe the Jewish people from the face of the earth. . . . In this sense, the Holocaust was manifestly unique: the darkest moment in the history of man." He concluded: "Likening Hiroshima to the Holocaust smacks of low-grade moral relativ-

ism." But consider the suggestion of Tuli Kupferberg in 1967 that "Auschwitz-Hiroshima" will become one word. W. J. Rorabaugh, *Berkeley at War: The 1960s* (New York: Oxford University Press, 1989), 169.

27. Quoted in James G. Hershberg, *James B. Conant: Harvard to Hiroshima and the Making of the Nuclear Age* (New York: Knopf, 1993), 241. This use predates by five years or more the citation in *Merriam Webster's Third International Dictionary* (1976) to Conant's phrase "an atomic global holocaust" (*President's Report*, Harvard University, 1953).

28. Vannevar Bush, *Modern Arms and Free Men: A Discussion of the Role of Science in Preserving Democracy* (New York: Simon & Schuster, 1949), 5.

29. In 1983 the Commission on Social Action of Reform Judaism published a workbook entitled *Preventing Nuclear Holocaust: A Jewish Response* (New York: The Commission, 1983). Nowhere does the commission elaborate on its title, but see 52, 59, and 177 for documents of American Jewish organizations and writers employing the phrase "nuclear holocaust." For the other view, see, for example, a plaintive letter to the editor (*New York Times,* 25 December 1993): "It is essential to have a museum [unlike the U.S. Holocaust Museum] that will present the Holocaust as something that happened to the Jews, at the hands of many nations. We must find another word, another viewpoint, to memorialize the horrors undergone by others in World War II." James Young's comment is most appropriate in this context (*Writing and Rewriting,* 91): "To leave Auschwitz outside of metaphor would be to leave it outside of language altogether."

30. For the Pisar, Hunthausen, and Rabi citations, see Lifton and Markusen, *Genocidal Mentality,* 8–9.

31. Carole Gallagher is author of the moving document *American Ground Zero: The Secret Nuclear War* (Cambridge, Mass.: MIT Press, 1993). Her comment is in the *Boston Globe,* 9 January 1994.

32. David E. Stannard, *American Holocaust: Columbus and the Conquest of the New World* (New York: Oxford University Press, 1992), 151–52; the controversy concerned the inclusion of Gypsies in the opening ceremonies.

33. Cf. Kurihara Sadako, "The Literature of Auschwitz and Hiroshima: Thoughts on Reading Lawrence Langer's *The Holocaust and the Literary Imagination*," trans. and ed. Richard H. Minear, *Holocaust and Genocide Studies* 7:1 (Spring 1993): 77–106.

34. For Hara, Ota, and Toge, see Richard H. Minear, ed. and trans., *Hiroshima: Three Witnesses* (Princeton: Princeton University Press, 1990); for Kurihara, see Minear, ed. and trans., *Black Eggs: Poems* (Ann Arbor: University of Michigan Press, 1994). The date of Kurihara's poem is December 1989.

35. On the Marukis and their art, see John W. Dower and John Junkerman,

eds., *The Hiroshima Murals: The Art of Iri Maruki and Toshi Maruki* (Tokyo: Kodansha, 1985), and the documentary film (also by Dower and Junkerman) *Hellfire: A Journey from Hiroshima* (First Run Features, 1986). The statement about painting people is from the book, 124. See also Lifton, *Death in Life*, 14: "And what did happen—what people in Hiroshima experienced and felt—seems to be precisely what we have thought least about."

36. J. Samuel Walker, "The Decision to Use the Bomb: A Historiographical Update," *Diplomatic History* 14 (Winter 1990): 110.

37. Hershberg, *James B. Conant*, 293; the date of this formulation is 20 January 1947. For the 1974 statement, see ibid., 818, n. 22 (emphasis added).

38. The term is Michael S. Sherry's in *The Rise of American Air Power: The Creation of Armageddon* (New Haven: Yale University Press, 1987), 251–255.

39. Paul Kennedy, *The Rise and Fall of the Great Powers: Economic Change and Military Conflict from 1500 to 2000* (New York: Random House, 1987), 352ff.

40. Paul Ramsey, *The Just War: Force and Political Responsibility* (1968; repr. Lanham, Md.: University Press of America, 1983), 273.

41. Michael Walzer, *Just and Unjust Wars: A Moral Argument with Historical Illustrations* (New York: Basic Books, 1977), 268.

42. Ibid., 262.

43. For the text, see, among others, Philip J. Murnion, ed., *Catholics and Nuclear War: A Commentary on the Challenge of Peace, the U.S. Catholic Bishops' Pastoral Letter on War and Peace* (New York: Crossroad, 1983). In Para. 147, the bishops quoted from the Second Vatican Council (1965): "Any act of war aimed indiscriminately at the destruction of entire cities or of extensive areas along with their population is a crime against God and man himself. It merits unequivocal and unhesitating condemnation."

44. Quoted in Hershberg, *James B. Conant*, 6. The context of this remarkable statement is apparently the 1954 controversy over the decision to produce the hydrogen bomb.

45. In *My Several Lives: Memoirs of a Social Inventor* (New York: Harper & Row, 1970), 304, James B. Conant offers a telling vignette:

> I have never been one of those who thought the use of atomic energy for peaceful purposes held such potential benefits for the human race that we should all rejoice at the discovery of atomic fission. To my mind, the potentialities for destruction are so awesome as to outweigh by far all the imaginable gains that may accrue in the distant future when atomic power plants may exist all over the world. I conclude this chapter by a reference to my visit to Secretary Stimson's office on the day after I returned from the Trinity Test. George L. Harrison . . . welcomed me with enthusiasm. "Con-

gratulations," he exclaimed as he shook my hand, "it worked." "Yes," I replied, "it worked. As to congratulations, I am far from sure—that remains for history to decide." As I write these lines in 1969, with American and Soviet aircraft and missiles poised to strike on a moment's notice, I can only regard my reply to Harrison as quite correct. The verdict of history has not yet been given.

The bombers and missiles may be standing down, but Conant's point remains valid.

46. It is not only textbooks. A recent collection of scholarly antirevisionist essays bears the title *From Pearl Harbor to Hiroshima: The Second World War in Asia and the Pacific, 1941–45,* ed. Saki Dockrill (New York: St. Martin's Press, 1994). An essay by Lawrence Freedman and the editor, "Hiroshima: A Strategy of Shock," includes this passage (212, n. 75): "More recently, a school of thought has suggested that while the Americans often say 'Remember Pearl Harbor,' the Japanese do not equate the causes (Pearl Harbor) and the results (Hiroshima)."

47. Even at the time, however, there were dissenting voices. Most notable in this context is Mary McCarthy's comment: "Up to August 31 of this year [1946], no one dared think of Hiroshima—it appeared to us all as a kind of hole in human history." The context is her scathing critique of John Hersey's *Hiroshima* (Letter to the Editor, *Politics* 3 [November 1946]: 367).

48. McGeorge Bundy, "Pearl Harbor Brought Peace," *Newsweek* (16 December 1991): 8. It is surely a question whether Japanese criticism of Japanese actions 1931–1941 "remains muted." And what, one might ask, has McGeorge Bundy, coarchitect of American policy in Indochina 1961–1966, had to say about that *American* record?

49. Kennedy, *Rise and Fall,* 356–357.

50. Lifton, *Death in Life,* 479.

51. Young, *Texture of Memory,* 21.

From Nuclear Patriarchy to Solar Community

MAYUMI ODA

I was born in Japan in 1941, right before World War II. I heard the news of the bombing with my mother in northern Japan, where we were evacuated from the air raids in Tokyo. I was four years old, and terrified by the news of hell; I heard that thousands of people were evaporated or scorched to death. Five years later, people were still dying, especially young children, from leukemia. The atomic bomb became my nightmare. I was very upset again when the United States started to test the atomic bomb on Bikini atoll in the South Pacific. As a child, I felt an anger toward the adults, but I did not know what to do. So we children folded origami paper cranes, thousands of them, stringing them together, sending them to the Hiroshima Peace Monument. Now, almost fifty years later, people are still dying from the effects of the bomb.

In 1992 I was back in Japan, and found out that my country was deeply committed to the use of plutonium by the electric utilities, which were building a fast-breeder reactor in Wakasa and a plutonium reprocessing facility in Rokkasho, a remote village of northern Japan. I also learned that we were about to transport 1.7 tons of plutonium (150 nuclear bombs' worth) from France. I was dumbfounded. How could the country that experienced the atomic bomb do this? What could we do to stop this?

I felt helpless. I visited the Tenkawa shrine with some women friends to pay homage to Sarasvati, goddess of prosperity, creativity, art, and music. In front of the shrine stood a huge ginkgo tree that was planted by our Buddhist saint Kobo Daishi twelve hundred years ago. Once this tree was two separate trees, male and female, but now the two have grown together into one big tree. I went to the tree and opened my arms and hugged it. I felt so connected to the tree and to the twelve hundred-year-old roots. So I asked the tree, "What can we do?"

When I was at home in California, meditating in front of a Sarasvati figure, I heard a voice saying, "Stop the plutonium shipment." It seemed to come from the goddess. I answered, "Why me? I am an artist." The goddess said, "Help will be provided on the way." The voice had irresistible power, so . . .

We formed a group, Plutonium Free Future, and worked hard with other nonprofit, nongovernmental organizations to let the world know about the Japanese government's nuclear policy and the plutonium shipment. We filed an international petition of objection in a Japanese court against the Japanese government. In three weeks, we collected over two thousand signatures from sixty-five countries, giving us power of attorney to make their objections for them in the Japanese court. Unfortunately, the shipment could not be stopped. But the plutonium ship *Akatsukimaru* was called a "floating Chernobyl," and acted as a catalyst bringing world attention to many of the nuclear issues that now face our world.

From Russia came news of mismanagement at nuclear production sites, the dumping of highly radioactive material into lakes and the ocean, and the continuing operation of dilapidated nuclear power plants in worse shape than Chernobyl was. In the United States, Hazel O'Leary, the Secretary of Energy, declassified a stack of documents three miles high, documents of American nuclear secrets, of human guinea pigs, of nuclear accidents and cover-ups, of the unsolved problems of radioactive waste, of the trillion-dollar cost to clean up Hanford and Savannah River. Finally, out came news of plutonium smuggling from the former Soviet arsenal.

General Charles Horner, head of the U.S. Aerospace Defense Command, has admitted to the world at large that nuclear weapons are obsolete. No civilized nation would use them on the cities of an adversary. But we all know that small bands of fanatics or terrorists might.

After more than fifty years of the Nuclear Age, and now that the Cold War is over, we are truly facing nuclear terror.

In 1941, American scientist Glenn Seaborg succeeded in isolating plutonium, an element whose nucleus can be split. Splitting the atom created extremely toxic by-products and released tremendous power. At that moment something happened to us. A thorn of violence stuck in the flesh of our Earth and started to infect us. Gaining the power of gods, we left a lethal legacy to our children and future generations, just as King Midas inadvertently sacrificed his daughter to his greed.

This lethal legacy is about to become out of control. Children have been living under the fear of the possibility of not being survived by anybody. We face the extinction of our species. Fear of total nuclear death is the source of the violence of our time. Until we remove the thorn of plutonium from the world, that wound of violence will fester and never heal.

Out of guilt, the scientists felt there had to be some peaceful use, some way to redeem the horror they had created. Thus, nuclear energy came to the world. Decades of research led finally to fuel reprocessing and prototype fast-breeder reactors that forever produce more fuel than they use. In Japan this is called "the dream energy." It is a dream of unending wealth and power, the oldest dream of mankind, an alchemy transmuting common lead into unlimited quantities of gold, the myth of Midas and of Faust.

At this moment, Japan is the last country still clinging to its Faustian bargain, causing tensions over nuclear proliferation throughout Asia, especially North and South Korea and China. Japan holds an important key to whether or not Asia goes nuclear. In addition, the world nuclear energy industry sees Japan as its only hope for survival. Japan's plutonium dream is the last clinging image of a crumbling patriarchal paradigm, which still seeks and believes in unlimited growth of power and wealth.

Patriarchal power, the control of the many by the few, and of women by men, requires control over information. Secrecy was the key to the development of nuclear weapons and energy. Secrecy was the way patriarchy held the power over us. We know now that we can go to our spiritual sources directly, to the goddesses, without going through any religious institution. There are no more secrets, and we can hear the voices of the goddesses without fear.

Nuclear patriarchy provided us our electricity at the price of high centralization, high fences, armed guards; it required an army of male experts who disregarded the safety of the future generations, without a thought of how to clean up the toxic mess—as if they never had to clean up their own rooms.

Nobody doubts that solar technologies will replace fossil fuels as they run out. The sun shines and the wind blows over us everywhere on this Earth. We can harvest energy from sun and wind. Using geothermal technology, we can send cold water to our Earth's belly, where it will boil and turn a turbine just as well as nuclear power can.

Using solar systems, individual homes, neighborhood communities, and villages in many regions can produce their own power. In addition, solar-hydrogen technology can turn water into fuel for trucks and airplanes. When energy for our daily lives—cooking, heating our homes, washing our bodies and clothes, and fueling our cars—comes directly to us from nature, it changes our relationship to each other. This is what I call solar community.

The solar community is also a community across generations. It takes almost nothing from future generations' resources, and it leaves behind no toxic waste. These technologies are here today. All we need is the political will and our commitment to a sustainable future.

First, we must put an end to the nuclear patriarchy immediately, and put all of our minds and resources together to figure out how we can safeguard and clean up the plutonium and other radioactive materials this patriarchy leaves behind. Otherwise, there will be no safe world for us to inhabit.

Then we can envision our solar community together. As an artist I have committed to use my creativity for this change. I hope we can work together.

Recommended Reading

Bartimus, Tad, and Scott McCartney. *Trinity's Children: Living Along America's Nuclear Highway*. New York: Harcourt Brace Jovanovich, 1991.

Bird, Kai, and Lawrence Lifschultz. *Hiroshima's Shadow: Writings on the Denial of History and the Smithsonian Controversy*. Stony Creek: Pamphleteer's Press, 1998.

Boyer, Paul. *By the Bomb's Early Light: American Thought and Culture at the Dawn of the Atomic Age*. New York: Pantheon, 1985.

——. *Fallout: A Historian Reflects on America's Half-Century Encounter with Nuclear Weapons*. Columbus: Ohio State University Press, 1998.

Bradley, John, ed. *Atomic Ghost: Poets Respond to the Nuclear Age*. Minneapolis: Coffee House Press, 1995.

Caufield, Catherine. *Multiple Exposures: Chronicles of the Radiation Age*. Chicago: University of Chicago Press, 1989.

Charman, Karen. "Block 'Mobile Chernobyl.'" *The Nation*, 8 February 1999, 6–7.

Clark, Claudia. *Radium Girls: Women and Industrial Health Reform, 1910–1935*. Chapel Hill: University of North Carolina Press, 1997.

Gallagher, Carole. *American Ground Zero: The Secret Nuclear War*. Cambridge, MA: MIT Press, 1993.

Garber, Marjorie, and Rebecca L. Walkowitz, eds. *Secret Agents: The Rosenberg Case, McCarthyism, and Fifties America*. New York: Routledge, 1995.

Ghosh, Amitav. "Countdown." *New Yorker*, 26 October–2 November 1998, 186–197.

Hales, Peter Bacon. *Atomic Spaces: Living on the Manhattan Project*. Chicago: University of Illinois Press, 1997.

Hersey, John. *Hiroshima*. New York: Vintage, 1989.

Hevley, Bruce, and John M. Findlay, eds. *The Atomic West*. Seattle: University of Washington Press, 1998.

Kuletz, Valerie. *The Tainted Desert: Environmental and Social Ruin in the American West*. New York: Routledge, 1998.

Kurihara, Sadako. *Black Eggs: Poems by Kurihara Sadako*. Trans. Richard H. Minear. Ann Arbor: University of Michigan Press/Center for Japanese Studies, 1994.

Lifton, Robert Jay. *Death in Life: Survivors of Hiroshima*. New York: Basic Books, 1967.

Lifton, Robert Jay, and Greg Mitchell. *Hiroshima in America: Fifty Years of Denial*. New York: Grosset/Putnam, 1995.

Linner, Rachelle. *City of Silence: Listening to Hiroshima*. Maryknoll, NY: Orbis, 1995.

Loeb, Paul. *Nuclear Culture: Living and Working in the World's Largest Atomic Complex*. Philadelphia: New Society, 1986.

Maclear, Kyo. *Beclouded Visions: Hirsohima-Nagasaki and the Art of Witness*. Albany: State University of New York Press, 1998.

Mesler, Bill. "Pentagon Poison: The Great Radioactive Ammo Cover-Up." *The Nation*, 26 May 1997, 17–20.

Minear, Richard H., ed. and trans. *Hiroshima: Three Witnesses*. Princeton: Princeton University Press, 1990.

Mojtabai, A. G. *Blessèd Assurance: At Home with the Bomb in Amarillo, Texas*. Boston: Houghton Mifflin, 1986.

NHK [Japanese Broadcasting Corporation], eds. *Unforgettable Fire*. New York: Pantheon, 1977.

O'Donnell, Joe. *Japan 1945—Images from the Trunk*. Japan: Shogakukan, 1995.

O'Neill, Dan. *The Firecracker Boys*. New York: St Martin's Press, 1994.

Rhodes, Richard. *The Making of the Atomic Bomb*. New York: Simon & Schuster, 1986.

——. *Dark Sun*. New York: Simon & Schuster, 1995.

Roy, Arundhati. "The End of Imagination." *The Nation*, 28 September 1998, 11–19.

Snider, Hideko Tamura. *One Sunny Day: A Child's Memories of Hiroshima*. Chicago: Carus Publishing, 1996.

Stone, Albert E. *Literary Aftershocks: American Writers, Readers, and the Bomb*. New York: Twayne, 1994.

Treat, John Whittier. *Writing Ground Zero: Japanese Literature and the Atomic Bomb*. Chicago: University of Chicago Press, 1995.

Williams, Terry Tempest. "A 'Downwinder' in Hiroshima." *The Nation*, 15 May 1995, 661–666.

Yamagata, Yosuke. *Nagasaki Journey: The Photographs of Yosuke Yamagata*. San Francisco: Pomegranate, 1995.

About the Contributors

MARILOU AWIAKTA remembers, "As a child, when I told my mother, 'I want to be a writer,' she'd say, 'That's good. And what will you do for your people?'" All her work, she believes, has been in response to that question. Awiakta's unique fusion of her Cherokee/Appalachian heritage with science has received international recognition. In 1986 the U.S. Information Agency chose her books *Abiding Appalachia: Where Mountain and Atom Meet* and *Rising Fawn and the Fire Mystery* for its global tour, "Women in the Contemporary World." Her third book, *Selu: Seeking the Corn-Mother's Wisdom,* applies Native American philosophy to contemporary issues. A poem from *Selu* is inlaid in the walkway of the Fine Arts Mall at the University of California, Riverside. Awiakta graduated from the University of Tennessee in 1954, with a B.A. in English and French. In 1989, she received the Distinguished Tennessee Writer Award. Her work is in many anthologies, including *World Without Violence: Can Gandhi's Vision Become Reality?* edited by Arun Gandhi. Awiakta's current research is on the healing power of the atom.

JOHN BRADLEY is the editor of *Atomic Ghost: Poets Respond to the Nuclear Age,* an international poetry anthology published by Coffee House Press. In 1995, he read from this poetry anthology in Hiroshima, Japan, at a ceremony commemorating the fiftieth anniversary of the atomic bombing of Hiroshima. The ceremony was organized by the World Friendship Center. With Bill Witherup, Bradley gave a presentation titled *Atomic Ghost* at the University of Missouri–Kansas City. Bradley has given other *Atomic Ghost* presentations at Goshen College, at Providence College, and at a conference held by the Snake River Institute in Jackson Hole, Wyoming. He is the author of *Love-in-Idleness: The Poetry of Roberto Zingarello,* which won the 1989 Washington Prize, and a recipient of a National Endowment for the Arts Fellowship in poetry. He received an M.A. in English from Colorado State University and an M.F.A. in Creative Writing from Bowling Green State University. He lives in DeKalb, Illinois, with his wife, Jana, and teaches writing at Northern Illinois University.

JIM CARRIER, a journalist for thirty-three years, has worked as a radio newsman, Associated Press editor and correspondent, newspaper managing editor, roaming columnist, and project writer. Of his thirteen years with the *Denver Post*, Carrier has written: "One million words, 500,000 miles, 7,665 sunsets, eighty-seven pairs of Levis—it was a glorious ride through the American West. I searched for the Marlboro Man, lived in Yellowstone, rafted the entire Colorado River, climbed the Tetons, chased racist cross burners, cried in Indian sweats, absorbed radioactivity, and howled with coyotes beneath a full moon." In 1998 he bought a sailboat, named it *Ranger*, and began to freelance. He has been published in the *National Geographic* and is a regular contributor to the *New York Times*. He is researching a book on responses to hate crimes for the Southern Poverty Law Center in Montgomery, Alabama.

ALISON HAWTHORNE DEMING is the author of *Science and Other Poems,* winner of the Walt Whitman Award from the Academy of American Poets; *The Monarchs: A Poem Sequence; Temporary Homelands: Essays on Nature, Spirit and Place;* and *The Edges of Civilized World*. She also edited *Poetry of the American West: A Columbia Anthology*. She is Director of the University of Arizona Poetry Center, where she also teaches creative writing. Currently she is working on a small book titled *Writing the Sacred into the Real* for the Milkweed Editions series "Credo: Notable American Authors on Nature, Community and the Writing Life." Of *Temporary Homelands,* W. S. Di Piero writes: "These essays, free of pieties and polemics, speak about love and the continuance of nature with humane moral fervor."

MARY DICKSON, a Utah-based writer, has had wide-ranging feature magazine articles, commentary, essays, and analyses published in a variety of publications. She has written extensively about nuclear radiation issues, women's issues, film, and the arts. A former newspaper journalist, she served for many years as the coeditor of the *Desert Sun,* a newspaper devoted to coverage of nuclear issues affecting states downwind of the Nevada Test Site. She has received a variety of writing awards, including those from the Society of Professional Journalists, the Associated Press, and the National Association of Women Journalists. Since 1988, Dickson has been the Director of Creative Services at KUED, Channel 7, the Utah PBS affiliate, where her work has been honored with awards from the National Broadcasters' Association, the Public Broadcasting Service, and the Rocky Mountain Emmy Association. She is the writer and coproducer of the PBS documentary film *No Safe Place: Violence Against Women,* which received an Emmy nomination and a Gold Award from the Houston WorldFest International Film Festival. She is a frequent commentator on public radio station KUER-FM. Dickson is a longtime community activist, serving on the boards of directors of nonprofit organizations, including the Utah Women's Forum, Women in News, the Utah Film and Video Center, and the Salt Lake Acting Company. She has been recognized for distinguished achievement by *The World's Who's Who of Women,* and is the recipient of the Quintus Wilson Distinguished Alumnus Award of the University of Utah.

EDWARD DOUGHERTY, after finishing his M.F.A. in creative writing at Bowling Green State University, in Bowling Green, Ohio, taught there and was poetry editor of the *Mid-American Review.* In 1993, he and his spouse went to Hiroshima as volunteer directors of the World Friendship Center, where they stayed for two and a half years, witnessing the fiftieth anniversaries of the atomic bombings of Hiroshima and Nagasaki. A bilingual collection of his poems, *Pilgrimage to a Ginkgo Tree,* appeared in 1996; it includes work by John Bradley (editor of *Atomic Ghost: Poets Respond to the Nuclear Age*) and Hiromu Morishita (poet, calligrapher, atomic bomb survivor, and chairman of the World Friendship Center). Some of Dougherty's essays about writing, peace, poetry, and faith have been published in *Peace Review, ELF, Writer to Writer, The Bookpress, Baybury Review, The Other Side,* and other journals. He has worked at a pizza shop, volunteered with the homeless, customized *The Cable Guide,* and coordinated retreats for young people, as well as taught writing and edited. Dougherty and his wife, Beth, now live and work in Elmira, New York, where they are active in the Quaker Meeting.

RAY GONZALEZ is a poet, essayist, and editor. He was born in El Paso, Texas, and received his M.F.A. in creative writing from Southwest Texas State University. He is the author of *Memory Fever: A Journey Beyond El Paso del Norte*, a memoir about growing up in the Southwest, and *Turtle Pictures*, a poetic/prose memoir. He is the author of five books of poetry, including *Cabato Sentora* and *The Heat of Arrivals*. He has edited twelve anthologies, most recently *Muy Macho: Latino Men Confront Their Manhood* and *Touching the Fire: Fifteen Poets of the Latino Renaissance*. His awards include a 1999 McKnight Land Grant Professorship from the University of Minnesota, a 1998 Fellowship in Poetry from the Illinois Arts Council, a 1997 PEN/Oakland Josephine Miles Book Award for *The Heat of Arrivals*, and a 1993 Before Columbus Foundation American Book Award for Excellence in Editing. He has served as poetry editor of the *Bloomsbury Review*, a book review magazine in Denver, for eighteen years and recently founded a new journal of poetry and translations, *Luna*. He is an assistant professor of English at the University of Minnesota in Minneapolis.

KARL GROSSMAN is a full professor of journalism at the State University of New York/College at Old Westbury who for almost thirty years has pioneered the combining of investigative reporting and environmental journalism. He is the author of *The Wrong Stuff: The Space Program's Nuclear Threat to Our Planet* and writer and narrator of the video documentaries *Nukes in Space: The Nuclearization and Weaponization of the Heavens* and *Nukes in Space 2: Unacceptable Risks*. His articles on the use of nuclear power in space have been repeatedly cited in the annual judging of Sonoma State University's Project Censored as among the issues most "underreported" or "censored" by the media. In 1997, Project Censored selected Grossman's articles on the subject as its "top censored story." He is the host of EnviroVideo's nationally syndicated weekly interview show *Enviro Close-Up*. He has received many citations for his journalism, including the George Polk and the John Peter Zenger Awards. Articles by Grossman have appeared in the *New York Times, The Nation, The Progressive*, the *Christian Science Monitor*, and the *Village Voice*, among other publications. He is coordinator of the media and communications major at SUNY/College at Old Westbury.

SONYA HUBER graduated from Carleton College in 1993 with a degree in sociology/anthropology. While at Carleton, she cofounded a political magazine and participated in many activist campaigns. Her writing has appeared in *In These Times, Sojourner, As We Are, Third Force, The Workbook, The Body Politic,* and many Midwestern community publications and student publications. In addition, her poetry has been published in small press magazines and anthologies across the country, and her fiction has won small press awards. She edited and wrote for *Infusion,* the magazine of the Center for Campus Organizing, from 1996 to 1998, on topics ranging from affirmative action to on-line education to low-income student organizing. She is currently the Associate Publisher at *In These Times.* Huber writes on issues of youth in society and women in the workforce, and reports on grassroots community efforts for social change.

BARBARA KINGSOLVER is the author of *The Poisonwood Bible, Pigs in Heaven, Animal Dreams* (awarded the 1991 PEN West prize for fiction), *The Bean Trees,* and the short story collection *Homeland and Other Stories.* She has also published the nonfiction book *Holding the Line: Women in the Great Mine Strike of 1983* and a book of poetry, *Another America.* Margaret Randall notes the following themes in Kingsolver's poetry: "what links communities of people, the misuses of power and empowerment that come from common struggles for justice, survival with dignity." Kingsolver is also author of a collection of essays titled *High Tide in Tucson.* She lives with her husband and daughter in southern Arizona and in the mountains of southern Appalachia.

VALERIE KULETZ grew up in the Mojave Desert as the daughter of a Cold War–era weapons scientist, within a Department of Defense scientific community devoted to the research, development, and testing of weapons. Her recent work on the transformation of the American Southwest under the influence of post–World War II nuclear and military activities describes how different groups constructed nature in the Cold War American West and the often tragic consequences of our creations— particularly for those outside the domain of state power. She is the author of *The Tainted Desert: Environmental and Social Ruin in the American West,* which won the 1997 American Sociological Association's award for technology and humanism. In 1998 *Choice* presented *The*

Tainted Desert with an award as the outstanding academic book of the year. *The Tainted Desert* also was a finalist for the C. Wright Mills Award of the Society for the Study of Social Problems. Kuletz is now engaged in researching nuclear colonialism in the Pacific Island region. She is currently lecturer in American Studies at the University of Canterbury. She lives with her husband, Richard Rawles, overlooking Pegasus Bay on the South Island of New Zealand.

MARY LAUFER has moved thirteen times, lived in eight states, and attended five colleges. She earned a degree in secondary school English education at the State University of New York at Albany and later taught in Orange County Public Schools in Orlando, Florida. Most of her adult life has been spent raising her kids, whose fascination with bugs and animals inspired several of her poems for children. "A Snail's Path" was recorded on cassette by *Shoofly,* a children's audiomagazine, and she is working on a collection of related poems that celebrate nature. The twelve years her husband was stationed on submarines kept her intensely aware that our government's decisions about nuclear weapons could easily erase the environment we take for granted. When their Navy life ended in 1996, the Laufers settled in Forest Grove, Oregon. The Hanford Nuclear Reservation in nearby Washington made newspaper headlines because of leaking fuel tanks, reminding Laufer again of the dangers of radiation. She tied herself to a chair and wrote "Imagine a World Without Nuclear Nightmares" by compiling old college papers and journal entries. Her other works deal with being a woman, a mother, a wife. Recently her poetry was published in *Earth's Daughters,* a short story in *Women's Words,* and creative nonfiction in *Coming of Age.* A poem titled "At the Top of the Food Chain" will appear in *Pemmican.* Laufer plans to continue writing literature with environmental and feminist themes.

KAY MACK is a poet, artist, and actor. Her poetry is published in several anthologies including *Buffalo Bones, Messages from the Heart,* and *Her Day Begins Flamingo Pink.* Scrapbook photographs from her summer stock, community theatre, and cellist days still make her smile. Mack earned an M. Div. from Yale Divinity School and a commercial art degree from the Colorado Institute of Art. She is a former state department of education Arts in Education consultant and a former coordinator for the northwest states' Alliance for Arts Education.

CRAIG McGRATH is a writer and journalist who has lived in Washington, D.C., since 1994. Born in Illinois, he is a graduate of the University of Illinois. He is the coauthor of *Consumers Guide to Alternative Health Care,* which is also available on the Internet. As a journalist, he has covered national think tanks, foundations, and media personalities for the *Texas Observer, New Times, Alternet,* and the *Progressive Populist,* among others. During 1988–1989, he was a staff member of the Minnesota Nuclear Weapons Freeze Campaign, and in 1991–1992 he was also on the staff of the Minnesota Peace and Justice Coalition. In 1989 he was lead organizer for the public signing of the U.S. Conference of Mayors' Nuclear Test Ban Resolution by the mayors of Minneapolis, St. Paul, and Bloomington, Minnesota. The resolution sought to put the U.S. Conference of Mayors on record in support of the International Comprehensive Test Ban as a means to halt the nuclear arms race. As part of his duties that year, he also organized the visit of Russian-Soviet writers to the Twin Cities.

BILL MESLER is a freelance journalist living in Washington, D.C. An Amerasian native of South Korea, Mesler has worked as an editor with the Seoul-based *Korea Economic Journal* and as a reporter with the weekly *San Francisco Bay Guardian* and *The Nation.* His stories have appeared in daily newspapers like the *Sacramento Bee* and magazines like *The Progressive.* He holds a degree in political science from the University of California at Santa Cruz. Readers interested in further information on depleted uranium will want to see Mesler's article "Pentagon Poison: The Great Radioactive Ammo Cover-Up," in the May 26, 1997, issue of *The Nation.*

RICHARD H. MINEAR, a specialist in Japanese history, is professor of history at the University of Massachusetts at Amherst. Born in 1938, he graduated from Yale College and got his Ph.D. in history and East Asian languages from Harvard. His previous works include monographs on Japanese constitutional law and the Tokyo war crimes trial, a book of readings for precollege use (*Through Japanese Eyes*), and translations from the Japanese of *Requiem for Battleship Yamato, Hiroshima: Three Witnesses,* and *Black Eggs.* He has conducted research in Japan on many occasions. His two monographs have appeared in Japanese translation, as has his essay "Atomic Holocaust, Nazi Holocaust: Some Reflections." This essay appeared originally in a symposium in the journal *Diplomatic History*; when the editor turned that symposium into a separate volume, he omitted only this essay.

RANDY MORRIS was born and raised in Richland, Washington. He received his B.A. in biology from Whitman College and M.A. and Ph.D. degrees in liberal studies from Emory University in Atlanta. After teaching children of all ages for ten years, including three years at the International School in Hiroshima, Japan, Morris returned to Washington State to work at Antioch University in Seattle. He is currently a faculty member in the B.A. Completion Program in Liberal Studies at Antioch, where he teaches classes in the history and philosophy of science, child and adolescent development, and various themes within the field of depth psychology, including the psychology of C. G. Jung, mythological studies, and dream work. He continues to research the effect of nuclear imagery on the human psyche, and he has recently published a collection of his essays on this topic in a book titled *Encounters with Hiroshima: Making Sense of the Nuclear Age.* Other research interests include ecopsychology, the idea of the *anima mundi* (the soul of the world), and the Sophianic imagination. Morris is currently editing a book on spirituality and higher education tentatively titled *Meditations on Spirituality and Adult Education.* He lives with his wife and two teenaged kids in Seattle, where he enjoys kayaking and attending basketball games.

MAYUMI ODA, an internationally recognized painter and printmaker, was born in 1941 to a Buddhist family in Tokyo. Her work has been exhibited throughout the world and is part of many collections, including those of the Museum of Modern Art, Yale University Art Gallery, Cincinnati Art Museum, Cleveland Museum, Portland Art Museum, Honolulu Academy of the Arts, Osaka Modern Art Center, and Tokyo University of Fine Arts, from which she graduated. Her book *Goddesses* has been widely acclaimed. In 1992 she founded Plutonium Free Future, an organization formed to publicize the nuclear program in Japan and to stop shipments of plutonium from France to Japan. She has lectured and held workshops at the United Nations NGO Forum and the Women of Vision Conference in Washington, D.C.

CATHERINE QUIGG, a graduate of Northwestern University, had a career in advertising and public relations in Chicago before becoming a free-lance writer in 1970. As research director for Pollution & Environmental Problems, Inc. (PEP), she was involved with information and action programs on recycling, pesticide control, nuclear safety, hazardous waste, alternative energy, and energy conservation. Under her guidance, PEP sponsored Illinois's first solar energy forum at Harper College, drawing more than four hundred solar experts and interested citizens. She was a founding member and past president of the Illinois Safe Energy Alliance, based in Chicago in the 1970s, an affiliation of twenty statewide environment groups dedicated to energy conservation and awareness of nuclear issues. She appeared as an invited witness before U.S. Congressional hearings on nuclear waste issues, and she has given seminars and workshops on the environment at colleges, universities, and community organizations. Her articles on health and environmental concerns have appeared in *The Progressive, Environment, Illinois Issues,* the *Bulletin of the Atomic Scientists,* the *St. Louis Post-Dispatch,* the *San Francisco Chronicle,* and other publications. She is currently working on articles to call attention to the need for nationwide distribution of potassium iodide pills to the public, especially children, as an antidote to potential releases of radioactive iodine in a nuclear reactor accident. She resides with her husband in Barrington, Illinois.

RICHARD RAWLES is an occasional journalist, essayist, and poet. His work has appeared in *Sierra, Spectacle,* and a variety of computer-related publications. His poetry has appeared in *White Heron Poetry Review, Café Solo, Outerbridge,* and *Bleating Hearts.* He is currently pursuing postgraduate studies in English at the University of Canterbury, New Zealand. His current research interests include the sociology of knowledge, critical theories of technology, hermeneutics, and Gnostic apocalypticism in English and American poetry.

KENNETH ROBBINS is a published novelist, produced playwright, and author of numerous short stories, essays, memoirs, and reviews. He completed "The Cenotaph" while living in Hiroshima, as part of a Japan

Foundation Artists Fellowship, during the summer of 1995. His play *Atomic Field,* written during the same time, is scheduled for production in Tokyo. Robbins holds a Ph.D. from Southern Illinois University and serves Louisiana Tech University as director of the School of the Performing Arts. His current writing project is a sequel to his published novel, *The Baptism of Howie Cobb.*

SCOTT RUSSELL SANDERS was born in Tennessee in 1945 and grew up in Ohio. He studied at Brown University before going on, as a Marshall Scholar, to complete a Ph.D. in English literature at Cambridge University. In 1971, he joined the faculty of Indiana University, where he is Distinguished Professor of English and directs the Wells Scholars Program. He has published twenty books, including novels, collections of stories and essays, personal narratives, and storybooks for children. His work appears in such magazines as *Orion, Audubon,* and the *Georgia Review,* and it has been reprinted in *Best American Essays, American Nature Writing, The Norton Reader,* and many other anthologies. His collection of essays *The Paradise of Bombs* won the Associated Writing Programs Award in Creative Nonfiction. *Staying Put,* a celebration of the commitment to place, won the Ohioana Book Award in 1994. *Writing from the Center,* a personal account of the quest for a meaningful and moral life, won the 1996 Great Lakes Book Award. His most recent book is *Hunting for Hope.* He has received fellowships for writing from the National Endowment for the Arts, the Indiana Arts Commission, the Lilly Endowment, and the Guggenheim Foundation. For his collected work in nonfiction, he was honored in 1995 with a Lannan Literary Award. He and his wife, Ruth, a biochemist, have reared two children in their hometown of Bloomington, Indiana.

DAVID SEABORG received a Master of Arts in zoology from the University of California at Berkeley, specializing in evolutionary biology and animal behavior. He founded and is President and Director of Research of the Foundation for Biological Conservation and Research (FBCR), which does research in evolutionary biology and works to save the world's rain forests under the World Rain Forest Fund, a branch of the FBCR. An award-winning wildlife and nature photographer, he has traveled to thirty countries, from Brazilian rain forests to African savanna to Caribbean coral reef. His research helped to conserve sea turtles in Mexico (leatherback turtle) and Florida (loggerhead turtle). He organized San Francisco Bay Area environmental leaders and organizations into The U-Turn Society, an organization dedicated to causing a U-turn from destruction of the planet to its conservation, preservation, and restoration. His talk show on environmental issues, *The Endangered Earth*, aired on KPFA, a public radio station in Berkeley. He has written poetry, as well as scholarly articles, dealing with the environment.

TERRY TEMPEST WILLIAMS was born in 1955 and grew up within sight of the Great Salt Lake. Her writing reflects her intimate relationship with the natural world. She is author of *Pieces of White Shell: A Journey to Navajoland, Coyote's Canyon, Refuge: An Unnatural History of Family and Place, An Unspoken Hunger—Stories from the Field,* and, most recently, *Desert Quartet—An Erotic Landscape.* Collaborations include *Great and Peculiar Beauty—A Utah Reader,* edited with Thomas J. Lyon; *Testimony—Writers of the West Speak on Behalf of Utah Wilderness,* edited with Stephen Trimble, and the forthcoming anthology *The New Genesis: Mormons Writing on Environment.* Ms. Williams has said that she writes "through my biases of gender, geography, and culture, that I am a woman whose ideas have been shaped by the Colorado Plateau and the Great Basin, that these ideas are then sorted out through the prism of my culture—and my culture is Mormon. Those tenets of family and community that I see at the heart of that culture are then articulated through story." Terry Tempest Williams was identified by *Newsweek* as someone likely to make "a considerable impact on the political, economic and environmental issues facing the western states in this decade." A recipient of the National Wildlife Federation's National Conservation Award for Special Achievement, she was recently inducted into the Rachel Carson Institute's Honor Roll. She has served as naturalist-in-residence at the Utah Museum of Natural History and is currently the Shirley Sutton Thomas Visiting Professor of English at the University of Utah. Ms. Williams has received a Lannan Literary Fellowship in creative nonfiction along with a Guggenheim Fellowship for 1997. She lives with her husband, Brooke, in Salt Lake City, Utah.

BILL WITHERUP, the contributing editor to this anthology, was also a contributing editor to *Atomic Ghost: Poets Respond to the Nuclear Age.* He is the author of *Men at Work* and *Black Ash, Orange Fire: Collected*

Poems 1959–1985. He is anthologized in *The Ahsahta Anthology: Poetry of the American West* (1996). His *Down Wind, Down River: New and Selected Poems* is presently being considered for publication. Witherup has been a volunteer member of Washington Physicians for Social Responsibility since 1990. He was consultant to the Nagasaki Broadcasting Company for the 1995 video *Living in the Nuclear Age,* which is available through the University of Washington Manuscript Archives. Along with his antinuclear activism, he has advocated for prison reform and is currently working on a biography of former convict Fred Markham, who is the business manager for *Prison Legal News,* published in Washington State. Witherup studied with Theodore Roethke and James Byron Hall at the University of Oregon. He counts these two literary men as important influences. A third and recent influence, especially in the area of labor ideas and labor history, is Dr. Fred Whitehead, publisher of *People's Culture* and *Free Thought History*. Bill Witherup is a freelancer and a member of the National Writers Union, Seattle Local.

PHIL WOODS has been active in the peace movement for over thirty years. He received his M.F.A. from the University of Oregon in 1983. He is the author of two books of poetry, *Waking the Woodcutter* and *The Good Journey,* and an award-winning letterpress broadside, *The Zodiac of Words*. Long Hand Press of Black Hawk, South Dakota, published his essay "Poetry as Witness" and some of his poetry in the anthology *On Fry Bread and Poetry* in 1999. Two new books of poetry are in the process of being readied for publication. Woods traveled to Spain in 1998 for the hundredth anniversary of the birth of Federico García Lorca. He recently presented his research in a talk at Telluride, Colorado, titled "Moistening the Soul: Garcia Lorca and Duende."

Acknowledgments

Marilou Awiakta, "Baring the Atom's Mother Heart," reprinted with permission from *Selu: Seeking the Corn-Mother's Wisdom*, by Marilou Awiakta, copyright © 1993, Fulcrum Publishing, Inc., Golden, Colorado. All rights reserved.

Jim Carrier, "Voiceless Victims," was originally published in the *Denver Post* in 1995. Reprinted by permission of the author and the *Denver Post*.

Edward A. Dougherty, "At the Crossroads," was originally published in *Peace Review* 10 (December 1998): 625–32.

Ray Gonzalez, "White Sands," was originally published in *Memory Fever: A Journey Beyond El Paso del Norte*, by Ray Gonzalez. Copyright © 1993 by Ray Gonzalez. Reprinted by permission of the author.

Karl Grossman, "Brighter than the Brightest Star," from *CovertAction Quarterly*, no. 60 (Spring 1997) (originally published as "Space Probe Explodes, Plutonium Missing"). Reprinted by permission of the author and *Covert Action Quarterly*.

Barbara Kingsolver, "In the Belly of the Beast," from *High Tide in Tucson*, by Barbara Kingsolver. Copyright © 1995 by Barbara Kingsolver. Reprinted by permission of HarperCollins Publishers, Inc.

Valerie Kuletz, "Tragedy at the Center of the Universe," from *The Tainted Desert*, by Valerie L. Kuletz. Copyright © 1998, reproduced by permission of Routledge, Inc.

Bill Mesler, "The Pentagon's Radioactive Bullet," reprinted with permission from the October 21, 1996 issue of *The Nation*.

Richard H. Minear, "Atomic Holocaust, Nazi Holocaust: Some Reflections," first appeared in *Diplomatic History* (Spring 1995) and is reprinted by permission of Blackwell Publishers.

Index

St. Paul (Minn.), 82
Savannah River (S.C.), 77, 218n. 18
Schell, Jonathan, 257–58
Seaborg, Glenn T., 33–41, 293
Shoshone Indians, 160, 162, 165, 176,
180; myths of, 174–75; and radio-
active contaminated food, 168–69
Silkwood, 94
Simpsons, The, 95
Sirota, Lyubov, xvii
Snyder, Gary, 70–71
solar technologies, 294
"Sorcerer's Apprentice" (*Fantasia*),
176–77
Soviet State Committee on Atomic
Energy, 38
Soviet Union and Nazi Germany,
compared, 72n. 11
Sputnik, 15
Star Wars, 84
State Radiation Protection Act of
1974, 114
Stimson, Henry L., 269, 284n. 4
Strategic Air Command (SAC), 57,
75–76, 123
strontium-90, 40, 64

Tainted Desert, The (Kuletz), 169
Teller, Edward, 62–63
Them! xv, 177
Three Mile Island nuclear power
plant, 46
Thresher (submarine), 44, 45, 46
thyroid cancer, 127, 128, 129, 130. *See
also* radiation: illnesses related to
Titan missiles, 97–107; accidents,
102–3, 104
Titan silo, 97–107
Toge, Sankichi, 235, 277

Tokyo Trial, 273–74
treaties: Comprehensive Test Ban, 41,
214; Limited Test Ban, 40; Ruby
Valley, 160. *See also* nuclear test ban
Trident submarines, 48, 51
Trinity, 20, 22, 119, 120
tritium, 54, 111, 114, 115–17
Truman (McCullough), 269
Truman, Harry, 278

UFOs, 13–14
undeveloped countries. *See* Fourth
World
Unforgettable Fire, 241
United States Holocaust Memorial
Museum, 267–68, 269–70
United States Radium Corporation,
113
University of California at Davis, 122
University of Utah, 122
uranium mines and mining: and
exploitation, 153–54; on Indian
land, 143–48
uranium mining: illnesses related
to, 141–42, 146–47, 149, 151, 152,
156n. 15; and scientific discourse,
148–53. *See also* radiation: illnesses
related to
USS *Jack* (submarine), 44
Utah: radioactive fallout in, 135; residents and cancer, 130–31, 135–36,
137

Vasilieva, Larissa, 79, 82, 83, 84
Veterans Administration, 183–84

Walker, J. Samuel, 278
Walzer, Michael, 278, 280
war, playing, 8–9, 11–14, 15–16
WarGames, 64

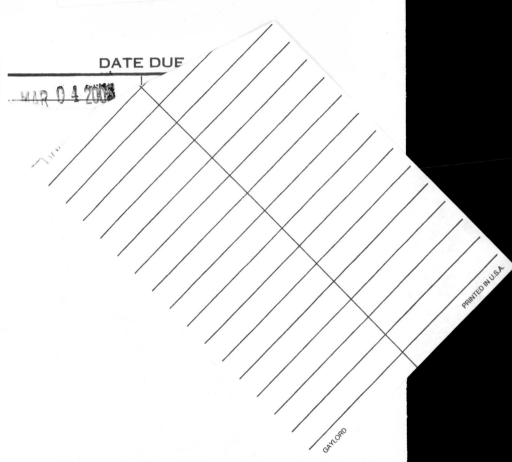